SAP® GRC

FOR DUMMIES®

by Denise Vu Broady and Holly A. Roland

WILEY

Wiley Publishing, Inc.

SAP® GRC For Dummies®

Published by
Wiley Publishing, Inc.
111 River Street
Hoboken, NJ 07030-5774

www.wiley.com

For general information on our other products and services, please contact our Customer Care Department within the U.S. at 800-762-2974, outside the U.S. at 317-572-3993, or fax 317-572-4002.

For technical support, please visit www.wiley.com/techsupport.

Wiley also publishes its books in a variety of electronic formats. Some content that appears in print may not be available in electronic books.

Library of Congress Control Number:

ISBN: 978-0-470-33317-4

Manufactured in the United States of America

10 9 8 7 6 5 4 3 2 1

WILEY

About the Authors

Denise Vu Broady: Denise is SAP's VP of Strategic Applications. She runs the SAP CFO Center of Excellence, a cross-solution team responsible for enabling customers to use SAP technology and products to transform the Office of the CFO. She has business development responsibility for the entire CFO portfolio of solutions, including Governance, Risk & Compliance (GRC); Enterprise Performance Management (EPM); and Spend Optimization. Denise has over 11 years of SAP-related experience. At SAP she has specialized in bringing new products to market; Denise played a central role in the launch of xApps, NetWeaver, Payroll Change Management, GRC and EPM. She came to SAP via the acquisition of TopTier where she was Product Manager. Earlier in her career, Denise gained hands-on SAP experience as a consultant on multiple R/2 and R/3 technical and functional projects. Denise has a BS in Management Science and Marketing from Virginia Tech and resides in New York City.

Holly A. Roland: Holly is the vice president of marketing for SAP's Governance, Risk and Compliance (GRC) business unit. In this role, she is responsible for product strategy and marketing for SAP's GRC products. Holly created the industry-leading executive advisory board for GRC, composed of customers, partners, and SAP executives, which facilitates collaboration among business executives and industry leaders to identify common GRC challenges, develop GRC best practices, and conceive of supporting technology solutions. Holly was instrumental in the integration of Virsa Systems and the successful design and execution of SAP's GRC product launch in 2006. She publishes articles and serves as an expert speaker for international events and forums on GRC topics. Holly has more than 15 years of experience in financial accounting and reporting, regulatory compliance, business analytics, and enterprise software marketing and development. Prior to joining SAP, she led product strategy, marketing, and product management operations at Virsa Systems, Oracle Corporation, Hyperion Solutions, and Movaris. Holly also served as a public accountant for PriceWaterhouseCoopers where she audited large public companies and provided business consulting. Holly graduated cum laude from Santa Clara University with a BS in Commerce. She is based in SAP Labs in Palo Alto, California.

Dedication

To my husband for always listening, no matter how long my stories take. And to Safra; my guiding light. —Holly

To Tsafi, my better half, who has been extremely patient and supportive with a hectic year of travel and work and letting many chapters of this book join us on vacations and weekends. —Denise

Authors' Acknowledgments

This book would not be possible without the help and support of many, many people. Our colleagues at SAP were very generous with their time and research materials, providing us with interviews, research materials, and even whole sections revised or written in their hand.

Special thanks are due to Gary Dickhart, who couldn't stop writing (we're waiting for your GRC book, Gary), David Milam and Dave Anderson, who helped us greatly improve our chapter on risk management (Chapter 2). Mark Crofton made important contributions to the financial compliance chapters in Part II. Marina Simonians and David Ahrens provided tremendous support for Part III, "Going Green." Paul Pessutti helped us with interviews, reviews, and revisions in the very complex area of global trade (Chapter 8), as well as our related Part of Ten (Chapter 17). Christian Berg, who is both a colleague and an expert in the area of sustainability, shaped Chapter 14. We would also like to thank Karan Dhillon for his excellent interview and research materials; his input can be seen throughout the book, as can the influence of Bob Crochetiere, whose interview was also formative. We also extend our appreciation to the following people who helped us in bringing this book together: Nenshad Bardoliwalla, Wolfgang Bock, Ben Cesar, Lee Dittmar, Ravi Gill, Marko Langes, Melissa Lea, Joe Miles, Phil Morin, Jim Mullen, Tom Neacy, Barry Nemmers, Eric Solberg, Axel Streichardt, and Greg Wynne. Thank you for the time you spent working with us, despite very hectic schedules.

We'd like to thank the writers at Evolved Media: Dan Woods, Deb Cameron, Charlotte Otter, D. Foy O'Brien, James Buchanan, Kermit Pattison, David Penick, and Justin Jouvenal.

We would also like to extend our sincere thanks to the great people at Wiley, especially Katie Feltman, Beth Taylor, and Linda Morris, for all their hard work, dedication, and perceptive editing.

Publisher's Acknowledgments

We're proud of this book; please send us your comments through our online registration form located at www.dummies.com/register/.

Some of the people who helped bring this book to market include the following:

Acquisitions, Editorial, and Media Development

Project Editor: Beth Taylor

Development Editor: Linda Morris

Senior Acquisitions Editor: Katie Feltman

Copy Editor: Beth Taylor

Editorial Manager: Jodi Jensen

Editorial Assistant: Amanda Foxworth

Sr. Editorial Assistant: Cherie Case

Cartoons: Rich Tennant
(www.the5thwave.com)

Composition Services

Project Coordinator: Patrick Redmond

Layout and Graphics: Stacie Brooks, Alissa D. Ellet, Reuben W. Davis, Christine Williams

Proofreader: Evelyn W. Still

Indexer: Potomac Indexing, LLC

Publishing and Editorial for Technology Dummies

Richard Swadley, Vice President and Executive Group Publisher

Andy Cummings, Vice President and Publisher

Mary Bednarek, Executive Acquisitions Director

Mary C. Corder, Editorial Director

Publishing for Consumer Dummies

Diane Graves Steele, Vice President and Publisher

Joyce Pepple, Acquisitions Director

Composition Services

Gerry Fahey, Vice President of Production Services

Debbie Stailey, Director of Composition Services

Contents at a Glance

Table of Contents

Part II: Diving into GRC...*87*

Chapter 4: How Sarbanes and Oxley Changed Our Lives 89

Chapter 5: Fraud, Negligence, and Entropy: What Can Go Wrong and How to Prevent It 105

Part V: The Part of Tens *295*

Chapter 16: Top Ten GRC Strategies 297

Chapter 17: Ten Best Practices in Global Trade 305

Introduction

GRC is an acronym that may be Greek to the uninitiated, but chances are if you picked up this book, you are at least interested in knowing what it means. And even if not everyone knows what GRC means, the concepts involved are ones that everyone understands.

The G is governance. In short, this means taking care of business, making sure that things are done according to your standards (and those of the ever-present regulators, not to mention your company's Board of Directors). It also means setting forth clearly your expectations of what should be done so that everyone is on the same page with regard to how your company is run.

The R is risk. Everything we do involves an element of risk. When it comes to running across freeways or playing with matches, it's pretty clear that certain risks are just not to be taken. When it comes to business, however, risk becomes a way to help you both protect value (what you have) and create value (by strategically expanding your business or adding new products and services).

The C is what everyone knows about — compliance with the many laws and directives affecting businesses (and citizens) today. One of the authors of this book would also like to extend that C to controls, meaning that you put certain controls in place to ensure that compliance is happening. This might mean monitoring your factory's emissions or ensuring that your import and export papers are in order. Or it might just simply mean that the same person is not creating vendors and cutting checks to her brother-in-law Frank on the sly. The C relates to laws as familiar as Sarbanes-Oxley (SOX) or as emergent as Europe's REACH (if we've got you on that one, see Chapter 12).

But when you put it all together, GRC turns out to be not just what you have to do to take care of business, but a paradigm to help you grow your business in the best possible way and — even more — to figure out what that way is.

About This Book

When we decided to write a book about GRC, we thought about writing a book for experts, a thought-leadership book. And although this book is no slouch in the area of thought-leadership (if we do say so ourselves), we decided that what was needed the most was a way to start the conversation about GRC. What are you doing, in terms of governance, risk, and compliance? What should you be doing? And do you know that it's a much bigger picture than you realize, encompassing areas like sustainability and dovetailing very nicely with developing and executing your key business strategies?

That's why this book was originally going to be called *GRC For Dummies*. But (as you can see by the title), it's *SAP GRC For Dummies*. That's a bit of a misnomer because unlike classics like *SAP NetWeaver for Dummies*, this book is not all about SAP software. It's mainly about GRC. But SAP has leading software for GRC, so at the end of relevant chapters, we tell you about products like SAP GRC Risk Management and how it can help you. This book could have been all about SAP GRC, easily — there are probably areas that SAP covers that you don't even know about. (For example, we bet you didn't know that SAP is a leader in the area of software for environmental management.) But just a disclaimer before we start—there's a lot more to learn about SAP GRC than we cover in this book. We focus on giving you the background to get started conceptually in the most important areas.

Now that we've explained a bit about the book, are you ready to get started and to become well-versed in GRC? That way, if you need a conversation stopper for Aunt Ida at Thanksgiving — or, better, a conversation starter when talking to almost anyone about what it takes to succeed in business today — you'll be prepared.

Foolish Assumptions

In writing this book, we made a few assumptions. If you fit one of these assumptions, this book is for you:

- ✔ You're interested in GRC from a corporate perspective. You can think about GRC from an individual perspective (paying your taxes, protecting your identity, and balancing your checkbook, for example), but this book talks about how to use GRC to improve your company, not your household.

- ✔ You have some background in common business terms like profit and loss and common accounting terms such as general ledger and purchase order.

- ✔ You're not adverse to acronyms. GRC can be a little like alphabet soup at times. For clarity, we provide a glossary to help you find your way through the more obscure TLAs (three-letter acronyms).

How This Book Is Organized

To help you get a better picture of what this book has to offer, we explain a little about how we organized it and what you can expect to find in each part.

Part 1: Governance, Risk, and Compliance Demystified

You need to have a good foundation in place to see how GRC can help you. Part I starts out with the ABCs of GRC to give you the big picture and then heads straight into risk and governance to round out your education.

Part 11: Diving into GRC

The C in GRC is for compliance, and Part II takes you through some of the regulations companies must comply with and the corporate scandals that led to those regulations. Once you know about them, what do you do about them? This part also addresses tools like access control and process control that can help you ensure compliance. And, since globalization has brought so many companies into the global trade arena, Part II provides details about the compliance-related issues you need to know about to effectively source goods from or sell goods to other countries.

Part 111: Going Green

Saving the planet is on everyone's minds these days, and it's not just good policy—it's good business, too. Part III addresses how you can ensure that your company's policies about people, processes, and products keep you compliant with the law and enable you to deepen your company's shade of green.

Part 1V: Managing the Flow of Information

GRC is strategic. It can provide you with new insights into how to run your business. Part IV first delves into the flow of information in the enterprise from an IT GRC perspective, ensuring that data is kept secure and private, for example. It then turns to the important area of sustainability reporting, the nonfinancial reporting that more and more companies are doing and which is so important to a variety of stakeholders, from employees to investors to nongovernment organizations such as Greenpeace. Finally, and perhaps most importantly, Part IV addresses how you can use what you learn about your company through a program of integrated GRC to help you envision and execute the best possible corporate strategy.

Part V: The Part of Tens

Maybe the Part of Tens are your favorite part in any *For Dummies* book (we always look for them). Here you'll find best practices for GRC implementation and best practices for global trade. You'll also find pointers to resources to help you in your quest to become an expert in the area of GRC, from books to blogs to web sites.

Glossary

As you read this book (or skip from chapter to chapter, section to section, looking over only those parts that interest you), you may have additional questions in some areas. That's why we include a comprehensive glossary, chock full of definitions of the many terms that you're likely to encounter as you learn more about GRC.

Icons Used in This Book

To help you get the most out of this book, we use icons that tell you at a glance if a section or paragraph has important information of a particular kind.

 This icon indicates information that is more technical in nature, and not strictly necessary for you to read. If technical jargon gives you a headache, feel free to skip these.

 When you see this icon, you know we're offering advice or shortcuts to quickly improve your understanding of GRC concepts.

 Look out! This is something tricky or unusual to watch for.

 This icon marks important GRC stuff you should file away in your brain, so don't forget it.

Where to Go from Here

If you're new to SAP GRC or GRC in general, your next step is to head straight to Chapter 1, which gives you the ABCs of GRC, as well as providing food for thought about what GRC can do for you.

If you're a professional in a particular area — such as global trade, risk management, or IT governance — you could decide to visit particular chapters in no particular order. But (and we're probably biased) we think the best way forward from here is straight into Chapter 1 (with a few intervening pages to entertain you on your way there).

Part I

Governance, Risk, and Compliance Demystified

The 5th Wave   By Rich Tennant

"We've got a machine over there that monitors our quality control. If it's not working, just give it a couple of kicks."

In this part . . .

You start your GRC education with the ABCs of GRC. Even if you're a GRC expert, Chapter 1 gives you the panoramic view of how GRC can help you run your business better. You then move into the all-important area of risk — nothing ventured, nothing gained. You find out that properly managing risk is one of the most important factors for business success today. And to put those management strategies into practice systematically, Chapter 3 lays a solid governance foundation, uncovering what governance means and all its implications.

Chapter 1

The ABCs of GRC

Governance, Risk, and Compliance, almost always referred to as GRC, is the latest addition to the parade of three-letter acronyms that are used to describe the processes and software that run the business world. The goal of GRC is to help a company efficiently put policies and controls in place to address all its compliance obligations while at the same time gathering information that helps proactively run the business. Done properly, GRC creates a central nervous system that helps you manage your business more effectively. You also derive a competitive advantage from understanding risks and choosing opportunities wisely. In other words, GRC helps you make sure that you do things the right way: It keeps track of what you are doing and raises an alert when things start to go off track or when risks appear.

This opening chapter takes you on a top-to-bottom tour of GRC to help you understand in greater detail what GRC means and what companies are doing to lower the costs and create new value.

Getting to Know GRC

GRC is not just about complying with requirements for one quarter or one year. Rather, those who are serious about GRC, meaning just about everyone these days, seek to create a system and culture so that compliance with external regulations, enforcement of internal policies, and risk management are automated as much as possible and can evolve in an orderly fashion as business and compliance needs change. That's why some would say that the C in GRC should stand for controls: controls that help make the process of compliance orderly and make process monitoring — and improvement — easier.

Some parts of the domain of GRC — measures to prevent financial fraud, for example — are as old as business itself. Making sure that money isn't leaking out of a company and ensuring that financial reports are accurate have always been key goals in most businesses—only recently have they attained new urgency.

Other parts of GRC related to trade compliance, risk management, and environmental, health, and safety regulations are somewhat newer activities that have become more important because of globalization, security concerns, and increased need to find and mitigate risks. For example, to ship goods overseas, you must know that the recipient is not on a list of prohibited companies. These lists change daily. Growing concern about global warming and other pressures to reduce environmental impact and use energy efficiently have increased regulations that demand reporting, tracking, and other forms of sociopolitical compliance. Companies are also interested in sustainability reporting, measuring areas such as diversity in the workplace, the number of employees who volunteer, and environmental efforts, so that companies can provide data about corporate social responsibility. Financial markets punish companies that report unexpected bad news due to poor risk management.

One simple goal of GRC is to keep the CFO out of jail, but that description is too narrow to capture all of the activity that falls under the umbrella of GRC. (It's also an exaggeration; the truth is that simple noncompliance is more likely to result in big fines rather than a long trip to the big house. But, that said, most executives prefer to leave no stone unturned rather than risk breaking rocks in the hot sun.) Most companies now face demands from regulators, shareholders, and other stakeholders. Financial regulations like Sarbanes-Oxley (SOX) in the United States and similar laws around the world mean that senior executives could face criminal penalties if financial reports have material errors. (For more on Sarbanes-Oxley, flip ahead to Chapter 4.) All of this means a lot more testing and checking, which is costly without some form of automation.

If GRC seems like a sideshow to your main business, remember you can't get out of it, so you might as well make it work for you, not against you. At first, especially in 2004 — the first year in which Sarbanes-Oxley compliance became mandatory — companies frequently engaged in a mad rush, throwing people, auditors, spreadsheets, and whatever resources were required at the problem. Although the rush to comply was heroic, it was far from efficient. Now companies are understanding how to turn GRC activities into an advantage.

The question every company must answer is the following: Will we do the bare minimum to make sure that we stay out of trouble, or can GRC become an opportunity for us to find new ways of running our business better?

Because it is concerned with creating a sustained stream of high-quality information about a business, GRC has a large overlap with Corporate Performance Management (CPM), a topic we cover in greater detail in Chapter 15.

If the burdens of GRC are a cloud, the silver lining is that in learning how to keep track of business in greater depth, GRC activities are transformed from an annoyance to a gateway to an expanded consciousness in a company, which can lead to better performance, reduced costs, and competitive advantage. GRC is part of the natural process of turning strategy into action, monitoring performance, and tracking and managing the risks involved. Choosing to see GRC as an opportunity can mean significant savings in auditing costs, creating new sources of information for improving processes, finding risks earlier, and most of all, avoiding those nasty surprises that spark a punishing reaction in the stock market.

Getting in the Business Drivers' Seat

In some ways, GRC is nothing new: Almost every activity under the bailiwick of GRC has been going on for quite some time in the business world. The segregation of duties that is required by Section 404 of Sarbanes-Oxley has always been part of an auditor's toolkit of recommendations when it comes to preventing fraud. Companies have always been under the obligation to report financial results accurately, to comply and report on their performance with respect to environmental, safety, and trade laws, and to identify risks as early as possible. Every well-run company — whether private or public — puts its own unique self-inflicted policies in place and makes sure that they are being followed. As times change, all of these measures must be updated.

What caused the birth of GRC as an area of focus for companies and those who provide consulting services and software was a perfect storm of urgency about various issues. Consider the following elements of that perfect storm:

- ✔ In the wake of the go-go culture of the Internet investing boom of the late 1990s, massive, systematic fraud was revealed at major companies such as Enron, WorldCom, Adelphi, and others. In many cases, the controls and external forms of scrutiny that were in place to stop such bad behavior had failed for many different reasons, including fraud, conflicts of interest, and other forms of malfeasance.

- ✔ At the same time, the terrorist attacks on September 11, 2001 led to a worldwide tightening of controls on trade, especially with respect to sales of certain types of products or materials that were deemed dangerous if fallen into the wrong hands. For example, ITT shipped night vision goggle components to China and other countries, resulting in a U.S. Department of Justice fine of $100 million.

✔ The third force driving the urgency of GRC is the rising concern about energy consumption and the environment. Instability in the Mideast, scarcity of oil supply due to increased consumption, and lack of new oil discoveries have driven oil prices to record highs. Worries about global warming have caused a new wave of demands for energy efficiency, reductions in environmental impact, and a desire for companies to demonstrate the long-term sustainability of their operations.

Lawmakers around the world awoke to this crisis and felt a burning need to DO SOMETHING! A debate still rages about the wisdom of the governmental response, but there is no mistaking the result: an across-the-board increase of the volume and urgency of compliance activities. But seeing GRC only in terms of Sarbanes-Oxley and financial compliance is a mistake. Although complying with Sarbanes-Oxley and other similar laws that have been enacted worldwide certainly spurred many companies to action, after they got started, companies realized that there was a whole other field of compliance, risk, and governance-related activities that needed to be performed with greater attention and efficiency.

Investors, along with governments and regulators, insurance companies, ratings agencies, and activist stakeholders have also joined in increasing the urgency with respect to transparency and accuracy of information about the company's operations and actions taken to mitigate risks and issues. Stock markets have dealt brutal punishment to companies that report problems with internal controls or other negative surprises. Consider these statistics:

✔ According to a McKinsey Study, investors in North America and Western Europe will pay a premium of 14 percent for companies with good governance, as shown in Figure 1-1.

✔ The difference in stock market value for companies that had good internal controls versus those that did not is 33 percent.

✔ AMR Research predicted that companies would spend $29.9 billion on compliance initiatives in 2007 alone, up 8.5 percent from the previous year, indicating that GRC spending continues to grow as companies cope with the myriad challenges in this area.

All of these forces combined led to the creation of the domain of GRC as companies realized that an ad hoc approach to meeting these demands was too expensive and actually increased risk for the companies because they couldn't mitigate issues they didn't know about.

The difficulty facing most companies right now is not how to meet these GRC challenges — the fact is, the forces that are driving increased attention to GRC are not optional for the most part and companies have no choice but to comply — but rather *how* to comply efficiently in a way that produces benefits. GRC shouldn't be just a cost that does nothing else for your business, but that may become your attitude if you want to be just good enough to barely meet minimum compliance standards.

Investors Reward Good Governance… and Penalize Poor Governance

Investors worldwide will pay a premium of 14% or more for shares in companies with good governance.

14% North America & Western Europe

25% Asia and Latin America

But companies with internal controls deficiencies experienced significant declines in their market caps:

39% Eastern Europe and Africa

McKinsey & Co. Global Investor Survey

Figure 1-1:
Rewards
for good
governance.

2004 Disclosure Examples: Company/Market Value		Disclosure	% / Mkt Cap Decline
Adecco SA $12.6 billion	Jan. 12	Company delays financial statements. Internal control deficiencies	-38% $4.9 billion
Goodyear Tire & Rubber $1.7 billion	Feb. 11	Company has not yet completed the implementation of its plan to improve internal controls	-18% $320m
MCI $5.4 billion	Apr. 29	Material weaknesses – lack of systematci and reliable internal controls	-17% $935m
INVESTORS FINANCIAL $2.9 billion	Oct. 21	Material weakness discovered during review of internal controls	-16% $475m
FLOWSERVE $1.3 billion	Oct. 27	Material weakness in internal controls; two quarterlies overdue	-11% $152m

One way of thinking of GRC is to compare the process of managing a company to driving a car. When you drive a car, you have a certain set of rules that you are expected to abide by. You have to have a driver's license and insurance. Your car must be inspected for compliance with safety and environmental laws. When you are driving, you are encouraged by law enforcement and penalties to drive within speed limits and other restrictions. You may have your own rules about driving, such as never driving while talking on your cell phone in order to be as safe as possible. Other activities such as maintaining the car are up to you and various drivers will have different approaches. Some will change the oil more often than recommended or rotate tires frequently, some will use premium gas, and so on.

What has happened with GRC, to use the driving analogy again, is that the laws for everything related to driving got tighter and more restrictive and the penalties got higher. In addition, the rewards for driving efficiently and safely became much higher. So, you can now figure out how to drive just to keep out of trouble with external watchdogs, or you can figure out how to drive in a new more efficient way that better helps your business win in the marketplace, while still playing by all the rules.

GRC is a new management mentality. The bad news is that more work is required to comply with regulations. More testing and controls have to be in place and the organization has to be carefully designed. As exceptions to policies occur, behavior must be checked and monitored. As people are promoted or job descriptions change, controls must be put in place so that compliance can be maintained. New forms of data must be captured and consulted. Risks must be proactively discovered while they are still small enough to manage. Without a doubt, this brave new world requires more work, and there is a shortage of trained people and expertise to carry it out.

The upside of GRC is that in addressing these issues systematically, the culture and performance of a company improves. In many ways, GRC is concerned with meta processes, which are those that look at the shape and flow of information in other processes in order to identify weak points. Controls and compliance are only one result of GRC: They put the C in GRC, if you will. When properly addressed, GRC helps identify ways that core business processes can be improved. Identification of risks also leads to discovery of opportunities. Governance processes can help create orderly ways to evolve a company, and improve program and change management across the board.

Getting Motivated to Make the Most of GRC

Although concern about GRC is growing, most companies that have engaged in a program of GRC are usually reacting to some pressure or concern that takes GRC from a necessary evil to an initiative that can really benefit the company if is executed thoroughly and efficiently. A serious approach to GRC may flow from any or all of these motivating forces that we discuss in the following sections.

Complying with financial regulations

New laws in the United States and in many other countries mean that if serious errors in financial reports are found, those responsible will face criminal prosecution. Section 302 of Sarbanes-Oxley says exactly this, and prosecutors around the nation have shown great eagerness to enforce this law.

It is not just American companies that are facing such dramatic penalties. See the "A global reaction to improve governance" sidebar later in this chapter for more on changes to GRC laws in other countries around the world. Governments of most of the largest economies have passed their own forms of legislation increasing the level of scrutiny about financial reporting and controls.

The driving force behind this regulation is the fear that inaccurate financial reporting will damage the financial system. Without accurate financial information, investors will have little to go on when making decisions about where

The march of the three-letter acronyms

The world of enterprise software has given birth to many Three-Letter Acronyms, called appropriately by yet another three-letter acronym: TLA. Here is a sample of the most common TLAs:

✔ Enterprise Resource Planning (ERP) software emerged in the 1990s to provide a complete financial model of a business along with tracking many other aspects. ERP was about closing the books faster and tracking the key financial and management processes of a business.

✔ Customer Relationship Management (CRM) software emerged in the late 1990s to give a name to software that tracked sales, service, billing, and other activities related to customer interactions with a business. CRM was about getting closer to the customer.

✔ Supply Chain Management (SCM) software emerged in the 1990s to track the flow of goods and manufacturing processes among a distributed network of partners working together. SCM helped manage increased specialization, outsourcing, and globalization.

✔ Product Lifecycle Management (PLM) software emerged in the 1990s to give a name to the processes related to creating new products, bringing them to market, and improving them. PLM was about helping increase the speed of product development.

✔ Governance, Risk, and Compliance (GRC) software emerged in the 2000s to automate controls to facilitate compliance with financial, environmental, health, and safety, and trade regulations, enforce internal controls, increase the efficiency of audits, identify risks, and employ proper governance procedures to keep all of these activities up to date and effective.

to place their money. If confidence drops too far, all companies, not just those who have engaged in bad behavior, will find it harder and more expensive to raise money. This is not the first time that such fears have been raised and reporting requirements have been tightened. Even the powerful tycoons of the Robber Baron era had bankers insisting on better accounting.

So, while compliance with regulations aimed at improving financial reporting and governance is really just one piece of the puzzle when it comes to GRC, fears related to such compliance are clearly the force that has driven most companies to action.

Failing an audit

There is nothing like failing an audit to spur companies to improve their GRC processes. In the wake of a failed audit, which must be reported in public financial statements, investors frequently lose confidence and sell stock.

Nowadays, audits can fail for more reasons than ever. Discovery of fraud or other bad behavior is of course the most dramatic reason. But in the face of tighter regulations for governance and reporting, audit problems can include the lack of adequate controls, improper segregation of duties, insufficient oversight of the creation of financial reports, and many other causes. So even if nothing is wrong, you can fail your audit for not having sufficient documentation.

In the wake of a failed audit, reporting requirements skyrocket. Controls, which are detailed reports of various types of activity that must be cross-checked for problems, may have to be run on a monthly or quarterly basis instead of annually. New controls are usually introduced. Other sorts of testing to discover problems will also usually result. The work related to all of this new activity must be staffed either from inside a company or by personnel from an auditing or consulting firm. Either way, costs rise.

A global reaction to improve governance

Everyone talks about Sarbanes-Oxley (SOX), but it's certainly not the only law shaping governance today. Numerous countries have enacted legislation to improve governance. As with the United States, many of these countries have passed legislation in response to the outcry over corporate scandals. Although they differ by name, the laws passed by various countries have similarities, namely with regard to establishing internal controls and effecting improved financial reporting:

✔ **Japan: J-SOX:** On June 7, 2006, Japanese legislators passed the Financial Instruments and Exchange Law, part of which includes the so-called J-SOX requirements. The two main components of the J-SOX legislation are the "Evaluation of and Reporting on Internal Control for Financial Reports," which forces management to assume responsibility for developing and operating internal controls, and the "Audit of Internal Control for Financial Reports," in which a company's external auditor, aside from its regular auditing duties, must conduct an audit of management's evaluation of the effectiveness of internal control for financial reports. The J-SOX requirements took effect starting in April 2008.

✔ **Canada: Bill 198:** Bill 198, also known as C-SOX, became effective on October 1, 2003. Its formal name is "Keeping the Promise for a strong Economy Act (Budget Measures), 2002." This bill requires companies to "[create and] maintain a system of internal controls related to the effectiveness and efficiency of their operations, including financial reporting and asset control." It also requires companies to place internal controls over their disclosure procedures.

✔ **Australia: CLERP 9 in Australia:** In 2001, Australia passed the Corporations Act, which governs corporate law. In 2004, a reform to the Corporations Act was passed, called the Corporate Law Economic Reform Program (Audit Reform & Corporate Disclosure) Act 2004 (or CLERP 9). CLERP 9 aims to make sure that business regulation is consistent with promoting a strong economy, in addition to providing a framework that helps businesses adapt to change. Three entities were created by CLERP 9: The Financial Reporting Council, the Australian Stock Exchange's Corporate Governance Council, and the Shareholder and Investors Advisory Council.

✔ **England: Combined Code of Corporate Governance:** In England, as in many other countries, legislation has been enacted as a response to corporate scandal. Two of the most famous scandals were Polly Peck and Maxwell of the late '80s and early '90s. These scandals led to the creation of quite a few reports that dealt with many governance issues. One of these reports, the Hampel Report, led to the Combined Code of Corporate Governance (1998). Some of the areas the Combined Code covers are the structure and operations of a company's board, its directors' pay, accountability and audit, and the responsibilities of institutional shareholders.

✔ **India: Clause 49:** Clause 49 went into effect in December 2005. Its main goal is to improve corporate governance for all companies listed on India's Stock Exchange. Clause 49 focuses on issues that are already implemented in many other countries, such as establishing a board of directors and appointing a managing director who reports to the board, in addition to the creation of an audit committee. A revised Clause 49 was released on October 9, 2004. This revision covers many areas, including a clarification and enhancement of the responsibilities of the board and the director and a consolidation of the roles of the audit committee as they relate to controls and financial reporting.

The rising costs that occur after a failed audit are a powerful motivator for a company to automate its GRC processes so that controls and testing are much easier and cheaper.

Experiencing a rude awakening

Another sort of inspiration for improved GRC performance comes in the form of outside scrutiny. When auditors come in and start asking questions, sometimes companies discover that they don't really have their GRC issues under control after all. Usually this happens because people do not deeply understand the demands that laws and regulations are placing on them or the complexity of meeting those demands using their current software systems.

Scrutiny can also come from senior management, the board of directors, new employees, auditors, and so on. The problem with GRC and the reason that it has become a new TLA is that it can be hard and complicated to get right. Companies that lack the knowledge and expertise may think they are safe when they actually are not.

Going from private to public

The imminent conversion of a company from a private form of ownership to a public form can be another driver of increased attention to GRC. An Initial Public Offering (IPO), in which a company sells stock to the public for the

Jail, schmail

The drumbeat of GRC consultants stating that "we'll keep you out of jail" has too long defined the conversation about GRC. It's time for a reality check.

Jail is a remedy for people who are engaged in criminal activity. But if you're entering a GRC program to stay out of jail, you're missing the point. The point of GRC is to run your business better, expand your consciousness of what is going on, and provide employees with guidance about what they should be doing and to find out when they're not doing it.

You can apply that knowledge to all sorts of areas: governance, risk, compliance, trade, environmental, data privacy, and much more. If you do it right, GRC can help you run your business better than ever before, gain competitive advantage, and increase the rewards to you and your shareholders.

From a shareholder perspective, which is worse: a CEO going to jail or an entire company running itself on stale data?

first time, is a common way for a private company to become a public one. But other events such as selling bonds or issuing other forms of debt can also initiate the same requirements to meet higher levels of reporting.

Private companies also seek to improve their GRC processes if they may be up for sale to public companies that have to meet more stringent levels of governance and reporting. Whether you're looking at a merger or acquisition or taking a company public, having all the ducks in a row, so to speak, can make the acquisitions process much smoother and can also make the difference between controlling the timing of an IPO or playing catch-up to try to get things in order.

On the other hand, even private companies can benefit from implementing the best practices highlighted by SOX. Private companies with government contracts get a favorable reaction from the government when they implement best practices based on SOX. There's certainly no harm in improving internal controls and corporate governance, and the benefits can be very real both in terms of clean financials and process efficiencies.

Managing growth

Smaller companies that are on a dramatic growth curve frequently use a GRC implementation as a way to make sure that as new employees are quickly hired, threats to the organization's financial health do not occur. With appropriate controls and tests, management can rest assured that the company is not at risk as more new people take over key tasks.

Smaller companies generally have more issues with segregation of duties for obvious reasons. Segregation of duties requires dividing key steps among employees to help prevent fraud that could take place if one person did all the tasks. But with fewer employees, there is less specialization and a single person may be doing many more tasks than in a larger company.

One common misunderstanding is that implementing GRC means that all potential conflicts are eliminated. Even in the largest companies, this is almost never the case. Usually, some employees are able to do things that might result in fraud. Such potential conflicts can be handled by adding controls and tests that reveal any bad behavior.

Taking out an insurance policy

When new owners arrive to take over a company, implementing GRC is one common way to make sure that everything is operating properly and that nothing fraudulent is taking place. GRC is like added insurance for the new owners: Adding the controls and testing that is part of a thorough GRC implementation provides added assurance that the financial management of a company is taking place in a proper way and that the condition of the company is accurately conveyed by its accounting reports.

Managing risk

Companies that have had a series of nasty surprises often improve GRC processes and automation as a way to create an early warning system to identify and manage potential operational risks. Unforeseen risks can lead to punishment in the markets as investors worry about what problems might be next.

As this chapter has noted, it is a mistake to think of GRC only in financial terms. Risks that have dire financial consequences can arise from a multitude of operational factors that never show up on a balance sheet. For example, in a manufacturing plant, what if spare parts inventory for a key piece of equipment drops to dangerously low levels? If someone notices this, how can they go on record to make sure that the significance of the risk is understood and that management knows that something must be done to avoid a huge problem? The risk management processes of GRC provide just such a solution.

Reducing costs

The desire to cut costs related to GRC is another major driver of GRC automation. In the mad rush to comply with Sarbanes-Oxley in 2004, many compliance activities were performed manually. Information was gathered, organized in spreadsheets or other simple ways, and then used to make sure that the company was complying with all requirements.

While this sort of manual work was inevitable the first time around, and perhaps even beneficial in that it gave those involved a hands-on understanding of what sort of work needed to be done and information needed to be assembled, it was not efficient.

Given the shortage of personnel trained in GRC and the expense of using external consultants and auditors to perform reporting and analysis related to controls and testing, many companies are seeking to implement GRC as a way to increase automation and cut costs. Some companies have reported reductions in auditing costs of more than 20 percent.

Struggling with the high volume of compliance

Risk goes way beyond financials and so does compliance. Globalization means that goods may be sourced from just about anywhere and shipped anywhere, and the compliance requirements for moving these goods are significant: each cross-border trade can involve as many as 25 different parties and generate 35 documents that must be tracked and saved. Furthermore, security issues have made the "anywhere" part of this more difficult as well; there are about 50 denied persons lists — lists of undesirable persons and companies that governments forbid shipping goods to — that must be checked before goods are shipped.

Environmental regulations are also increasingly the focus of compliance. The number of environmental regulations companies must comply with is constantly growing, both at the state and national level, particularly relating to hazardous substances. In many cases, the sheer volume of compliance activities forces automation because no other approach is feasible.

Introducing the GRC Stakeholders

No matter what the motivators and how much automation you may apply, the essence of GRC is to change the hearts and minds of the people in a company. The responsibility for GRC enforcement and implementation is spread across a variety of different stakeholders, each of which plays an important role. Understanding the interactions between these stakeholders is a key element of a successful program of GRC improvement.

GRC stakeholders inside a company

Like every other major trend affecting business, increased attention to GRC concerns is having its effect on the organizational chart. Of course, the ultimate responsibility for all corporate issues resides with the board of directors and the CEO, and then devolves down through the organization. At most companies, the operational responsibility for implementing a program for improving GRC performance resides with the COO or CFO. The consequences of inadequate attention to GRC processes are so extreme that interest from senior management is at an all-time high.

The need for effective management of GRC has led to the creation of a new set of titles that may include any of the following:

- ✔ Chief Compliance Officer, Vice President of Compliance
- ✔ Chief Risk Officer, Vice President of Risk
- ✔ Chief Sustainability Officer, Vice President of Sustainability
- ✔ Manager of
    - SOX
    - Compliance
    - Risk
    - Sustainability
    - Trade Management
    - Environment, Health, and Safety

Some analysts recommend that companies keep any organization dedicated to GRC as small as possible. From this point of view, GRC should be something for which every line of business is responsible. The creation of a separate department dedicated to GRC is an invitation to empire building. After a department dedicated to any specific purpose is created, it tends to grow. The ideal way to implement GRC is to make compliance efficient and easy through controls, training, and automation so that improved business processes make the process easy, a part of everyone's day-to-day work, instead of creating a large cost center.

GRC stakeholders outside a company

Investors and shareholders have perhaps the most to lose monetarily from failures of GRC processes. When a stock price drops after a company reports an audit failure, a material breach of compliance with regulations, or any other sort of negative event that could have been foreseen, investors are demonstrating their profound concern.

Besides investors, the other important external groups are institutions inside and outside of government that set rules that must be followed. This group includes all of the following types of organizations:

- ✔ Legislative bodies that make laws that must be complied with.

- ✔ Government agencies responsible for carrying out laws, such as OSHA, the EPA, U.S. Customs, and many others.

- ✔ Financial regulators that set standards for financial reporting, such as the Securities Exchange Commission, Financial Accounting Standards Board, Federal Reserve, Bank for International Settlements, and others.

- ✔ Non-governmental Organizations (NGOs) charged with setting policies that govern how business is done, such as the United Nations.

- ✔ Trade organizations such as the World Trade Organization, World Intellectual Property Organization, NAFTA, CAFTA, and others.

- ✔ Auditing firms that certify the correctness of procedures and policies used for financial reports.

This list of stakeholders is constantly changing as new issues arise and new laws and regulations are created to address them.

Understanding GRC by the Letters

So far in this chapter, we've treated GRC like a large black box: a mysterious container full of improved processes and software for automation. Now it is time to open that box and look inside at all the moving parts. The challenge in moving to a more detailed discussion of GRC is that the meaning of the terms and the actions required are different depending on the nature of the business. GRC activities at a stock brokerage firm will be quite different from those at a chain of grocery stores, for example, although the goals at the highest level are the same.

This section breaks down GRC into its component parts by looking at the meaning of each of the three words that make up the acronym: *governance*, *risk*, and *compliance*. The challenge here is that these words are general terms as well as terms of art applied to GRC, so we start our discussion by separating the informal meanings of the terms from the precise way these words are used with respect to GRC.

Governance

Governance is a general term. The way that a board of directors works with a CEO is a form of governance, for example. The governance in GRC is that which is exercised by the CEO on down. How are you going to do what you must do to execute on a strategy? How is the CEO making sure that the right policies and procedures are in place to run a company? How are those policies communicated? What sort of checking is done to make sure that the policies and procedures are being followed? How are the policies and procedures updated? What controls are in place? How can methods of checking and confirming that policies are being followed be improved?

Risk

The word *risk* is the trickiest of the three that make up the GRC acronym. All of GRC, for example, can be seen as an exercise in understanding and controlling the risk of running a business. So a program of GRC improvement helps reduce the risk of failing to comply with regulations for financial reporting, trade, environmental protection, or safety. GRC also deals with the risk of not having adequate governance structures to keep a company under control and effectively managed. Every business strategy runs certain risks that can be identified at the outset and must be monitored. There is also the risk of not identifying operational risks that may have significant impact on a business early and dealing with them adequately. The R in GRC includes all these risks, in fact, any risk the business faces.

Compliance

Compliance is the term that has a general meaning that is closest to the way it applies specifically to GRC. Compliance in general means that you are satisfying a set of conditions that has been set forth for you. Compliance implies that someone else has set those conditions up and that you must meet them. That's exactly what's going on in GRC. Most of the time, when people talk about compliance, they are referring to external standards for which compliance is mandatory. The word compliance also sometimes refers to internal standards as well.

Defining the C in GRC as standing for *controls* can broaden the discussion. Compliance is what we have to do, and controls are the way we do it. Furthermore, controls are a way to monitor that the business is compliant, and also efficient and orderly in every way.

Figure 1-2 shows the way that the three core activities of governance, risk management, and compliance interact.

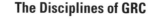

The Disciplines of GRC

Figure 1-2:
Interaction
between
processes
for
governance,
risk, and
compliance.

Figure 1-2 shows GRC from the top down. Governance guidelines, which are the policies and rules of the game for a company that explain how the company will be run to best meet its obligations and pursue the business strategy, are set forth by senior management. The operational executives then carry out programs and put in place controls that ensure compliance, frequently with the help of consultants or auditors who are expert in applying GRC. Risk management results in the creation of mechanisms so that risks can be brought to the attention of senior managers who then take steps to reduce them.

So although Figure 1-2 shows a top-down structure, in most companies, GRC is actually implemented from the bottom up, like this:

1. The company puts in place controls to make sure that compliance requirements are satisfied so that no laws or regulations are violated.

2. After the controls are in place, which may take a year or more to achieve, the next task is to analyze what has been done to make it more efficient and effective and to reduce costs associated with compliance.

    At this stage processes for governance may begin to be developed as internal policies are added to external requirements and the company looks at its compliance activities from the top down.

Risk management processes may be added at any time during this cycle, depending on how worried a company is about risks connected to a particular strategy or about unforeseen risks. With this cycle in mind, in the next few sections, we explain the activities involved in each area of GRC in greater detail. In preschool, you may have learned letters by remembering that A is for apple: The same approach can be taken with GRC. We take the bottom up approach in our explanation and work through the acronym from right to left.

C Is for Compliance: Playing by the Rules

The goal of the compliance process is to make sure that a company meets or exceeds all of the demands that are placed on it by external institutions that make laws and regulations for various purposes. Compliance is also concerned with self-inflicted rules; in other words, policies related to how a company does business. Financial compliance is the one that has gotten the most attention in the past couple of years, but trade management and environmental, health, and safety compliance are also always key concerns. These areas are all interrelated and provide companies a set of guidelines to follow from a perspective of best practices and processes. Each of these areas will be covered in detail later in this section.

Some regulations require that reports of activities are created and may set thresholds for acceptable financial ratios or amounts of emissions, for example. Others require that a company's processes have a certain shape or follow certain guidelines so that certain types of bad behavior become impossible or extremely difficult. But by far the most frequently mandated item from a compliance perspective is the mandate that a company have sufficient controls to detect bad behavior. A complete grasp of what controls are and how they work is key to a complete understanding of GRC.

Controls: Mechanisms of compliance

Controls are the means by which bad behavior or violations of policies are discovered. Controls also provide companies with an alert mechanism for highlighting what processes are working well and which areas need to be improved. By finding out what's working and what's not, companies can optimize all their processes through the enterprise.

Some controls are *preventative*, meaning that they stop you from doing things that are not allowed. Preventative controls are frequently part of access control, which is the discipline of allowing people to have access only to transactions and capabilities that they need to do their jobs and to limit the potential for bad behavior. Access control is key to managing segregation of duties, which is one of the most important mandates of Sarbanes-Oxley. See Chapter 5 for more information about segregation of duties.

Although stopping people from bad behavior is a great idea, preventative controls are too blunt an instrument to enforce complex policies that may prohibit actions that take many steps to complete. Most of the controls that are used to enforce policies in a company are *detective controls*, which analyze what has gone on in a company and reveal policy violations or bad behavior after it has happened. Although in some ways it seems like creating a system that makes bad behavior impossible is preferable, in practice, the processes in a business are too complex and fluid to be automated in such a rigid way. When implementing policies and enforcing them with detective controls, you never stop people from doing what they need to do to keep the business running. You do, however, detect the problems after they occur and then come up with remedies of various sorts to mitigate the problems and prevent them in the future. *Mitigating controls* are those controls that are put in place to fix any problems created by violations of policies. Mitigating controls are descriptions of steps that need to be taken to fix problems.

Detective controls can either be automated or manual. For a *manual control*, someone may have to scour through the logs of various types of activity to find certain types of transactions and record them in a spreadsheet. Then the collected transactions are analyzed to see if any of the transactions have violated a policy. *Automated controls* gather the information and check for the violation automatically. Automated controls can also generate alerts and cases that can be assigned to the appropriate manager for remediation. One of the key methods for making GRC processes more efficient is through the application of automated controls. Given that most companies have around 500 controls in place, improving the efficiency of controls can mean significant savings. (For more on access control, see Chapter 6; turn to Chapter 7 for more on internal controls.)

Controls are determined by the direction provided by corporate governance and risk management and then are applied to the most important processes of the enterprise. One common control is to check the credit of each new customer before doing business with them. A control could take the form of looking at each new customer record and then examining activity to see if a credit check was performed. If new customers have been created without credit checks being performed, a mitigating control may need to be executed, perhaps to perform the credit check after the fact. Then the control may analyze why the credit check was not performed. Perhaps the problem is systematic, resulting from inadequate training, for example. Maybe the people creating new customers did not know that a credit check was required. Perhaps the problem was that the system used to check credit is unreliable so that credit checks cannot always be performed. Whatever the reason, the control can discover a problem that must be dealt with to comply with a policy or regulation.

Some controls are run once a year; for example, to check whether policies for capitalizing equipment are followed. Other controls may be run once a quarter or once a month. One of the things that usually happens when problems are discovered in an audit is that controls are run more frequently. If the controls are manual, this means that someone must be doing a lot more work, which can drive up auditing and personnel costs (and the cost of doing business). Replacing manual controls with automated controls is one way to allow controls to be run more frequently — in some cases, continuously — without large additional costs. That way, if 1 in 100 transactions violates a control, an automated control will catch it every time without incurring the cost of checking the 99 transactions that did not violate the control. A manual control that tests every transaction would find such a problem, but the more common approach — sampling transactions — is unlikely to find needles in haystacks. Automated controls save money, run 100 percent of the time, and allow you to practice exception management.

In the process of designing, applying, and analyzing controls in a business, you develop a deeper understanding of the processes of your business. Problems discovered by controls can lead to the redesign of processes to better meet both business and compliance goals. To get the most out of GRC, the insights gathered in compliance activities must be shared with managers in each department so that compliance can become part of the process of continuous improvement.

Domains of compliance

The sorts of controls just described are used in numerous domains of compliance: financial management, global trade, and environmental, health, and safety. In each of these areas, different external regulators have set forth increasingly complex rules and regulations. Proof of compliance with these regulations may be required in the forms of controls, reports, and certifications to the veracity of reported information. The section below summarizes the sorts of compliance that are required in each area. For much more information, see the following parts of this book:

- ✔ Financial compliance is covered in Part II.
- ✔ Trade management is also covered in Part II.
- ✔ Environmental and safety concerns are covered in Part III.

In addition to these traditional domains of compliance, some newer compliance domains also fall under the GRC umbrella:

- ✔ Privacy regulations
- ✔ Risk management regulations
- ✔ Sustainability
- ✔ Internal policies

In the following sections, we discuss each of these domains in detail.

Financial compliance

Financial compliance these days is dominated by the regulations that have been introduced by Sarbanes-Oxley. Section 302 of the law makes it a crime to certify financial statements that have material errors. Section 404 requires strict segregation of duties to prevent various forms of bad behavior including fraud, inaccurate reporting, and other forms of malfeasance.

Section 302 requires that CEOs and CFOs literally sign on the dotted line on annual and quarterly reports and certify that the information is true. Behind that signature are many other levels of signatures of everyone in the chain of command, stating that they vouch for the numbers they provided for this report. Controls designed to monitor key processes are one of the ways that executives and managers feel comfortable putting their signatures on these reports: Controls help to verify that the numbers are accurate and not inflated.

If a CEO knows that processes like order-to-cash, revenue recognition, and procure-to-pay are all being monitored closely through a comprehensive set of controls, the CEO (and those under him or her) can feel comfortable certifying that there is no fraud or inaccuracies in financial reports. If errors do show up, everyone involved will be more understanding if a full set of compliance and information quality procedures are in place and diligently enforced.

Section 404 is handled through putting access control mechanisms in place. When someone is given access to a computer system, a role is usually assigned to them. That role has a set of permissions that grants that user access to a certain set of transactions. In a modern computer system like SAP ERP, for example, there can be more than 20,000 transactions and more than 100,000 data elements. Each company has hundreds of roles in place. It is impossible to manually check that the roles assigned to any one individual do not grant access that would violate any reasonable segregation of duties schemes. Depending on the nature of a business, a company may have to provide other forms of reporting, such as levels of capital for banks or other indicators of financial health.

Modern GRC systems help automate the process of implementing, running, and analyzing controls, performing segregation of duties checks, and creating regulator reports of all kinds.

Trade management compliance

Compliance with trade management regulations was never simple and has only become more complex in the post-9/11 era. If you're doing business with someone overseas, you must document the answers to the following sorts of questions:

- Who is it acceptable to do business with?
- Which goods can be sent to which countries?
- What are the limits on amount of goods sent to each country or buyer?

✔ What goods qualify under trade agreements?

✔ How must goods be labeled?

✔ What information is required to clear customs?

✔ Is a license required?

✔ Is a letter of credit required?

Each country has its own regulations. For example, worldwide there are approximately 50 different lists of denied persons or companies that countries prohibit sending goods to. Many of these lists change daily. Although U.S. exporters are mainly concerned with the lists of denied persons from a U.S. perspective, best practices state that they should also check the lists for the countries to which they are shipping the goods. Also, governments are starting to use more advanced methods of providing information and are requiring electronic submission of global trade documents. Globalization and outsourcing mean that more and more goods are moving across borders. When products are shipped, regulations of the receiving and sending countries must be satisfied as well as any countries that the goods pass through.

Companies at one time left many of these tasks to the shipping and freight-forwarding companies. But now compliance is so challenging and the penalties so severe that this is less often a viable solution. The latest trade management systems help automate these activities as much as possible through integration with internal systems like ERP (Enterprise Resource Planning) and SCM (Supply Chain Management) and external sources of information.

Environment, health, and safety compliance

Environmental, health, and safety regulations are constantly moving forward as new dangers are identified and new concerns arise. OSHA and the Clean Air Act in the United States, the RoHS act and REACH acts in Europe, and standards for labeling of hazardous materials, are just a small sample of the sort of regulations in effect.

For example, for companies that create and ship hazardous materials, labeling requirements differ throughout the world, as do requirements for the data sheets that accompany such materials.

Risk management compliance

Although laws regarding risk management are not yet mainstream compliance requirements in the U.S., risk management is increasingly becoming a compliance issue as well. Switzerland and Germany already have laws mandating risk management. In the U.S., official recommendations indicate that compliance for risk management may not be far away: the U.S. Amended Sentencing Guidelines state that organizations must take reasonable steps to ensure that their compliance and ethics programs are followed, including monitoring and auditing to detect criminal conduct and to evaluate periodically the effectiveness of their compliance and ethics program. Although risk management is not explicitly stated in the guidelines, what is required to meet them is basically, in fact, a systematic approach to managing and monitoring risks. Also, the Public Company Accounting Oversight Board (PCAOB) and the Securities and Exchange Commission (SEC) recommends a top-down, risk-based approach to organizations' SOX compliance requirements.

Data privacy and security compliance

The problem of identity theft is driving increased regulation as well, both in the areas of data privacy and computer security, which go hand in hand in protecting sensitive data. Regulations are on the rise in this area, whether it's laws regarding how sensitive data must be protected or laws that kick in if a security breach has occurred (for example, the California Security Breach Notification Law). In the healthcare industry, HIPAA has strong implications for how data is handled. The COBIT framework helps companies organize their compliance in this area; Chapter 14 covers the important topic of IT GRC.

Sustainability reporting

A new horizon in this area is the domain of sustainability, which doesn't yet fall in the realm of compliance, but one day might. Companies are increasingly being asked to demonstrate that their operations do not have long-term damaging effects on the planet and that they practice good corporate citizenship. The United Nations releases a list of 230 sustainability indicators that companies may one day be required to report on. Chapter 13 discusses the topic of sustainability.

R Is for Risk: Creating Opportunity

Risk management is the process of uncovering what *could* go wrong for the express purpose of making more things go right. All strategies and all opportunities worth pursuing involve risks that must be monitored and managed. Racecars win not just because of their gas pedal but also because of their brakes, which help drivers deftly maneuver around corners and other obstacles. In the same way, risk management can help companies identify potential pitfalls and thereby optimize their opportunities for success.

Many types of operational risks don't appear on the balance sheet but can have disastrous consequences. Risks in this category include such hazards as

- Environmental catastrophes
- Difficulties with integration of acquisitions
- An aging workforce
- Extreme weather
- Currency fluctuations

✔ Kidnapping

 ✔ Terrorism

For example, if a key supplier is going to be taken over by a competitor, the sooner a company knows about it, the better. Or perhaps, a major customer has indicated they are in big financial trouble and may cut back on orders. Or, what if replacement parts for a critical piece of equipment are no longer being produced? A well-run company has a way for its employees to identify such risks and raise the alarm so that the risks can be prioritized and mitigated.

Unmanaged risks increase the potential for unpleasant surprises. Thinking that risk management is only about catastrophic risks is a mistake. A series of unanticipated smaller risks can have an equally devastating effect, especially if they cause targets for financial performance to be missed, even by a small amount.

Risk management, though it initially sounds negative, has great potential for helping companies maximize their opportunities. Reporting mechanisms to raise alerts about risks may also be used to identify opportunities. When done properly, risk management can be like a crystal ball that helps you get a vision of the future, tweak it according to your strategy, and make that improved vision come true.

G Is for Governance: Keeping Focused and Current

Governance is about the big picture, about steering a company in the right direction and evolving policies, procedures, and processes as needed. Governance is about how you are doing what the strategy of your business demands that you do. Governance is about establishing the larger goals, the top-down perspective that organizes compliance and risk management activities as well as everything else a company does. Governance is also about how the data gathered by GRC processes is analyzed and used to improve a business.

At the highest level, governance is about steering the corporation: making sure that a company is selling the right products in the right markets. Governance exists to translate the strategy set by the board of directors and CEO into the actions that will bring that strategy to life.

The first step most companies take with respect to GRC is to put in place controls that ensure the firm is complying with external requirements. But after that has been accomplished, the sort of self-governance shown in Figure 1-3 becomes an issue.

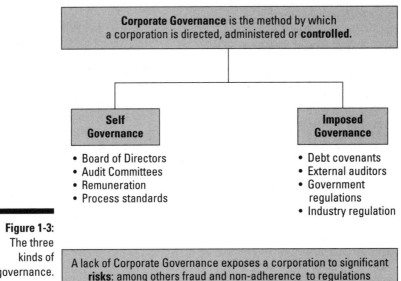

Corporate Governance

Corporate Governance is the method by which a corporation is directed, administered or **controlled.**

Self Governance
- Board of Directors
- Audit Committees
- Remuneration
- Process standards

Imposed Governance
- Debt covenants
- External auditors
- Government regulations
- Industry regulation

A lack of Corporate Governance exposes a corporation to significant **risks**: among others fraud and non-adherence to regulations

Figure 1-3:
The three kinds of governance.

Self-governance means adding policies, procedures, and controls to enforce them to those already imposed by external parties. Self-governance helps create a continuous feedback loop of information to improve the operations of a company and to make sure that any important operational processes take place as desired by the board and CEO.

One of the most important governance activities is to look at the existing set of controls for both imposed and self-imposed governance and ensure that they have the proper scope and effect. In performing this analysis, a company frequently gains insights into how to redesign its processes to increase efficiency and better align them to corporate goals. After new ideas for improvements have been discovered, they must be implemented in order to take effect. In other words, governance, when properly implemented, helps guide the evolution of a company. For this reason, there is a natural link between governance and program management.

Hitting the Audit Trail

Increased attention to GRC has been a boon for auditing firms as companies have hired them to help make sure they are complying with Sarbanes-Oxley and other regulations. Auditors have been asked to help design and implement controls and to perform other forms of testing to ensure compliance.

Most auditing activity involves examining the transactional record of a company that is kept in various sorts of audit trails that record corporate activity. When this work is performed manually, it can take an enormous amount of time to carry out. One of the goals of most GRC improvement programs is to automate as many controls as possible, which means that audits can become more efficient. This can mean a reduction in certain kinds of auditing fees, but it also means that auditors can spend more time on higher-value activities. With more automation, the costs of audits drop but the benefits of audits rise.

Designing Your Approach to GRC

Each company approaches GRC differently depending on its needs and circumstances. Some firms find that focusing on compliance is all they want to tackle. Firms in this group may not have trade management or environmental, health, and safety problems to deal with and may feel that their existing processes for identifying risks are working adequately. Other companies may feel they have a good collection of compliance processes in place already and just want to improve their risk management.

But no matter where a company started from and where it is at now with respect to its GRC processes, the cost of compliance is large and growing. Some analysts estimate that companies spend $1 million on compliance for every $1 billion in revenue. Eventually, the board of directors and CEO will want to reduce GRC costs, or maybe another of the motivators we mentioned earlier in this chapter kicks in. That's when a program of GRC improvement begins.

After the rush to clean up

The most common pattern that leads to a desire to reduce GRC costs was caused by the rush to comply with Sarbanes-Oxley in 2004 (see Figure 1-4).

Growing imperative to achieve process-oriented improvements and automation

Year One	Year Two	Year Three and Beyond
• Comply at whatever cost	• Focus on cost reduction and control rationalization	• Automate to reduce burden

Figure 1-4: The phases of GRC adoption.

✔ In 2004, companies went through the sprint phase. Risks were identified and managed with appropriate controls. Roles and user access were cleaned up.

✔ In 2005, the marathon phase began. Companies focused on staying clean and lowering the costs of compliance.

✔ In 2006 and beyond, companies started to focus on automation to bring costs down to the lowest level possible.

Another, no doubt oversimplified, way of putting it is that companies rushed to get clean regardless of cost, and then sought to stay clean as cheaply as possible.

Stages of GRC adoption

Observers and analysts watching the progression of GRC adoption have identified four stages of growth and maturity that companies move through as they improve their GRC processes: reacting, anticipating, collaborating, and orchestrating. As shown in Figure 1-5, the first step is *reacting*, which is the rush to get things done.

The second step, where most companies are now, involves *anticipating* needs and increasing automation. The third step involves higher levels of *collaboration* in which GRC awareness is propagated throughout an organization. In the fourth phase of GRC adoption, a company seeks to better *orchestrate* and optimize its activities based on greater visibility.

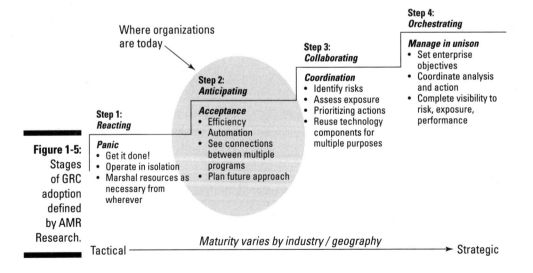

Figure 1-5: Stages of GRC adoption defined by AMR Research.

As companies grow in their maturity, they cut costs for compliance and auditing, increase the scope of activities that are monitored by GRC processes, and make better use of existing systems for GRC purposes.

What GRC Solutions Provide

Companies have found that the ad hoc approach that was used in the sprint to get clean is expensive and unwieldy. Manual processes that use spreadsheets to gather and analyze information work to establish compliance, but drive costs up as the same manual work is repeated again and again. Executing controls through armies of testers has the same problem. With an ad hoc approach, there is no common repository for GRC information and little benefit from GRC activities. An integrated approach to GRC allows for risks from one side of the business to be reviewed by the other side, helping to quickly build a corporate knowledge base of best practices. The benefits of an integrated approach to GRC can best be accrued by implementing an integrated GRC solution.

For example, sometimes companies briefly give super-user control of their systems to people who otherwise don't have that level of access, perhaps for year-end processing or because key personnel are on leave. Such access must be tracked and later carefully revoked. The ad hoc approach to access control can get you clean, but it doesn't keep you clean: It's hard to remember to revoke that access after the stress of year-end processing has passed. Smaller companies take the approach of having their audit partners run a one-time testing to identify access control risks annually. The problem is that this provides only a snapshot, and without a GRC solution to help monitor this on a day-to-day basis, problems may go unnoticed for nearly a year before they are uncovered.

Vendors of GRC software such as SAP have created products that are aimed at making GRC processes as efficient and inexpensive as possible. Companies are increasingly adopting GRC solutions because doing so saves money through automation and provides a consistent context for management of GRC processes. Using GRC software is especially advantageous in today's environment in which there is a shortage of people with GRC skills and experience.

GRC solutions provide a common language and ready-made policies and controls that are built to work with the systems you have in place. A large part of the value of GRC systems comes from the content that such solutions provide. For example, a good global trade solution should come with real-time checks of denied parties lists and a way to generate the proper customs documentation to ensure that goods cross borders as quickly as possible.

Integrated GRC systems not only have a system for managing access control but they also have rules that take into account the thousands of specific transactions inside an ERP system so that segregation of duties conflicts can be avoided. In addition, GRC systems not only have systems for automating the collection of information and the analysis of that information for controls, but they come with a large set of commonly needed controls that are ready to implement.

Perhaps the largest benefit of GRC systems is that they come with a step-by-step approach of the sort shown in Figure 1-6 that is proven through the experience gathered at numerous companies.

The general approach of one component of SAP's solution, SAP GRC Process Control, is to follow these steps:

1. **Document the control environment.**

   What are you doing? What are your processes? Where are the risks?

2. **Test: Implement the process and access controls needed to address the risks identified.**

3. **Remediate: Resolve exceptions found by the controls.**

4. **Analyze: Use the information gathered to gain a deeper understanding of the business.**

5. **Optimize: Improve both GRC and business processes as insights are gathered.**

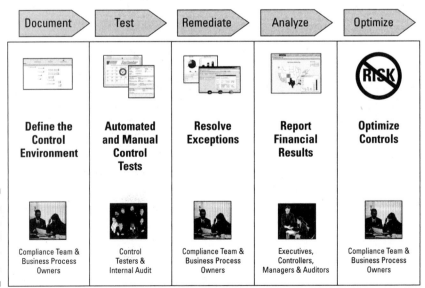

Figure 1-6: The steps to GRC implementation.

Systematic application of a GRC solution leads to a process that constantly deepens management's understanding of what is going on in a business and increases their confidence that risks are being managed. Figure 1-7 shows how this leads to a closed-loop system of constant improvement of GRC processes.

With such a process of continuous improvement in place, companies get the most important benefit that they are seeking from GRC—the peace of mind that comes from knowing that financial information is accurate, risks are being managed, regulations are being complied with, and that the probability of nasty surprises is as low as it can be.

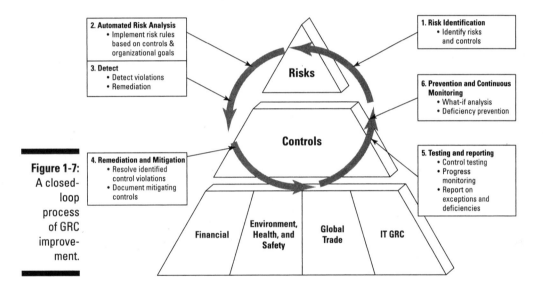

Figure 1-7:
A closed-loop process of GRC improvement.

2. **Automated Risk Analysis**
  • Implement risk rules based on controls & organizational goals

3. **Detect**
  • Detect violations
  • Remediation

4. **Remediation and Mitigation**
  • Resolve identified control violations
  • Document mitigating controls

1. **Risk Identification**
  • Identify risks and controls

6. **Prevention and Continuous Monitoring**
  • What-if analysis
  • Deficiency prevention

5. **Testing and reporting**
  • Control testing
  • Progress monitoring
  • Report on exceptions and deficiencies

Risks

Controls

Financial | Environment, Health, and Safety | Global Trade | IT GRC

Chapter 2

Risky Business: Turning Risks into Opportunities

Risk is a fact of life. No matter what your plans are, whether it's crossing the street, going on vacation, or buying a subsidiary — risk is inevitably involved. However, not all risk is bad. Effective risk management can allow you to protect the value that you've worked to build within your organization and can also allow you to create new value by identifying opportunities to build growth, increase competitive advantage, and drive efficiencies throughout your organization.

In this chapter, we talk about risk in a new way and discuss how you can use risk management to both protect value and create new value. This new approach to risk management enables you to embed a strategic risk methodology across your enterprise, at all levels, from operational management, to line of business owners, risk managers, and senior executives and directors. This approach to risk management can help enhance performance and innovation for new products, new processes, and new strategies and can allow risk to become an additional driver of business change.

Discovering Enterprise Risk Management

Enterprise risk management provides a framework for your business to identify your risks and decide which risks are likely to happen and what the associated impact will be for your business. By managing this type of information, you can better protect the value that you have created across your business because you are more aligned with your risks and can mitigate the potential impact of those risks.

Enterprise risk management also allows you to become more strategic and proactive about how your business operates. By using technology to track, monitor, and even model key risk indicators directly against business performance, you can begin to implement change across the enterprise to increase efficiency and improve business processes. This can lead not only to cost savings and an improved bottom line, but also to a higher degree of performance within your business, and a higher level of competitiveness within your industry.

In Chapter 1, we talked a bit about compliance and how you can make sure that you're following all the laws that apply to businesses. By complying with laws, you avoid fines and ensure that your business processes and policies are effectively implemented. Profits increase because fraud is eliminated, or at least detected and remedied quickly. In a sense, compliance — the C in GRC — is nonnegotiable: You have to make sure that you do the things that you have to in order to comply with regulations that govern your business.

The R in GRC, for Risk, is more strategic and its potential impact on the bottom line is greater as well. With effective risk management, you can both help *protect* value — your brand name, your quarterly earnings, your sales — and *create* value, evaluating the impact of risk on strategy execution as well as finding new opportunities and evaluating them from a risk-intelligent perspective. How you manage risk can literally revolutionize the way you run your business. The R in GRC is sometimes seen as optional, after all, we have to comply, and we have to govern well in order to comply. Not everyone realizes that managing risk is every bit as important. As we discuss in this chapter, risk management is far from optional. In today's environment, evaluating everything from a risk-intelligent perspective can help you win against the competition and protect your brand at a time when news travels around the world at the speed of light. And because risk management takes into account what could go wrong, your risk-adjusted strategy has a much greater chance of being executed effectively.

Defining Risk

Risk is typically defined as the potential for loss caused by an event that can adversely affect the achievement of a company's objectives. That's true enough, but it's only part of the story. Risk awareness can also inform strategy, helping companies select the opportunities to pursue that are most likely to succeed and that offer the most bang for the buck. That's why we say that risk can both help you protect value — protect what you've got — and create value — help you figure out the best way for your business to go in the future.

Figure 2-1 lists some types of risks that businesses should think about. Now that we've got you uptight about risk, don't worry: In this chapter, we also lead you through some ways to deal with these risks. Thinking about them may seem like courting failure, but it is in fact one of the best ways to improve your chances of success.

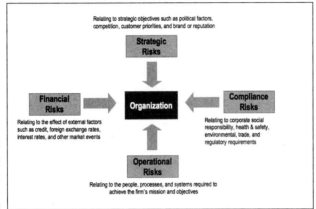

Figure 2-1:
Classes
of risk.

Although some of the risks illustrated in Figure 2-1 might be considered negative, keep in mind that some risks can also result from success. You could have a product launch where demand is much greater than anticipated. Your founder may be a great entrepreneur and company starter, but not have the skills to keep the company growing at that initial pace (partly because the best starters of companies are so good at starting things that they are not very excited about keeping them going; they start itching to start something else). Just as both positive and negative events produce stress in our lives (for example, weddings and new babies are positive events, but undeniably stressful), so business success can bring stress and associated risks as well. The risks of success must also be taken into account in order to protect value in the present and create value in the future.

You have likely heard the sayings, "no risk — no return" or "nothing ventured, nothing gained." Taking smart risks is part of being a successful businessperson. Rather than not taking risks, systematically cataloging, evaluating and managing your risks, as we discuss in this chapter, can be thought of as helping you to take the *right* risks, the ones most likely to pay off. Furthermore, rather than running around and gathering information about *all* your risks — which is difficult to manage and keep updated — technology can help you out by monitoring and reporting on the risks you want to manage closely.

Ignoring Risk (At Your Peril)

If you *really* wanted to ignore risk, you probably wouldn't be reading this chapter. Because you are reading it, we assume you're at least a little willing to think about it. There are two approaches to handling risk: You can think about risk and try to reduce the chances of the risk becoming reality, or you can choose to not think about risk and just let things happen.

If you notice that the wiring in your house is starting to be a little unreliable, you might call an electrician. For example, if you're in the basement and the children run upstairs, and you see sparks fly, you call an electrician. If you didn't pay attention to that risk, when your house catches on fire, you call the fire department. The risk became a reality — "a loss event." You might call this approach firefighting. But wouldn't it be better to call an electrician before the situation got to that point? Of course it would. In order for that to happen, you have to notice the problem and do something about it. You can prevent that risk and avoid going into firefighting mode.

Many people — and companies — find themselves in a similar type of fire-fighting, or crisis, mode. Crisis mode is expensive, and depending what the crisis is, you might have losses from which you can't recover (old family pictures burned in the fire, for example). An electrician's bill is lower than the loss associated with losing your photo albums and other treasures, not to mention the potential harm to family members and the cost of rebuilding after the fire. It's clear that while an electrician's bill might be high, it's nowhere near as high as the cost of the house burning down. In other words, the electrician's bill offers a good return on investment relative to the risk, which is an important consideration when evaluating responses to risks.

An effective risk management program helps you foresee problems and prevent or mitigate them. But without effective risk management, the financial impact can be severe when risks become reality; that is, when incidents or loss events occur. A recent Deloitte Research study found that in the past decade, nearly half of all Fortune 1000 companies experienced a loss event that caused their stock price to decline by 20 percent in one month. Recovery took a long time — more than a year for half of those affected. Another 22 percent of the companies never recovered their stock value.

Upon further examination, Deloitte found that the loss of stock value was not the result of a single incident; rather, 80 percent of the losses occurred when two (or more) risks in different areas of the company turned into loss events at the same time. Here are some examples of these types of situations:

- ✔ A new competitor enters the market at the same time that your supplier can't deliver

- ✔ A sharp rise in customer returns and complaints occurs at the same time a competitor introduces a product upgrade

✔ Production is stalled because permits for air, water, or waste are exceeded at the same time that inventory is at a record low and demand is high

Only through systematic monitoring of risks can you see two or more events coming at the same time and recognize that, if they're not mitigated in some way, together they form a real threat to the company's financial and competitive position. If the number of accidents in a factory is rising at the same time the scheduled maintenance of equipment is being neglected, the ingredients for a disaster are brewing. By systematically monitoring risks, you can see the train wreck before it happens and prevent it.

Sorting Through the Approaches to Risk Management

If you really take a firefighting approach to risk, you probably won't be successful in the long term. But in practice, many companies do take risk seriously and try to evaluate their risks in one way or another — they just don't do so in a systematic way. In this section, we look at some of the possible approaches to risk management.

The ad hoc approach

The ad hoc approach means that some of the people are thinking about risk, some of the time. With this approach to risk management, risk assessment is mainly intuitive. Much of the company's knowledge about risk is kept in someone's head, and no validation of the assumptions surrounding the risk can be made. If the expert gets a better job offer somewhere, or even changes teams, all of the risk information is lost. With this approach, you can't learn from the mistakes of others. This type of risk management is better than nothing, but because there's no shared information, this approach offers no common vocabulary, it isn't formalized, and your mileage — and value — will definitely vary.

The fragmented approach

Another way of thinking about the fragmented approach is that lots of people are thinking about risk in different ways. In this approach, managers generally are looking at risk, but they are using their own tools and their own vocabularies or terminology to manage their own organizational or departmental risks. And in doing so, their management approach is often very informal.

Who cares about risk?

In addition to business owners, a variety of other stakeholders are concerned about risk and how risks are managed. Here are some of them:

- **Boards of Directors.** Boards of directors worry about risks. You tell the board the plan, and they ask you, what are the risks? What do we know about them?

- **Investors.** Investing is all about risk. Is investing in this company a good bet, or is it too risky? If investors are confident that the company is assessing its risk accurately, they will be more willing to invest in and support the growth of the company.

- **Companies that provide data for investors.** For example, Standard & Poor's issues credit ratings for companies. These ratings determine how much their bank will charge them to loan money. Standard & Poor's now includes the company's approach to risk in its evaluation, so whether a company conducts risk management affects whether it will be able to borrow money and at what rate.

- **Managers.** Good managers also care about risks: they are often compensated based on their group's performance, and risk management will maximize that performance.

- **Regulators.** Although the R in GRC has traditionally been separate from the C (compliance), risk-related regulations are on the rise:

  Switzerland has passed a law that requires boards of directors of publicly held companies to describe their procedures for conducting risk assessments in the notes to their financial statements. Companies may instead list the significant risks that they face.

In Germany, the Act on Control and Transparency in Enterprises (KonTraG) specifies that companies must perform risk management, and they must do so in a way that allows them to address the risks before they turn into incidents. Furthermore, they have to address the risks in a way that aligns with their corporate objectives.

In the United States, the Public Company Accounting Oversight Board (PCAOB) and the Securities and Exchange Commission (SEC) has published Auditing Standard No. 5, which recommends a top-down, risk–based approach to organizations' SOX compliance requirements (assessment of internal control over financial reporting). As such, companies are implementing a risk-based methodology to implement and maintain their policy and control environment.

Even where risk management is not directly named by regulators, it turns out that you need effective risk management as part of the underlying business environment. The U.S. Amended Sentencing Guidelines state that organizations must take reasonable steps to ensure that their compliance and ethics programs are followed (including monitoring and auditing to detect criminal conduct) and must periodically evaluate the effectiveness of their compliance and ethics program. Although risk management is not explicitly stated, analysis of the guidelines shows that what is required to meet the guidelines is basically, in fact, a systematic approach to managing and monitoring risks.

Commonly, these managers keep Excel spreadsheets filled with risk information, but each manager does things differently, making comparisons difficult or impossible. Furthermore, the frequency of updates may vary widely, with the sales department conducting risk assessments quarterly while the development organization does them once a year.

This siloed approach means that you have no way of aggregating data about risk. Because you can't aggregate the data, you can't really gain an enterprise view of risk, either. There is no transparency of the risks at an enterprise level, and generally any formal focus on risk management is on the negative aspect of risk, rather than a proactive approach to strategic risk management.

This fragmented approach to risk, with everyone doing their own thing, creates a false sense of security. You think your organization is managing risk, but in fact, the organization lacks any visibility or insight into common business situations with regard to risk. With this approach, you can't really protect value or create value. The only real perspective offered is historical, and managing a business based solely on a historical perspective doesn't allow a business to move forward.

The risk manager's job approach

With the risk manager's job approach, some people are appointed to think about risk some of the time. With this approach, the company believes it is taking risk seriously because it has hired or appointed a risk manager. The risk manager then has the job of gathering information from all the line of business managers, meeting with them to discuss their risks, and working with them to provide ongoing risk-related information. This approach does have some merit because it indicates that risk is taken seriously and is given the support of management. If this is the only approach your business takes, however, it can lead to isolated support for risk management, which at best can yield only isolated benefits. Another danger of this approach is that line of business experts generally only *communicate* their risk information rather than *taking responsibility* for managing their risks: They report the information up the chain and then consider their job done. They don't take responsibility for mitigating and managing the risks; after all, they think, that's the risk manager's job.

The systematic, enterprise-wide approach

Another way of thinking about the systematic, enterprise wide approach is to say that this approach means that the right people are thinking about the right risks at the right time. The infrastructure and processes that have historically served risk management are now straining under the weight of a global economy in which change is a constant and information travels at the speed of light. Companies are increasingly putting into place an enterprise-level methodology for thinking about risk.

Such an approach provides a framework for analyzing and managing risks in the context of corporate strategy and performance, for gaining an understanding of the true exposures relating from risk correlation, and for complete transparency so that risks can be effectively managed at the right time. By agreeing on a common vocabulary, a unified catalog of risk types, a common methodology for assessing the probability of risks occurring and a formal remediation or response methodology, companies can take a more strategic view of their risks, and risk can become a driver of the business to help enable performance and innovation.

Without the help of a system that can help you automate monitoring of risks, however, even a common methodology and a risk-aware culture won't really help you protect your brand value, let alone create value. If the market finds out about loss events before or at the same time that you do, and that news is published through the media, it's already too late. Risk management today needs to provide automated monitoring of key risk indicators as soon as certain thresholds are reached so that relevant risk information is constantly being identified, analyzed, and managed before the risks become loss events and negatively impact the business.

With this type of automated risk monitoring, different scenarios can be modeled for future projects or products and these scenarios can be effectively risk-adjusted and managed, supporting intelligent choices about strategic directions. For example, if a salesperson enters a large quote, there is a risk that the sale won't close (and an even bigger risk if we are counting too much on the success of that sale). With automated risk monitoring, that large quote can trigger an e-mail to the salesperson with a few questions to help characterize the risks associated with the deal. In this way, risks can be collected and updated as part of standard operating procedure, rather than relying on someone to get around to updating their risks.

A cultural approach

In a cultural approach, all of the people thinking about risk some of the time. Face it: line of business managers and their teams have the best view of the risks in their particular areas. Creating a culture in which risks are reported, managed, and monitored by each of the business units is powerful, particularly if reporting is easy to do. The responsibility for managing risks — because they have a direct impact on business performance — must stay with the line of business.

Part of this involves instilling in the culture a way to think about risk. It's clear that we live in uncertain times. By taking this uncertainty into account — rather than ignoring it — we can incorporate risk into the complete business cycle of strategy- and objective-setting, business planning and budgeting, executing against plan, and measuring performance.

Identifying the Critical Components of a Successful Risk Management Framework

As you might have guessed, all of the approaches to risk management that we discussed in the previous section are not mutually exclusive. In this section, we combine the best of these approaches to see what it takes to build a successful risk management framework. A successful enterprise risk management framework requires four components:

- Making risk part of the culture from the top level down
- Building an organization to help with risk
- Instituting a systematic framework for dealing with risk
- Using technology to automate the monitoring and the management of risks

In the next few sections, we unpack each of these components in more detail.

A culture that takes risk seriously, from the C-suite down

Building risk into the culture doesn't mean having employees hang-gliding off the roof of corporate headquarters. What it *does* mean is that there is support for risk management that starts at the top with the C-level executives, including the CEO, CFO, and COO. This level of risk buy-in is critical. Further, if the company puts a policy in place and an employee violates it, a response from C-level executives to the whole company helps to clarify that this initiative is to be taken seriously. C-level execs have to hold themselves to the same standards that they expect of their employees; they must build risk analyses into their own decision-making.

One effective way for the C-suite to help build a culture of risk management is in creating a formalized risk policy — communicating their expectations to all employees and setting standards for how often risk management and reporting must be done.

Reticence about risk

Not all corporate cultures are willing to talk about risk. Here are some attitudes that prevent frank discussion of risk:

Risk is negative. Some people think that risk is negative and so, in order to be "positive," they avoid discussions of risk. Such thinking reflects an outdated understanding of risk in which risk is viewed as something bad rather than as a positive force that can both protect value and actually create value by helping companies find new opportunities and manage those opportunities effectively.

I don't want to be the bearer of bad news. If we have a corporate policy of shooting messengers, there will be some fear about bringing up what can go wrong. This requires cultural reinforcement that we want to know what the risks are: how the deal could possibly fall through, what factors might cause the product to be late, or whether our supplier is showing signs of instability and may not be able to supply. The point to make here is that we are trying to take into account all risks at an early stage to see how we can mitigate the risk and increase our chances of success. Remember that even promising new business opportunities can be a risk if we don't prepare for the increased capacity that success will require.

If you know my risks, you know my strategy. Who wouldn't like to be in the other team's locker room and find out what plays the coach is planning to use in the Super Bowl? Information about risks is strategic, so it must be treated as privileged information, just like any other aspect of corporate strategy. For this reason, although you want risk to be part of the culture, you have to think about who is trustworthy enough to have the complete picture of all the risks. Educating people about risk should include a vetting process that employees go through before being included in risk management discussions. Furthermore, risk information may sometimes fall under attorney-client privilege and thus must be managed within the legal department; it's important to support this kind of clear authorization.

I can't let my risk managers network. Risk managers obviously must be discreet and savvy enough to know what they can network about and what they can't. Although risk information is strategic, competing companies face many of the same risks, particularly regarding compliance with the ever-increasing number of regulations. Networking about best practices — while not revealing corporate secrets — is key to developing in-house expertise in risk management.

The C-level executives guide the company regarding its objectives and plans. This information is critical in developing an effective risk management framework. After all, if you don't know where you're going, it's hard to figure out what might try to stop you or slow you down.

Strategy and planning starts at the top, but it builds on input from the whole company. Line of business executives do their budgets as input to the corporate budget. Plans and objectives are set at the top, but also at the departmental level.

In much the same way, line of business managers generally can see certain risks most clearly. That's why managing risk is *everyone's* business: The composite of all those unique perspectives creates the most complete picture of the risks that the company faces and helps pinpoint the most strategic risks to consider.

To get even more specific about what moving risk into the culture really means, Table 2-1 lists various roles and responsibilities to consider for helping them integrate risk.

Table 2-1	Moving Risk into the Culture, Role by Role
Executives	Executives should view risk management as a critical part of performance management. Risk should be considered when deciding which corporate strategies to pursue (such as mergers and acquisitions, new product development, and the like). Once the strategy is set, executives need to review the top risks and monitor the key risk indicators for meeting each of the company objectives. Based on the new transparency of risks across the enterprise, create risk-adjusted proformas for what-if analyses and scenario testing. Benefit: Executives gain transparency across all enterprise risks that can help them be proactive, because they can view the most up-to-date risk data in dashboards, reports and alerts.
Risk managers	Risk managers are able to leverage all the data currently in their enterprise systems so the risks can be automatically identified and monitored. The professional risk management team needs a single platform to automate risk management processes across the disparate systems within their enterprise. They need an open framework to integrate other systems to provide an end-to-end risk process across the extended enterprise of customers, suppliers, and partners. This also includes manual processes. Rather than trying to fight collaboration done manually using the phone, email, and spreadsheets, the risk management processes should incorporate these tools automatically into risk management processes. Benefit: By taking this approach, risk managers will be able to focus on collecting and analyzing important risk information, and become strategic advisors to the business units.

(continued)

Table 2-1 *(continued)*

Line of business managers	Line of business managers need tools to be able to drive their performance and respond to their top risks to help them achieve their objectives. They need company- and role-based risk best practice playbooks. Line of business experts should be provided with guides that help them identify risks that often occur within business processes, provide potential mitigation and management strategies, and include benchmark assumptions and setup of risk monitoring processes. Companies can learn from the experiences of these users, examining which responses were effective in the past so that they can avoid making mistakes twice. Benefit: Line of business managers start to own and drive risk management for their areas, a true sign that risk management is now part of the culture.

A risk management organization: Distributing responsibility throughout the culture

Even if risk is part of the company culture, someone needs to be minding the store, ensuring that risk information is being gathered and updated so that it can properly inform corporate decisions large and small. Appointing a corporate risk manager can help ensure that risk management is given the attention and focus it requires.

As with any type of corporate messaging, having someone in charge helps ensure that the message is delivered and is owned by the business units. Risk managers should have as part of their objectives the goal of building a risk-aware organization. Effective risk management should permeate the organization, providing vertical visibility from the top management to the line of business managers and their workers. Risk management professionals should push responsibility for risk down to the level of line of business owners. In this way, risks can be rolled up and monitored at other levels as needed.

You can easily see how risk managers can help the company manage risks by pushing responsibility down into the organization. What's a little more subtle is the horizontal visibility that this ultimately provides.

By monitoring, managing, and documenting risks and risk response actions, the company builds a pool of experience in managing risks. Managers can learn how to better manage, and even model, risks in their own organization,

Regulatory risks are diverse: All hands on deck

Companies today must comply with many different regulations, and that means monitoring many kinds of risks to achieve a holistic approach to GRC. Because the risks are so diverse, neither corporate risk managers nor the C-suite executives can have a complete handle on them. Line of business owners must monitor and manage these risks, often with the help of experts in the organization. Here are some of the types of risks that must be monitored:

Environment, Health, & Safety Risks

The environment, health, and safety (EH&S) umbrella contains many risks that pose potential threats to your employees and your company. If you don't comply with EH&S regulations, not only do you expose your employees to unnecessary harm, but you potentially face significant fines and penalties, disruption to production, and damage to your company reputation. However, if you manage EH&S issues effectively, you can lower your operating costs and ensure the safety of your employees. See Chapter 10 for more details on this type of risk.

The Risk of Noncompliance with Emissions Regulations

A related operational risk for many companies is emissions control. The potential for political, financial, and public image fallout for noncompliance with regulations such as the Kyoto Protocol, the U.S. Clean Air Act, or the EU IPPC Directive is enormous. Noncompliance with greenhouse gas emissions regulations poses an even greater risk to brand image and corporate goodwill for companies that operate complex, multifaceted manufacturing facilities. See Chapter 11 for more details on this type of risk.

The Risk of Noncompliance with Financial Regulations

The passing of the Sarbanes-Oxley Act (SOX) means that institutional investors, rating agencies, and regulators have started assessing GRC management as part of their evaluation of companies. Furthermore, the stakes for noncompliance with financial regulations such as SOX have become more than just fines and penalties. Stock valuations and credit ratings can be affected by your inability to comply with mandated regulations. There are numerous other laws to consider as well in this category, including those dealing with security and privacy, as well as your responsibility for your partners, such as the Foreign Corrupt Practices Act. See Chapters 4 through 7 for more information on this type of risk.

Global Trade Risks

Security concerns of the post-9/11 era have spawned a host of new trade and transport regulations. To ensure that you are not trading with any entities on government-issued "watch lists" or "sanctioned party lists," you need to identify your business partners — and their outsourcing suppliers — throughout your global supply chain. Noncompliance with these trade regulations can be expensive; in extreme cases companies have even had their trade licenses or privileges revoked. See Chapter 8 for more information on global trade risks.

but also the experience of how one division can benefit another. A manager in one division can learn from the experience of those in other parts of the company. Risk expertise accrues and the experience of the company as a whole is leveraged. Managers learn not only from their own experience but also from the experience of others in a very real and tangible way.

The risk manager's role, then, becomes like that of another business owner, helping the organization improve its wall-to-wall risk awareness and risk management approach. The risk manager can also help develop best practices.

It's important to send a message that risk managers support the corporation in risk management, not that they "handle" risk management. Human resources supports the organization with detailed information about health insurance and the like. But employees have to file their own health claims and know what coverage they have. Similarly, risk professionals support risk management but they cannot possibly have the breadth of knowledge of all the risks that people across the organization have. Risk is everyone's job.

A systematic framework in place

Because you're looking for consistency and comparability in your approach to risk management, you need a systematic approach to gathering and managing that information. One way to do this is by adopting an enterprise risk management framework that leverages technology to collect, monitor, and manage the key risk information. The important factor here is to put measures in place that drive consistency so that everyone is not out there creating apples-and-oranges spreadsheets that, though perhaps wonderful on a departmental level, are impossible to compare with the kumquats-and-cucumbers spreadsheets produced by another division.

This systematic framework also sets boundaries for the type of risk management the company will do. It answers the following types of questions:

- How quantitative does the analysis need to be?
- Which areas of the business are we going to include?
- Which types of risks are we going to monitor?
- What are the key risk indicators associated with those risks?

Technology that creates a risk picture

The final component you need is a technology infrastructure that provides an ability to manage and communicate all components of risk and response. A good technology infrastructure should

- Automate the collection, analysis, monitoring, and response of risk-related information

> ✔ Monitor key systems across business processes to ensure real-time iden-
> tification and management of key risks. Raise alerts when key figures
> reach preset thresholds (for example, a 5 percent increase in use of a
> single-sourced material)
>
> ✔ Incorporate risk evaluation into corporate strategy and planning so busi-
> ness units have visibility into key risks before it is too late

A risk management technology platform provides the foundation for stronger
collaboration and understanding across the enterprise. By having a common
set of risk content embedded in the technology solution, lines of business
managers can now manage risk by using a common system to classify risk.
Doing this drives more strategic integration across departments in managing
the interdependencies of risks. Each department is now working against
aligned risk management goals and objectives, which are enforced at the
underlying technology layer. Such a technology infrastructure can help a corporation manage risk as it seeks to protect value (by monitoring and mitigating its risks) and create value (by marrying risk information to strategy).

Taking the Four Steps to Enterprise Risk Management

Enterprise risk management means that risk management is not an isolated
activity: An enterprise-wide approach includes all risks and takes input from
across the enterprise. Enterprise risk management also means that risk is also
seen as a strategic opportunity, not just a tactical program to mitigate the
effect of loss events. Managing risks can be aligned with corporate strategy:
Rather than reviewing an endless list of risks and developing tactical remediation plans, risks can be proactively and strategically managed in light of what
the company is trying to achieve short-term and long-term.

With that framework in place, you're ready to get down to the process for
enterprise risk management, which is comprised of four large steps:

> ✔ **Risk planning:** For each business activity, what are we trying to achieve,
> what are the assumptions and constraints, and what risks do we want to
> monitor?
>
> ✔ **Risk identification and analysis:** For each business activity, we identify
> the risks. For each risk we look at the nature of the risk, its probability of
> occurrence, and the quantitative and qualitative aspects of the risk.
>
> ✔ **Risk response:** Is there anything we can do to reduce, mitigate, or even
> remove the risk? How much will this cost? What is the potential ROI of
> taking this step? Who's responsible for making sure that the response
> happens?

✔ **Risk monitoring:** In this step, we continuously track and monitor each of the risks and analyze any risks that, despite our efforts, turn into incidents.

Unlike other processes where you follow the steps and you're done, enterprise risk management is an ongoing and perpetual process, so the final step circles back to the first step, as shown in Figure 2-2.

The bottom line is that this process provides you with "news you can use": actionable information that helps you make better decisions and removes roadblocks from the projects that are important to you.

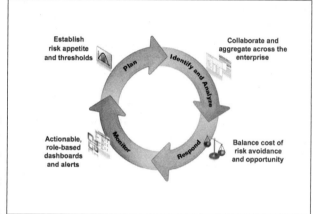

Figure 2-2:
The Risk Management Process.

Risk planning

Risk planning is a first step in any enterprise risk management process. It typically involves defining the boundaries of the risk assessment, deciding who should participate, and capturing any assumptions or constraints about the business activity. The planning process also helps organizations establish their risk appetite and risk thresholds and helps them define their process to manage their risks more strategically and effectively.

Proper risk planning helps drive consistency across the organization in terms of how risks are defined and managed. Part of the planning process is to ensure that risks are aligned with corporate goals. A historical challenge of risk management was that risks have not been aligned with corporate strategy, and therefore management of these risks did not proactively and strategically support the enterprise.

Risk identification and analysis

The next step is to identify and analyze all of the risks to the business. For each risk, the goal is to analyze the impact of the particular risk occurring and quantify the risk, both in terms of likelihood (probability) and in terms of potential loss (impact). It is important in this phase to collaborate and aggregate across the enterprise to ensure that all risks are identified, as well as ensuring an understanding of the impact of the risks and any associated loss event.

You should consider two key attributes when analyzing risk:

- ✔ **Probability:** How likely is it to happen? Think about the weather as an example. A popular weather site includes an hour-by-hour probability of precipitation. But some possible weather conditions are, well, less possible than others. On a dry July day in Washington, D.C., for example, the risk of heavy rain is characterized as minimal. But the risk of heavy snow and ice buildup is also said to be minimal. In D.C., rain is far more likely than snow in July, but these events are categorized as being equally probable. Assign a probability to your risks as accurately as you can. (Perhaps because of its sensitivity to the issue of quantifying risks, this same weather site now assigns a percentage probability to various weather events, listing a 0 percent chance of snow in July in Washington, D.C.)

- ✔ **Impact:** What will happen if this risk becomes reality? What will be the consequence? It could be significant; it could be catastrophic. Where possible, estimate the risk in terms of monetary value. Bear in mind that some risks, like possible loss of human life, are qualitative instead; you can't put a price on someone's life (unless you're an insurance company).

By quantifying the risks and determining a probability of their occurrence, management can see what risks are either most likely or are associated with the highest potential loss. Identification and analysis yields a short list of your most critical risks, the ones that really have an impact. If those risks can be reduced or mitigated in some way, the bottom line will look a lot healthier. Risk response is the next step to consider.

Risk response

After you know what the risks are and what the potential losses could be, you have to think about what you can do about them. The risk response phase primarily deals with balancing the cost of risk avoidance and opportunity. Risk response allows you to develop and manage resolution strategies for critical risks that could significantly impact the business. Part of this is being able to identify interdependencies between risks across the organization. For example, a risk of a supplier going bankrupt could cause associated risks within the sales and marketing organizations. A response process also allows the line of business owners to effectively manage their risks. Risk response helps business owners identify and implement the appropriate technology or processes to manage the impact of a loss event to their line of business. Now, there are some risks you can't do anything about if you didn't anticipate them, such as an earthquake, hurricane, or a big change in the economy: These you just have to accept. But in many cases, you can select a response that allows you to better manage the impact of these risks. In fact, when submitting risks to managers, employees may also provide what they view as some possible responses and even quantify how those responses could help.

The type of quantitative analysis mentioned in the identification and analysis step can be used to compare the return on investment of various responses, which may be used in combination or separately. Based on the return on investment, you may decide to choose one response over another.

Every response is recorded in the enterprise risk management framework, whether it actually prevents the risk or not. The next time someone is faced with a similar question like this, she can look at the experience of others to discover whether hiring more people, one possible approach to a project in trouble, actually helped. (Hiring people doesn't always help; for example, consider the classic question: If one woman can have a baby in 9 months, can 9 women have a baby in one month?) If your organization is using spreadsheets, this information might be on someone's laptop rather than in your enterprise risk management framework, where it can be informative to others who are managing similar risks.

Part of managing risks is looking at what best practices suggest. If you don't have much experience yet, consultants can be helpful in providing input. But with enterprise risk management, whether you get outside help or not, you begin to harness everyone's experience in a systematic way, building your own database of best practices.

Any risk response has a status. It's all well and good to say that you will hire three more people to help with a project, but if you don't have three people to hire, the status has to reflect this fact. Depending how hard it is to find qualified help, the response might not be as effective as you had hoped. The status of the risk has to be updated periodically so that the risk can be properly monitored, which is the next phase to consider.

Risk monitoring

After you've decided what kinds of risks you want to consider, quantified them in terms of likelihood and potential loss, and considered your responses, the next step is to monitor them, analyzing the information you have from a number of perspectives.

For example, what classes of risks are causing the most problems? This may point us in a strategic direction for change. Are there any changes in the risk levels? Are some business units going beyond the risk appetites or thresholds set for them by management? Is the information on the risks being monitored?

Monitoring can happen in several ways, but one popular way to present it, if you are using enterprise risk management software, is through a risk dashboard. Risk dashboards can be presented at multiple levels based on the target audience, including C-level executives, risk managers, or even line of business owners. The information contained within the dashboards can be aggregated to track and monitor multiple risk elements or can present only the risk information that a given role needs to monitor or is interested in.

Risk monitoring frequency depends on many things, but here are a few to consider:

- ✔ Priority of the risk ("high priority risks could be updated or monitored daily or weekly, depending on the impact")
- ✔ Company or regulatory policy ("all risks are reviewed every quarter")
- ✔ Frequency of new information ("earthquake" (no new information) vs. "product development timeline" (new information after each R&D team meeting))

Analyzing What Went Wrong: When Risk Becomes Reality

A certain proportion of risks are going to become loss events: That's just how life works. Products are delayed, some sales are lost, a new competitor steps in on the scene, or a key component for our product is stuck in customs somewhere.

Enterprise risk management can help you understand and better manage a loss event. By analyzing this incident and reviewing what went wrong, you can see whether the risk could have been prevented or its impact reduced if certain measures had been taken sooner. By analyzing and managing these incidents in a systematic way, you have the opportunity to avoid additional problems in the future.

With incident analysis, you look at factors like:

- ✔ What went wrong?
- ✔ What caused the problem to occur?
- ✔ Was this a risk that was even being tracked?

✔ What were the costs of managing the risks and implementing a response plan compared to the costs of the incident?

✔ What was the nature of the loss? Was it a financial loss? An opportunity loss?

✔ What was the root cause? Is our product out of date or not suited for the current market? Were our people (sales or support) unfriendly or unhelpful?

✔ What response strategies did we try and why didn't they work? Maybe they did work, but not as well as you hoped. In either case, you need to know what went wrong where and how you can do better next time.

Incidents have much to teach you, and doing an analysis of what went wrong is important to making more things go right in the future.

Automating the Risk Management Cycle

So far in this chapter, we've talked about managing risks in a manual way. However, the process of monitoring risks can be automated as well by implementing an enterprise risk management software application. For example, if you enter a lead for a potential sale with a dollar value above a certain amount, the enterprise risk management software could alert the key participants about the risk, or even implement a workflow to send a survey to document the key risk information regarding the deal. Once submitted, that survey could be sent to the risk manager or to your manager, depending on how it has been set up, and key risk indicators against this risk could be automatically monitored. This implies a level of integration between the software you use to track leads and your enterprise risk management software.

Taking the SAP Approach: SAP GRC Risk Management

The SAP application that supports this enterprise approach to risk management is called SAP GRC Risk Management. This application is integrated with all other SAP applications, making it easy to raise alerts about key business processes right from the software itself. Monitoring these risks is a key feature of SAP GRC Risk Management.

SAP GRC risk management and key risk indicators

You may have heard of KPIs — key performance indicators — that help companies and employees track progress toward their goals. Key risk indicators (KRIs) provide the same kind of metric, but in the realm of risk. KRIs tell you that if a certain risk is realized, it represents a significant problem. SAP GRC Risk Management provides automatic KRI monitoring. Furthermore, as shown in Figure 2-3, KRIs are related to risk targets and thresholds, making it very concrete that if a certain metric reaches a certain level, the risk owner must be notified.

Figure 2-3 highlights how KRI monitoring helps drive and automate the risk management process.

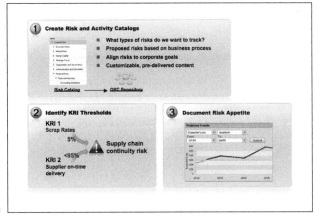

Figure 2-3: Automatic KRI monitoring with SAP GRC Risk Management.

The process of KRI monitoring starts with identifying the key risk indicators:

✔ What are the top key risk indicators that could affect your business processes?

✔ Which of your business processes or activities are "worth" tracking from a risk management perspective?

✔ What are your company's goals and how do risks align to those? How do they differ by line of business?

The next step is to set thresholds for each KRI using configurable business rules. For example:

✔ Setting a level (for example, more than three injuries in a quarter)

✔ Monitoring percentage increase or decrease (for example, a 5 percent increase in unplanned manufacturing downtime) or percentage by volume (more than 0.5 percent customer complaints per product shipped)

If any of these thresholds are reached or exceeded — more than three injuries in a quarter for example — an alert is raised so that the situation receives immediate follow up.

Finally, the risk appetite for each line of business and for the enterprise as a whole needs to be documented. How much loss can the business absorb based on current capitalization? It may make sense for some parts of your business to take more risks (in a product line, for example) while other lines of businesses, which provide a steady revenue stream — your cash cows — will be managed more conservatively.

Monitoring risks and key risk indicators with SAP GRC Risk Management

Here are some situations where you could use SAP GRC Risk Management to monitor risks and the associated key risk indicators:

✔ **Mass exodus.** SAP GRC Risk Management integrates with SAP Human Capital Management so that you can generate an alert if key people from the same group are leaving the company, perhaps because they are being wooed by a competitor.

✔ **Accidents on the rise.** SAP GRC Risk Management integrates with SAP Environment, Health & Safety, so you can raise an alert if an accident (or two of the same type) occurs, indicating a safety problem.

✔ **Projects are late; deals hang in the balance.** The new product release is key to several important sales deals. SAP GRC Risk Management integrates with SAP Project System and SAP Customer Relationship Management so you can receive alerts both on the status of the project and on the revenue that depends on its timely delivery.

✔ **Supplier reliability on the wane.** Maybe your suppliers usually deliver on time, but that on time delivery is slowly falling behind. SAP GRC Risk Management, working with SAP ERP, can alert you to this trend — before it becomes a problem.

✔ **Entering a new market.** One possible risk is noncompliance with trade regulations for that market. SAP GRC Risk Management integrates with SAP Global Trade Services, so you could choose to receive alerts when export declarations are being rejected due to improper product classifications for customs.

✔ **Maintaining a safe working environment.** For example, a mining company is required to maintain equipment according to safety standards. Safety equipment is scheduled for periodic inspections. SAP GRC Risk Management integrates with SAP ERP, so you could choose to receive alerts when inspections are not conducted on time.

✔ **Meeting government reporting requirements.** Think of a pharmaceutical company that is required to follow FDA regulations, including procedures on how to conduct clinical trials. You could choose to set up an alert that monitors data in SAP HCM that shows whether each relevant employee has successfully completed training in clinical trial document submission.

✔ **Changes in your competition.** Your largest customer is going through a merger and acquisition process and the merging company buys from your biggest competitor. You need to get an alert of all sales activities and start to determine ways to manage the risk of losing this customer due to the merger. SAP GRC Risk Management is integrated with SAP CRM, so it can alert you to all relevant sales activities.

✔ **Market fluctuation.** You do 25 percent of your sales in Brazil and need to monitor the fluctuation rate of the real (BRL). You set up a key risk indicator to monitor the risk of booking a deal on a day when the real is below the monthly average so that you are alerted about how currency fluctuation impacts contract bookings. This could represent a difference of $1 million in the contract booking, so you might want to wait until the rate is more favorable to book the contract if you can.

Using SAP GRC Risk Management: A Fictional Case Study

To see how SAP GRC Risk Management works in the real world, we've created a fictional case study. Plastic Time, a fictional plastics manufacturing company, produces styrene, and the CEO has been asked if they can fill an order for 2 million pounds in 30 days — a tight deadline that requires a quick answer. Because Apslcom (a fictional customer) is a prospect the company has been pursuing for some time, Plastic Time is very interested in making the sale. But to evaluate the opportunity intelligently, Plastic Time's CEO asks the management team to factor in all the risks so that he can give the client a solid answer to its inquiry. He also asks them to include the corporate risk manager in the analysis process.

Where should we produce?

Three possible plants could produce the styrene: one in China, Romania, and in the U.S. Whichever plant is chosen, Plastic Time needs assurance that it can ramp up production very quickly and get the necessary supplies. The planning team performs a quick analysis of the ramp-up scenarios and from a pure cost standpoint, China seems to be the best choice. The general manager assembles the management team to quickly convene and evaluate the Chinese plant from a risk standpoint.

Considering China

At the meeting, the Chief Risk Officer shows the management team the GRC Risk Management Dashboard. The dashboard shows how all the risks affect each other and provide a complete picture of the risks the Chinese plant faces. All the risks are linked to KRIs that the software automatically updates, so the management team is viewing the latest risk information for the plant.

The CRO uses the assessment capability to see the impact of adding a job for producing 2 million pounds of styrene in 30 days. She also sends out a survey by e-mail to the key line managers to get their input on the risks involved in giving this job to the Chinese plant. It appears that high-level risks such as the global economy are under control for that timeframe. The survey results indicate that the risks in the area of suppliers will require further assessment. After all, suppliers are key to filling the order on time. The CRO asks her team to conduct a fast assessment that includes suppliers, timeframes, deadlines, and deliverables and all the risks related to these factors.

The additional assessment shows that increasing staffing and responsibility will not be a problem for this plant. However, the results also show that the Chinese plant is currently struggling with a key supplier, and shows a 58 percent probability risk that the key supplier will not be able to meet this new demand, which would incur a loss of $15.6 billion due to penalties and unsaleable inventory if the decision were made to produce there.

The management team asks about alternative suppliers for the plant, but the Chinese team has already started working with a new supplier, which is currently ramping up production and is expecting to come online in about four months — too late to help with the Apslcom deadline. Considering yet another supplier would require getting import licenses, and given the timeframe, that won't work either. The CRO shows how GRC Global Trade Services shows that the cost of an expedited effort in China makes China actually the most expensive location for the job — the opposite of what the initial calculations showed. (For more on SAP GRC Global Trade Services, see Chapter 8.) In addition, SAP GRC Risk Management shows that there's a 50 percent chance that the job wouldn't get done on time, regardless of the cost.

Considering Romania

China is clearly not the best choice, and the U.S. plant is both costly and over-booked by comparison, so the team looks at the plant in Romania. The Chief Risk Officer reviews the top two risks for Romania, which are financial and environmental. Data for this plant indicates a lower level of supply chain risks, and the line of business managers there do not indicate any additional production problems. However, the increased revenue from this job will put the plant over the compliance audit threshold, placing higher compliance costs on the company; however, U.S. compliance processes and controls will be leveraged to minimize the risk and the impact of the additional compliance requirements. The increased revenue substantially offsets the cost of the additional compliance requirements, given that these requirements can be met efficiently because of the SAP GRC implementation that is already in place.

The second risk to be considered is environmental. What are the current carbon targets in Romania based on the new production limits? SAP GRC Risk Management automatically monitors the key environmental risk indicators and shows that the Romanian plant falls below emissions permit limits even with the expected increase in production. There is no risk of having to apply for new permits or buy emissions credits.

After finishing this evaluation, the team settles on the Romanian plant and creates a draft of the operational plan. The CRO then works to get all of the risks and mitigation plans into GRC Risk Management so that progress on the job can be monitored.

The bottom line is that Plastic Time can make a confident reply to Apslcom, assuring the client it can handle the job (and confident that it makes good business sense, too).

Using SAP Risk Management: An SAP Case Study

When Henning Kagermann became CEO of SAP AG, he wanted to know how risks were being identified, reported, and managed within the company. What he found was pretty typical. Everyone at SAP said, yes, we track our risks, and here are the spreadsheets we use.

As you might suspect, risks were being managed in a fragmented and ad hoc manner. Everyone did it in their own way, and in most cases, their methodology was sound, but the result was far from systematic or even comparable in any rigorous way.

The idea for creating SAP GRC Risk Management was born, to give SAP the ability to identify and manage their own risks within their own business. The benefits SAP realized by implementing SAP GRC Risk Management solutions are quantifiable in several ways:

- ✔ **Cost savings:** Time is money, and now SAP spends approximately 30 percent less time managing risk activities centrally and throughout the business (previously, SAP employees spent this time manually completing and tracking risk assessments, consolidating assessments, and rolling up and generating reports).

- ✔ **Reduced insurance premiums:** Because SAP is monitoring its risks systematically, insurance companies can reduce their premiums. Using SAP GRC Risk Management drove down insurance costs, saving the company $4 million annually in insurance premiums. Because of automatic KRI monitoring, fewer risks result in incidents, and there are fewer claims. "Prior to the implementation, we had an average of 7 to 10 claims per year within our Americas region alone," says George Haitsch, Vice President Corporate Risk, Global Risk Management, SAP AG. "Now we average just 2 to 4 claims annually for the entire SAP Group."

- ✔ **Risk management as competitive advantage:** SAP GRC Risk Management has made SAP AG a tougher and savvier competitor. "All loss events impact the bottom line, making us less profitable," states Phil Morin, senior director of risk management, SAP AG. "If we reduce the number of loss events, we have more money to invest in areas such as research and development @md and that's got to be good news for our customers."

- ✔ **Monitoring important KRIs:** Part of the competitive advantage derives from the ability to important information such as the sales pipeline, new project launch status, and the effectiveness of internal controls.

Gleaning the Benefits of SAP GRC Risk Management

SAP GRC Risk Management enables businesses to understand the true nature and exposure of enterprise risks. Benefits include increased visibility into risks, the ability to leverage existing data throughout the enterprise, the ability to align risk management with strategy, and the ability to make better decisions.

- ✔ **Increase visibility:** SAP GRC Risk Management enables and automates the cross-enterprise identification, monitoring, and mitigation of risks across lines of business. It provides visibility and transparency of risks across the enterprise to allow organizations to be more accountable and make more effective risk-based business decisions.

- **Leverage all the information, everywhere:** SAP GRC Risk Management taps into the vast data stores of the systems in your SAP landscape, but doesn't stop there. It can embrace information in non-SAP enterprise applications as well as incorporating unstructured risk information held in other ERP systems, e-mail systems, spreadsheets, and documents. It automatically collects and aggregates all risk-relevant information at an enterprise level, creating a single repository for ERM. This consolidated information matures over time into a database of the company's experience, learning, and best practices for dealing with risks, helping you avoid making the same mistakes twice, even in different divisions.

- **Consolidate risk management and strategy management:** SAP GRC Risk Management aligns risk management with corporate strategy. Effective strategy management requires a consolidated view of objectives, underlying strategy execution initiatives, KPIs, and related risks. The synergy between risk management and strategy is further considered in Chapter 15.

- **Better, more informed decision-making:** SAP GRC Risk Management provides you with the information you need to make better decisions that take into account important risk factors. SAP GRC Risk Management allows you to conduct what-if scenarios, allowing you to factor in multiple scenarios to help you see how various market conditions and other variables could impact your plans. Relationships between data elements are dynamic; adjust the KRI thresholds for various areas and the risk forecasting automatically adjusts itself. Constant, real-time monitoring of KRIs provides confidence that the risk information you use to help you make solid decisions reflects the current state of all risks.

SAP GRC Risk Management gives you proactive and risk-adjusted management of enterprise performance, providing the tools you'll need to compete effectively in the future.

Chapter 3

Governance: GRC in Action

In This Chapter

▸ Getting to know the ropes of governance

▸ Creating a governance plan

▸ Maintaining a good governance framework

*I*n the past few chapters, we examined the R (risk) and the C (compliance) of GRC. In a nutshell, risk not only deals with what could go wrong, but also where a sophisticated and enterprising company might be able to divine opportunities. Examining risk involves finding the lemons and maybe some water and sugar to make fresh lemonade. Compliance, on the other hand, is doing what you are supposed to do from a regulatory standpoint. Simply put, comply or pay the consequences.

On their own, the two legs of risk and compliance make something of a fairly wobbly stool. They are all talk and no action. They are a car with no engine. It's the third leg, governance, that allows the stool to stand, or the car to drive, depending on which analogy you favor.

In this chapter, we show you the benefits of good governance, how to create a blueprint for it, and how to make sure that you maintain a positive approach to governance over time. We also take a look at the importance of automation in executing your governance plan and examining the details of the SAP solution.

Getting to Know Governance

So, what is governance? Avoiding risk and trying to make lemonade out of lemons seem like pretty good ideas. So, too, is complying with relevant rules and regulations rather than paying fines, risking the company's brand and reputation, or worse.

However, without the governance component, compliance and risk are merely ideas floating around the boardroom. It's a classic stereotype: white-haired corporate leaders sitting in the boardroom congratulating themselves because they know what the risks to the company are and have identified how to comply with various laws and regulations. Meanwhile, the company falls into a giant hole of risks and is as lawless as Bonnie and Clyde with regard to compliance because no one has taken management's knowledge and acted on it. The corporate execs may be aware of risk and compliance issues, but without governance, there is no framework within which to establish a risk and compliance program.

Generally, *governance* is thought of as the activities and responsibilities undertaken by the CEO and all of the other bigwigs to run and oversee the company. Within the context of GRC, governance means doing all of the work to understand risk and compliance issues and then creating policies and procedures that *act* on that knowledge to ensure that risks are avoided, opportunities are acted on in a timely manner, and compliance to internal and external laws and regulations is actively pursued throughout the company. Governance is also about establishing what should happen if a risk scenario occurs or some unit of the company, intentionally or accidentally, violates internal or external regulations. In brief, governance is the structure any company implements to succeed in achieving its operating goals in the manner that it defines as the right way from a risk and compliance perspective.

One way to delineate the boundaries and relationships between governance, risk, and compliance is to think of owning a home. Compliance is the legal side of governance, which means you have to comply with all local ordinances, pay your property taxes, get approval for improvements from the planning board, be a good neighbor, appropriately dispose of garbage and other waste, and hold homeowners' insurance. Risk is identifying where and when noncompliance of the law could occur and identifying risk factors associated with homeownership, such as maintenance issues, threat of fire, illegal behavior on the property, loss of value due to an external action such as a change in zoning ordinances, and failure to comply with zoning ordinances.

Governance is everything you do to achieve those goals: You have taxes automatically paid from an escrow account, find good homeowners insurance, keep the yard clean, recycle, install smoke detectors, keep a regular maintenance schedule for repairs, and ensure everyone living in the house follows the law. Further, a few of these governance initiatives, such as smoke detectors, an escrow account, and a regular maintenance schedule function as *controls* (the tools of governance) in that they are the means to achieve governance goals. (For more on controls, flip to Chapter 7.)

Governance is not about creating a slow-moving internal bureaucracy. Far from it: Governance is about creating a fast-moving, disciplined, agile, and continuous enterprise-wide initiative centered on the areas of risk and compliance. You may not be able to control government regulations or forestall events such as the loss of a single source supplier or a natural disaster, but governance is where the corporation and its leadership are in the driver's seat. Corporate leadership identifies risks and compliance issues and then establishes the governing framework to ensure that the company manages risk and compliance in a way that helps drive it toward meeting its goals and objectives, while also remaining alert to opportunities and agile enough to act on them. The goal of governance is to break down barriers so that implementation of GRC is not done in a piecemeal fashion. GRC is not G or R or C separately, but a unified and enduring system that is adopted throughout the enterprise. The goal is to create a management system where all compliance and risk structures, such as policies, processes, risk monitoring, controls, test plans, remediation cases, and documentation are centrally managed to break down obstacles that could hamper an integrated implementation of GRC.

Further, a strong governing framework takes into account the value of implementing proactive and collaborative processes that balance opportunities with financial, legal, and operational risks in a transparent manner.

Gleaning the Benefits of Good Governance

A strong governing framework has many benefits. Here are just a few:

- **Increased shareholder value:** A properly functioning and documented governing framework can provide corporate leaders with an increased sense of security as they reflect on the efforts they are making toward managing compliance and risk issues. Governance can also provide reassurance to those outside of the company by demonstrating the organization's capacity for understanding the need to manage risk and compliance issues as well as its ability to institute a functioning GRC system. The result can be measured in the strengthening of the company's brand and reputation, which translates into stronger shareholder value.

- **Lower overall costs:** A unified and holistic approach to GRC also helps to lower the overall yearly costs to managing a company's risk and compliance activities. For example, a GRC approach increases efficiency, allowing a company to reduce the number of people dedicated to this function and the number of hours required to carry out risk and compliance duties.

- **Improved financial performance:** A strong governing framework facilitates transparency, giving company leaders a logical and structured process to proactively and more effectively address risk scenarios and compliance issues. Further, by providing the tools to mitigate risk and manage compliance, companies can reduce performance variability and increase overall financial performance.

- **Sustainability of efforts:** Because a systematic framework is more efficient and functional than a piecemeal approach, it is also far more sustainable because it is less expensive from a human resources point of view and is better able to adapt to an ever changing and increasingly complicated business environment.

✔ **Greater agility:** In addition, as a company adapts and alters its business model to reflect changes in the market or evolved goals, it will be better able to evaluate how those changes will affect its risk and compliance landscape and how individual scenarios interrelate. As a result, the company will be more adept and faster at developing processes and policies to address these issues.

Drafting Governance Blueprints

To stick with our house metaphor from earlier in the chapter: Before you can build the house, you need a blueprint, which may include quite a bit of customization to meet the tastes of an individual homeowner. Governance is no different in that it must start with a plan, but that plan will be different for individual companies and industries due to the idiosyncratic nature of a company, its regulatory environment, and the need to create a specific area of practice for the governance organization.

For example, the pharmaceuticals and life sciences industries have strict compliance requirements from the FDA; therefore, a governance structure for this sector would need to incorporate the rules for FDA validation.

Given that variation, here's an overall design map to consider following as you develop your specific blueprint:

✔ **Create a governance office.** Creating a dedicated office eliminates the notion that governance of risk and compliance issues is some sort of sideline job such as "Hey Ted, why don't you organize Mary's retirement party, and, by the way, could you set up a governance structure for risk and compliance?" It takes this issue and makes it part of the company's structure rather than allowing it to languish as an ad-hoc effort among individual units.

The governance office is in charge of helping to populate and support the company's code of conduct and all risk- and compliance-related policies. For example, the office could be in charge of investigating violations with regard to segregation of duties policies and enforcing those policies. The governance office is also something of a go-to point where employees and line managers could bring questions about how to resolve issues when two policies conflict or where a policy conflicts with a stated company objective.

Functions of the governance office could also include fraud reporting and prevention, diffusing and communicating policies, training on policies and conduct, regular reporting, and coordinating compliance functions among varying business units, to name a few.

It is also important to note that if your company operates in more than one country or in subdivisions with distinct sets of regulations and rules, it would be a good idea to create a centralized governance office with satellites localized to each geographic or relevant subdivision.

✔ **Localize offices and policies.** If your company needs to create satellite offices for geographic areas, each of these subsidiaries should be able to make changes to the overall set of policies as they relate to local laws and regulations. However, as much as possible, changes should attempt to stay close to the central framework to maintain consistency across the enterprise.

Localized changes and exceptions as well as all other policies and procedures, should be stored in a centralized and accessible database so that they are available to employees.

You should also sprinkle local governance officers throughout the organization where it makes logical sense to do so. The intent is to make following the governance framework as easy and accessible as possible.

✔ **Ensure partner and third-party compliance.** Create a structured and standardized means to describe and communicate internal policies that partners must follow. You must also make sure that you have a way to verify that those partners are living up to your standards.

Be sure that as the relationship unfolds, there are documented processes that can be used for internal and external audits.

✔ **Communicate.** Employees *must* feel empowered to report when violations to policies have occurred or when they have identified previously unknown risk scenarios. They must have access to several ways for such communication to occur, such as a unique and standard GRC e-mail address, phone number, or even via Web forms. The governance office should also maintain an open-door policy for employees.

Be aware that if you allow anonymous communication, you run the risk of false reporting. Creating the position of ombudsman, which is essentially an advocate for employees making a report of a violation or inconsistency in a policy, helps to alleviate this worry while also helping employees feel more secure because a dedicated officer is in charge of representing their interests.

Creating a Framework for Great Governance

After you understand that you need a governance structure in place, you're probably starting to wonder what a strong governing framework looks like. Simply speaking, it is a unified approach where strategy is set at the top and disseminated down to corporate vice presidents, line managers, and

Executives are key to the G in GRC

As discussed in Chapter 4, corporations have had to incorporate compliance with numerous regulations and laws since nearly the dawning of civilization. However, Sarbanes-Oxley (SOX) altered the landscape in a very significant way by placing responsibility and accountability for a company's financial reporting squarely on the shoulders of executives and board members.

Further, accountability includes making sure the opportunity for a violation does not exist. As stated in the law, executives and board members are responsible for instituting effective internal controls to ensure that the corporation — and by extension, stockholders and investors — is protected from malfeasance throughout the enterprise. (Simply put, an employee or department manager cannot do bad things, or if they do, processes are in place to detect it and policies exist to address it.)

On this last point, take the example of the store clerk who, when handed cash at the register, is faced with a choice — pocket the cash or place it in the till. If there are no company rules or processes (a tool of governance) in place, the clerk may keep the cash and simply adjust the register totals to avoid being caught.

In this case, the clerk is stealing, but in the context of SOX, the fact that the opportunity for the clerk to steal existed (ineffectual controls) is the fault of executives and is something they are liable for. By having lax governance, executives are allowing employees to make a choice and have the opportunity to take an action that could hurt the company and its investors, and are therefore liable.

employees (wisdom can flow downhill too). At each level, VPs, managers, and employees are responsible for the individual roles they are assigned in order to implement and carry out on an ongoing basis the tactical initiatives necessary to achieve the strategic goals. Essentially, the top-level management creates a culture that is managed by a governance structure and creates a report card that gauges the effectiveness of the governance model.

Further, the size and scope of a corporation's GRC efforts are determined by the industry it is in, its relative regulatory environment, and the idiosyncratic tendencies of its board and executive level leadership. However, some conventions as to the establishment and structure of a governing framework apply across industries and regulatory environments.

Either the board or the CEO might initiate a GRC program, but whatever the spark, after the need for a systematic approach to GRC is identified, the CEO generally examines governance issues with the board. Such governance issues might include establishing a risk committee, if one does not already exist, or to place this role under an existent committee, delineating in general terms the risks the company should examine such as operational, compliance, trade regulations, financial, external scenarios, and so on, and then making a recommendation for how the board (company) should proceed. One hallmark of companies that take governance seriously is the appointment of a Chief Compliance Officer to own and manage the overall governance structure.

Roles of the board and audit committee

With the explicit declaration in SOX that corporate leaders carry responsibility and accountability for the integrity of information provided to investors and regulators, they must understand what their role should be within a governance framework in order to comply with the expectations created by SOX.

Board of Directors: In what has come to be known as the Caremark case (Caremark International Inc. Derivative Litigation; 698 A.2d 959; Del. Ch. 1996) former Delaware Supreme Court Chief Justice E. Norman Veasey established what is commonly termed the Caremark Standard for Corporate Compliance programs. Essentially, Veasey is answering the following questions for the board of directors: What kind of compliance program needs to be established to fulfill the duty of oversight? And, how far must directors go to fulfill the duty of disclosure?

Veasey then established the following seven protocols:

- The board must truly be independent.

- The board should engage in governance, not merely be advisors.

- Quarterly meetings on the topic of compliance (GRC) should be held and directors should expect to spend a minimum of 100 hours per year on these issues.

- There should be a regular evaluation of the CEO and independently advised audit, nominating, and compensation committees on the board of directors.

- The board should establish and monitor compliance programs.

- There should be a limit to the number of boards that directors may serve on.

- The board should carefully review disclosure documents to make sure that relevant audiences and materials are made reasonably available.

Audit Committee: For those who draw the short stick and are assigned to the audit committee, the following are questions you should consider when measuring potential risk to non-compliance. These also directly relate to how this committee should operate within a functional governing framework.

- Are you in control of the agenda or are management and the auditors?

- Do you know the effectiveness of internal controls?

- Do you recognize or know about off-balance sheet financing practices or past history at the company?

- How do you find out about third-party transactions?

- Do you know what the fees for non-audit related services by the audit firm are — the amount and what services are involved?

- What credentials do auditors and internal control personnel have to evaluate ramifications on financial, technology, legal, and operational decisions affected by internal control weaknesses?

- Do you understand the business areas and inherent risks associated with the company?

- Is there a process for acquiring independent information on risks and major decisions?

- Do you have a handle on management practices and culture that encourage or discourage integrity breaches in the company?

- Does compensation encourage risk-taking or conservatism among corporate officers?

After the CEO examines governance issues with the board, the CFO and COO are brought into the process. Risks (including compliance issues) have been identified and a plan of action has been drawn up, which leads to the creation of an implementation plan. The challenge here is expressing and implementing the strategic initiatives throughout the company while also translating those strategies into tactical actions that need to be taken at the managerial and employee levels. The implementation plan must include how to assess the way all levels of the company are following through on the agenda. In other words, you have to find a way to tell people what you want them to do, what they need to do in specific terms, and then make sure they are doing it.

To do this, the governance office should write down the policies and processes (governing frameworks) and communicate them by dashboard, Power Point presentations, strategy documents, or in any other manner that would work for your company (a GRC clown, billboards, blimp, fun tattoos . . . let your imagination run wild.) These policies and processes are then translated into various types of plans (that is, tactics), such as management-by-objectives, key performance indicators (KPIs), controls such as access control and process control (see Chapters 6 and 7 for more on these), and other oversight and operational tools. In other words, use what works for you to get people to do what needs to be done.

As the implementation plans are drawn up, the CEO, along with the CFO and COO, may determine that their efforts would be strengthened by creating a high-level officer — with a title such as Chief Compliance Officer (CCO) — who is given the job of overseeing that the company is complying with external regulatory requirements as well as internal policies and procedures (the captain of a tight ship).

CCOs are responsible for the ethical conduct of a company and are a recent creation that has come in the wake of the passage of SOX. Additional offices and departments can also be created depending on the needs of the individual corporation.

Depending upon the company, the CCO role could include managing policy development; implementing and enforcing policy, which includes training, communications and investigating policy misconduct or violations; assuring corporate compliance with third-party (vendor or customer) guidelines and policies, managing internal audits, facilitating external audits, and responding to various requests from and required reporting to regulatory agencies.

Another important role played by a chief compliance officer, and one that would translate to any company and industry seeking to strengthen its GRC efforts, is to identify compliance violation trends.

Identifying compliance violation trends is distinct from efforts such as preventing employees from downloading objectionable material from the Internet. Rather, it involves scanning a number of resources — news media, industry journals, regulatory Web sites, speeches by regulatory officials, and

Controls: Tools of governance

Controls are one of the more powerful tools of governance. They encompass all of the actions, processes or physical barriers that direct or guide a resource or person to achieve a desired result. Although there are many methods, they all pretty much can be placed in the following three categories:

Preventative controls: Preventative controls are used to prevent an identified risk scenario from actually occurring. For example, Segregation of Duties (see Chapter 5 for more on that) is a preventative control because, among other things, it seeks to ensure that no one person can establish a vendor relationship and then make a payment to that vendor. Preventative controls are considered to be the most effective controls because they help deter malicious behavior or avoid risks and alert management in a timely fashion.

Detective controls: Detective controls are used to determine if any bad behavior or risk scenario has occurred or is occurring. They are also used to validate that monitored processes — such as payments to vendors, financial reporting, or regulatory compliance — are being performed within certain tolerances. For example, within SAP's GRC solutions, tolerances for financial reporting can be set so that if one unit is reporting a drop or increase in net sales that exceeds set tolerances ("why are we selling so many shorts in January?"), which could indicate a reporting issue ("Actually, one division has transferred a bunch of shorts to another division and someone is labeling those as sales") and/or a business issue ("We may not be producing enough shorts to meet demand"), a report is created and appropriate personnel are notified in order to set the response plan into action ("We need to label the transfer appropriately and increase shorts production"). These controls are important because they provide information to help a company understand where it is within the risk and compliance spectrum and what actions, if any, should be taken at any given time.

Corrective controls: Corrective controls are policies and procedures that lay out what actions are to be undertaken if a risk scenario occurs ("Why did Bob set up a vendor relationship with a company named Bobcom and then approve a check to be sent to a private residence?"). These provide the methods necessary to correct whatever condition may exist ("We need to talk with Bob"). Within the SoD example, if an individual is found with conflicting roles — establish a vendor and then make a payment ("Bob?") — that person's roles are redefined to remove the exception ("Bob, we still need to talk").

If a net sales tolerance is exceeded and a report is generated, actions such as an internal audit of that particular unit could be undertaken to understand why the tolerance may have been exceeded, and justify and document it (i.e., more people are buying shorts in January because more people are going on vacation to Florida at that time).

so on — for enforcement trends that could help the company focus its efforts and highlight new risk scenarios. For example:

> ✔ **Responsibility for partners:** A few years after enactment of SOX, regulatory watchers were surprised to discover that the regulatory agencies had held a few companies liable for the actions of their partners or third-party organizations. To respond, some companies began an internal

> analysis of how they interact with their partners and third-party organi-
> zations and for any scenarios that could possibly place them at risk of
> being held accountable for the actions of others. In this way, the efforts
> to seek out trends helped these companies enact preventative controls
> to address the new risk scenarios they had discovered.
>
> ✔ **Conversations between partners:** Another compliance violation trend
> to consider is scrutiny of the collaboration between two partner compa-
> nies. It is not hard to imagine that conversations that unintentionally
> veer into the area of unit costs could be interpreted as attempts at price
> fixing. To react to this kind of risk, a company could enact an initiative
> to examine how conversations between partners are carried out and to
> establish a system of procedures to ensure regulatory compliance.

Evaluating Your Governance Framework

After a governing structure is in place, you must still evaluate whether it is
performing well and ensure that it is capable of achieving the company's
goals. These two questions could prove helpful in assessing the strength
of a governance framework:

✔ What is the structure of the risk management process from a strategic
and operational perspective?

✔ What's the structure of the legal and regulatory compliance department?

From a strategic and operational perspective

When evaluating the structure of the risk management process from a strategic and operational perspective, what you're hoping to find is that the risk
management process is relatively sophisticated and somewhat self-managed
so that it could be relied upon for data that is accurate and thorough in its
nature and scope. The bottom line is that strategic and operational risks are
vital bits of data for a company to know, so therefore the company should
allow the experts to run and develop that data with little or no interference
(in other words, keep micromanagement to a minimum).

For example, in the case of a large software implementation deal, risk management would and should have the expertise to make sure the salespeople
are not over-committing the company to something it cannot deliver on, or
that the implementation may in some way as yet unseen cause the company
to lose money, displease the client by not meeting the deliverables, cause a
legal risk (such as a compliance infraction), garner negative publicity, or
some combination of the above.

So, if you feel that your risk management efforts follow the model outlined in Chapter 2, it is likely that risks are being identified and that the company is able to develop a plan to mitigate those risks, which is the essence of good governance — managing risk and compliance within the company's business environment.

From a legal and regulatory compliance perspective

The second question to answer when evaluating your governance framework is, "What are the tasks that the legal and regulatory compliance department should perform?" The tasks for this group fall into the areas of setting, communicating, and enforcing policies. More specifically, the group tasked with compliance should do the following:

- ✔ Identify legal and regulatory risks
- ✔ Evaluate policies from the standpoint of completeness, especially regarding whether they are complete (or whether a new policy is needed)
- ✔ Evaluate policies from the standpoint of enforcement. Are the policies being enforced the way they should be?
- ✔ Evaluate policies from the standpoint of effectiveness. Are the policies achieving their stated goals? Are they effective?
- ✔ Decide on and implement a strategy for communicating policies and governance initiatives
- ✔ Assess where and whether training is necessary and if so who should receive training and how often (for example, new hires receive training and company wide refreshers are held quarterly on various topics)
- ✔ Make sure that staff is available to answer questions about policies and that everyone knows how and where to report policy violations if necessary
- ✔ Decide how to respond to any violations of policies
- ✔ Establish a performance metric so that it can demonstrate what the group has done and communicate the value of its work to the company

In all, the evolution and ongoing efforts toward a strong governance regime are part of an iterative process that involves as much intuition and learning through experience as it does an application of long established business practices.

Perhaps, though, the best way to test for the effectiveness of the company's governance efforts is if every employee at any level of the organization knows what the company expects of them, they know what the policies are, they know where to find them, and have been trained on those relative to their function. (Sounds like the perfect employee, doesn't it?)

Hurdles to Instituting and Maintaining a Good Framework

With any project that is worth doing, there are going to be a number of challenges and hurdles to overcome at implementation and throughout the life of the initiative. Establishing and maintaining a good governance framework is no different because there are a number of ways for a company to go astray. In the next few sections, we give a few examples of issues to be considered.

The Open Compliance and Ethics Group

For those seeking a good resource to help them get started on the journey toward GRC or for those seeking to better hone their efforts, the Open Compliance and Ethics Group (OCEG) provides quite a bit of information at its Web site www.oceg.org. The OCEG is a nonprofit organization dedicated to helping companies align their GRC efforts in order to drive business performance and promote integrity.

To this end, the online magazine *Compliance Week* published a series of articles by Scott L. Mitchell, chairman and CEO of the OCEG. These articles are intended to help companies put the goals of GRC into practice. (The series can be found online at `www.complianceweek.com/index.cfm?fuseaction=Page.viewPage&pageId=345`.) Throughout the 11 part series, a number of best practices are highlighted that relate directly to the governance function of GRC (many of these overlap with the information provided above).

Here is a summary of a few of Mitchell's points:

- ✔ Corporate culture is a safety net for the company facilitating information sharing

- ✔ Talented individuals should drive the governance initiative and should occupy decision making roles

- ✔ The governing framework ensures that objectives (strategic, operational, financial, and compliance) can be achieved; problems being detected in a timely manner; when detected the response is timely and effective; and the framework complies with internal and external regulations

- ✔ Information should be able to easily reach relevant external stakeholders

- ✔ Technology should be used appropriately

- ✔ Process and nomenclature should be ubiquitous among the company's units and reflect industry norms

- ✔ Valid tests and metrics should be in place to validate the framework is functioning as intended and detect issues

Avoiding GRC silos

For most companies, compliance issues and risk analysis have been done on something of a case-by-case basis. For example, a new regulation is enacted, causing the company to respond by assigning its legal team to establish what the company's responsibilities are in order to comply. A plan of action on that one issue is then created and implemented.

As time goes by, the company, wittingly or unwittingly, creates a variety of piecemeal structures to address individual risk and compliance issues rather than creating a unified and efficient enterprise-wide approach. In this way, the company has established numerous GRC-related silos under a plethora of issue areas. Such efforts are inefficient, carry a higher degree of risk, lack visibility, and miss out on opportunities that could be created using a more holistic approach.

As Scott Mitchell writes in the first segment of his series for *Compliance Week*, "How Do We Align Our GRC Initiatives?" many organizations operate between three and 15 GRC silos divided among various business segments, such as financial, human resources, billing, and so on. He notes that with the above issues of a segmented GRC approach, these companies also place a significantly greater compliance burden on their core business functions. These companies may recognize the need to make investments to manage compliance and risk, but because they have established a segmented rather than unified governing structure, they are mismanaging their investments.

Making GRC strategic

As the previous example demonstrates, many companies have perceived GRC (though they may not have thought of compliance and risk management in terms of GRC) to be an adjunct project rather than an ongoing and iterative process integrated into the company's operations.

In the years following the passage of SOX, many companies considered compliance and risk to be tactical issues rather than a unified strategic initiative, which, in many cases, led to over-reliance on third-party contractors (primarily audit firms operating outside of their regular audit functions) to carry out the controls necessary to comply with the new regulations (and, by extension, assess risks in this area). In this manner, auditing firms were able to grow revenues from non-audit clients by providing controls, doing all of the testing of those controls, and then telling the client what controls they should have in order to comply with the requirements of SOX.

Not only is this expensive (auditors were more than happy to bring in teams to perform these functions and then reap significant fees for these services), but the knowledge of how to establish a compliance system and create the governance framework around it was left with the auditors — the company likely retained very little of this "how to" knowledge. It was the equivalent of receiving a fish someone else caught rather than learning how to catch it yourself.

The solution is for companies to start perceiving GRC as more than just addressing separate issue areas and perceive it as a strategic initiative rather than a set of tactics to be applied on a piecemeal basis. As such, a company should integrate this knowledge and function into its day-to-day operations rather than having an outside firm carry out the process for them. A company could hire an auditing firm to consult on what controls are needed, how to test them, and help document the process. At that point, however, the process should be brought in-house. Third parties can still be helpful to periodically evaluate how well the GRC initiative is being carried out, however, and to suggest improvements.

Justifying the cost of GRC

The fact that cutting costs equals increased profits, all other things being equal, is a very simple formula for people to understand. You can easily see that executives and managers face huge pressures to make sure that costs are as low as they can be. In many ways, cost control is their number one imperative. Within the context of GRC, though, top-down pressures could push some managers and executives to cut GRC-related investments to the point that the company's exposure to risk and compliance violations is increased.

For example, think back to the homeowner's analogy we mentioned earlier in this chapter. When a person buys a house, they have it inspected to ensure that the roof doesn't leak, the electric system is up to code and safe, the exterior walls are painted and there are no signs of rot, the septic system is in good working order as is the rest of the plumbing, and that the foundation is solid.

However, as time goes by, a certain amount of wear and tear occurs on the house. Without continued investments to replace the roof before it leaks, update the electric system, maintain the plumbing, and fix cracks in the foundation, there is a risk of failure with profound consequences to the house and the people living in it. Further, a lack of investment may cause the home to violate certain municipal codes or ordinances. And of course, the batteries in the smoke detectors need to be regularly checked and replaced.

GRC for a company is no different: It has to be an ongoing investment. Therefore, it is important to incorporate within the governing framework a means to rationalize and communicate the need (risks and benefits) to *maintaining* investments in GRC in an enterprise-wide and sustained manner.

One solution to this issue, writes Scott Mitchell, is to develop a thorough and logically argued business case for GRC investment that can be easily accessed and communicated to all levels to assure enterprise-wide understanding of the importance of maintaining the GRC home and what that entails.

The challenge, though, is that many of the benefits to GRC and a strong governing framework are difficult to quantify because they either prevent a risk scenario from occurring or are difficult to measure and report. One example of a factor that's difficult to report is the fact that if employees are better at their jobs, the brand and reputation of the company are more highly regarded, better decisions are being made at all levels, and so on. Further, some in leadership may not view GRC as a high priority worthy of continued investment.

As Mitchell writes, "An effective business case will communicate GRC's strategic value by showing key components of the GRC program support or enable overall strategy." An effective business case should also quantify the problems and issues that are being avoided by showing the costs of non-compliance, costs of minimally complying (that is, inefficiencies caused by silos, duplication of efforts, errors, visibility, etc.), and miscellaneous risks such as unethical behavior by a single or small group of actors within the company. It should then explain the benefits of GRC, and explain the journey to GRC.

Applying GRC too narrowly

It may be obvious that the framework and tools of governance should be applied to resolve SoD issues and to ensure SOX compliance, among others, applying the framework and tools (controls) across *all* activities of the company, even in areas that may at first glance seem to be outside of the scope of GRC is also important.

For example, charitable contributions may seem like a relatively benign area. However, suppose that a company contributes a certain amount to a number of charities in a year and payments on that commitment are made in three installments.

A company with lax oversight (lack of controls or too narrowly applied) on how those payments are made is establishing the opportunity for a number of risks to occur, such as employee fraud and/or noncompliance with tax laws and financial reporting requirements. If a payment isn't made because an employee managed to divert it or a mistake occurs, and the company claims it as a deduction, that contribution, rather than serving the greater good, could create a significant financial risk and sully the company's reputation and brand.

Within a broad and strong governance framework, these payments would be established within the system in the same manner as a vendor contract. Controls would be in place to prevent or identify an issue and report it to the appropriate person, and a process to react and mitigate the impact of the event would exist.

Setting up checks and balances

Within any governing structure, a robust set of checks and balances must be in place to ensure that the system is operating as intended and to make sure that there is little chance a risk or compliance issue could be missed.

At a company that perceives its risk management and compliance efforts as a strategic initiative designed to drive company performance and integrates a broad and strong governance framework, controls would be in place to document and send an alert if income from operations deviates from set tolerances. And policies and processes would be in place to address the alert limiting the company's risk exposure and liability.

Further, and importantly, within this type of framework, systems would be in place to check the checkers. A good governance framework addresses the question of what happens if the manager who receives the alert does not act on it.

Governance includes creating a strong and responsive corporate culture that can overcome the social, financial, and career pressures to act irresponsibly that may be experienced by any individual. Essentially, it is policy with some controls to establish culture and enforce behavior.

Just as checks should be placed on individuals within the system, there should be checks on the system as a whole as well. This is where a mix of technology and external oversight can be used to enhance internal oversight. In the case of Enron, they did have limited external oversight in the form of Arthur Anderson, but this proved to be dysfunctional in terms of providing the type of oversight the company needed to avoid the risk scenario that played out. A proper governance framework includes some degree of external oversight that is qualitative and has the independence to be effective, ask difficult questions, and hold the company accountable to its own GRC goals.

Making the Argument for Automation

Within a governing framework, tactical software has an important role to play. After all, when considering the complexity and scope of a company's activities that would fall under the domain of GRC, and in particular governance, it is easy to see that manual processes and self-reporting by employees would fall short. For this reason, automation of critical functions is key to achieving the goals of efficiency, transparency, uniformity, data collection, reporting, and documentation, to name a few.

For example, would a manual process detect if ten payments to one vendor for $10,000 each are entered into the system, yet are totaled out at less than

$100,000? Or would a manual process be able to generate an automatic report if an important disbursement step is being manipulated or accidentally missed?

The answer to these questions is a profound maybe.

As companies see the need for a unified and holistic GRC strategy, they are also seeing the need to weave technology into the mix at every level of the organization. And they are looking for products that not only match their business model, but also the compliance and risk scenarios for their respective industries. They want IT solutions that can decidedly answer the preceding questions in the affirmative and do so in a manner that reflects the environment they operate in.

Therefore, they are looking for IT solutions that facilitate a unified corporate strategy, incorporate the three control classifications (see the sidebar "Controls: Tools of governance" elsewhere in this chapter), aid in discovering new opportunities where GRC can align with the overall business goals of the organization, and reduce the potential for loss or mitigate scenarios as they may occur across the enterprise. Further, the benefits derived from this approach would extend to partners, suppliers, and customers in a truly systemic approach.

Just as you should avoid implementing a governance framework in a piece-meal fashion, the same is true for GRC IT applications. Fragmented or segmented automation efforts only confound the overall goal of a unified and systemic governing structure.

The SAP Approach: Integrated Holistic IT for GRC

As one example of an integrated IT approach, SAP provides a suite of integrated solutions that are intended to support a holistic approach to GRC by automating end-to-end GRC processes, which includes corporate governance and oversight, risk management, and compliance management.

The primary motivations behind SAP's unified platform approach flow directly from established GRC goals, which, in a general sense, are to effectively govern GRC activities from a system-wide and integrated perspective. Embedded in the platform architecture is the intention to treat GRC as being one piece of the company's core business processes so that it can be integrated within the day-to-day activities of the company.

The applications within the suite are each targeted towards a particular aspect of GRC with one each for governance (SAP GRC Repository, shown in Figure 3-1), risk (SAP GRC Risk Management), and a number targeted toward

**GRC Repository - Central System of Record Drives
Governance, Increases Transparency**

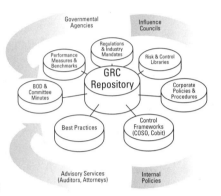

Figure 3-1:
The SAP GRC
Repository
centralizes
all relevant
policies and
information
for a unified
approach to
governance.

- Correlates regulations with internal compliance policies and procedures as evidence of compliance

- Centralizes knowledge base of content contributed from GRC Ecosystem

- Rationalizes controls against multiple frameworks

compliance (SAP GRC Access Control; SAP GRC Process Control; SAP GRC Global Trade Services; and SAP applications for environment, health, and safety compliance management).

Further, harkening back to the beginning of this chapter, as governance seeks to break down barriers between risk and compliance activities, each of the SAP GRC applications is designed to support the overall goals of the company's governance framework. For example, SAP GRC Risk Management provides support for best practices such as collaborative risk analysis, predefined risk responses, and continuous monitoring and reporting. The SAP GRC Global Trade Services application embeds regulatory and corporate compliance into core logistical processes. And the applications for environment, health, and safety align business processes with environmental, occupational safety, and product safety regulations as well as internal policies to make management of all three sharper and more efficient.

From a governance perspective, these applications feed into the SAP GRC Repository — the central IT tool for governance — in order to centralize management in terms of documentation, testing, remediation, and control monitoring. As such, the SAP GRC Repository centrally documents and stores all governance, risk, and compliance information for enterprise-wide and industry specific needs, and provides the means to centrally manage compliance structures, policies, processes, risk and control libraries, test plans, remediation cases and evidence.

In addition, the application links risks and controls to multiple external security and control modalities — such as the Committee of Sponsoring Organizations and Control Objectives for Information and Related Technologies — as well as to financial reporting requirements and health, and safety regulations.

In short, the intent is to desegregate disparate GRC structures in order to reduce system complexity and ensure the company is maximizing its return on investment (ROI) for its GRC efforts.

Coming to Grips with Governance

It's easy to view GRC as something of a burden because, on its surface, it appears to come with costs and seems to be placing constraints on the core functions of the company. This is especially true of the governance part of it because this is where you actually have to go and talk to people and change what they are doing, and as we all know, change is hard.

However, if you look past the surface, you will find that GRC is only a constraint to those activities and potential actions that could cause the company harm. And governance is the mechanism by which a company frees itself of risk and takes on its regulatory responsibilities — in other words, does its chores — in the best way possible.

So it is even easier to accept what may at first glance seem to be a contrarian point of view, which is that an integrated and holistic governing framework — and GRC system in general — can liberate corporate resources by automating its risk and compliance management and placing related functions within a highly efficient and cost effective system. And on top of that, governance initiatives can play a significant role in helping a company find and create opportunities to enhance core functions.

Far from being a burden, governance can be, and often is, an agent for change and for systematically helping an organization achieve its goals.

Part II
Diving into GRC

The 5th Wave   By Rich Tennant

"Thanks to Sarbanes—Oxley, we've got more internal controls than a warehouse full of Imodium."

In this part . . .

You plumb the depths of everyone's favorite GRC regulation, Sarbanes-Oxley, and then take a step back to examine how fraud can happen and the segregation of duties that can prevent it. You'll then jump into the important areas of controls: access control, making sure that roles don't conflict in ways that promotes violations, and process control, whereby you put in controls to watch over key business processes, making them efficient, compliant, and easy to monitor. Taking all this in, you then look at one of the most complex areas of compliance: global trade, where hundreds of regulations govern imports and exports and acronyms abound.

Chapter 4

How Sarbanes and Oxley Changed Our Lives

Sarbanes-Oxley, otherwise known as SOX, is a law passed in 2002 that is changing the way companies and their senior executives behave. Some say it is the most important securities law since the 1930s, when legislation was enacted after the Depression and the subsequent banking crisis. SOX was passed in response to the corporate and financial scandals of the early 2000s, when companies such as Enron and WorldCom covered up or misrepresented a variety of questionable transactions, resulting in a crisis in investor confidence and huge losses to their shareholders. The US government responded quickly, passing the Sarbanes Oxley Act, which holds up a mirror to the way corporations do business. Spawned from scandal, SOX is an attempt to find the moral compass that businesses lost in the 2000s.

In 2000, 2001, and 2002, the stock market finished lower than the year before for three years in a row: a feat that hadn't occurred since the 1930s. When you consider the snowballing effect of company scandals, the loss of billions of investor dollars, and a huge decline in investor trust, it was clear that something needed to happen. The Public Company Accounting Reform and Investor Protection Act of 2002, or SOX, is that something. In this chapter, we look at the events that led to the creation of SOX and the ramifications the law has for your business.

Figuring Out Whether SOX Applies to You

SOX applies to you if you are:

- ✔ A publicly traded company, a division of a publicly traded company, or a wholly owned subsidiary of one
- ✔ A non-U.S. public multinational engaging in business in the U.S.
- ✔ An audit firm that works for either of the above

If you don't fit in those categories (but you are a private company or a not-for-profit), two parts of the Act still apply to you:

- ✔ By law, you are not allowed to punish whistle-blowers. (In other words, don't shoot the messenger.)
- ✔ You may not alter, cover up, falsify, or destroy any document to prevent its use in an official investigation. (To put it simply, stay away from the shredder.)

SOX Online (www.sox-online.com), shown in Figure 4-1, is a great source for news and information about SOX; it will keep you laughing, too (believe it or not).

Figure 4-1:
SOX Online (www.sox-online.com) provides a wealth of SOX information along with humor for good measure.

Discovering Why SOX Became Necessary

In the late 1990s, a stock market bubble was created: More and more companies were going public, and the share prices of listed companies kept going up. Some companies forgot to serve their shareholders and instead focused on the numbers. They were more interested in making analysts happy than making their shareholders happy. In addition, extreme competition for experienced executives pushed company leadership to offer shares as part of their compensation, which meant there was more of a drive to keep the prices going up. Enron, for example, threw any bad deals into off-the-books partnerships to hide their bad assets, and their accounting practices no longer represented the reality of their finances. Then there were conflicts of interest for companies such as Arthur Andersen, which provided consulting services and audit services to Enron at the same time. Still, as the gatekeepers, Arthur Andersen should have drawn attention to the corporate fraud that was taking place (in fact, however, Arthur Andersen went out of business partly because its employees gave the order to shred documents at Enron.) When it became public knowledge that companies were indulging in willful fraud and corruption, there was a decline of public trust in accounting and financial reporting. People were losing billions of their investment dollars. In 2000, 2001, and 2002, the stock market ended every year down compared to the previous year. The US government needed to make investors confident in the market again, and so SOX was born.

Have corporate scandals such as those seen at Enron happened before? In his book *The Complete Guide to Sarbanes-Oxley* (Adams Media), UCLA law professor Stephen M. Bainbridge says that they have, many times:

"History teaches us that market bubbles are fertile ground for fraud. Cheats abounded during the Dutch tulip-bulb mania of the 1630s. The South Sea Company, which was at the center of the English stock market bubble in the early 1700s, was a pyramid scheme. Fraud was rampant before the Great Crash of 1929. Hence, it was hardly a shock to find fraudsters and cheats when we started turning over the rocks in the rubble left behind when the stock market bubble burst in 2000."

After the 1929 stock market crash and the resulting Great Depression, Congress passed several statutes to regulate the securities markets. In 1933, it passed the Securities Act, which legislated against fraud in the sale of securities, and allowed issuers to sell any securities, even unsound ones, provided they gave buyers enough information to make an informed investment decision.

The content of these 80-year-old laws requires companies and auditors to maintain strict financial controls. However, because this was clearly not happening, it became necessary for the US government to re-release the laws. They did just that in 1992, reinstating the older laws.

The scandals: How bad were they?

The names *Enron* and *WorldCom* have become synonymous with scandal, and for good reason: The scope of their misdeeds is staggering. The Enron debacle is estimated to have wiped out some $60 billion in shareholder value, whereas WorldCom lost roughly $175 billion worth of investors' money. WorldCom's $103 billion bankruptcy filing in 2002 was the largest in U.S. history; Enron's $63 million filing in 2001 was the second largest.

In the wake of the scandal, Enron laid off nearly all of its 22,000 employees, and WorldCom cut its staff by 5,100 before heading into bankruptcy. Many of those employees lost pensions, retirement savings, and college tuition funds.

And because many pension funds around the country had invested in Enron and WorldCom, the ripples from the scandals spread far and wide. For example, the Florida's state pension fund lost $335 million when Enron went bankrupt. The Oklahoma Teachers Retirement System lost $17 million before selling its holdings in WorldCom.

The scandals also set off a wave of investigations into the accounting practices of other corporations including Tyco, Qwest, and Coca Cola. The scandal even had political ramifications. Many questioned the Bush administration's close ties to Enron officials; California residents recalled their governor, Gray Davis, and elected Arnold Schwarzenegger in part because of the state's power crisis, a crisis in which Enron played a role.

Historian Joel S. Seligman told *The Washington Post* that Enron "was the most important corporate scandal of our lifetimes. It was one of the immediate causes of the Sarbanes-Oxley Act, the governance reforms of the New York Stock Exchange and NASD, and the most consequential reorientation of corporate behavior in living memory."

Being SOX-compliant means that companies are allowing investors to make informed decisions with clean, up-to-date, and management-certified information. Misinformation, whether intentional or not, is now punishable by law. This insistence on clean information levels the playing field for investors and shareholders. Instead of operating in the dark, they can now see the light.

Who Are Sarbanes and Oxley, Anyway?

The Sarbanes in Sarbanes-Oxley, is Paul Sarbanes, a lawyer and Democratic senator who represented Maryland in the Senate from 1977–2007. Elected to the House of Representatives in 1970, Sarbanes sat on the House Watergate Committee in 1974 to introduce the first Articles of Impeachment for obstruction of justice against President Richard Nixon. In 2002, he was the Senate sponsor of the Sarbanes-Oxley Act. Michael G. Oxley was a Republican member of the House of Representatives for Ohio, from 1981–2007. In 2002, he was chairman of the House Financial Services Committee, giving him primary responsibility for Sarbanes-Oxley on the House side.

Alphabet soup: Your handy guide to SOX terminology

Here are some of the many acronyms you'll hear tossed around when discussing SOX, and what they stand for:

- ✔ **COBIT:** Control Objectives for Information and Related Technology

- ✔ **COSO:** Committee of Sponsoring Organizations of the Treadway Commission

- ✔ **FASB:** Financial Accounting Standards Board

- ✔ **GAAP:** Generally accepted accounting principles

- ✔ **IFRS:** International Financial Reporting Standards

- ✔ **ITIL:** Information Technology Infrastructure Library

- ✔ **PCAOB:** Public Company Accounting Oversight Board

- ✔ **SEC:** Securities and Exchange Commission

Sarbanes and Oxley, whose pictures appear in Figure 4-2, both retired from public life in 2007.

Figure 4-2:
The infamous Sarbanes and Oxley.

Breaking Down SOX to the Basics

SOX aims to restore investor confidence and enhance corporate governance by using a series of internal checks and balances. The goal is to ensure transparent financial reporting. SOX consists of 11 titles and 65 sections. Instead of quoting you the full letter of the law, we have selected a specific group of important sections related to compliance to give you an overview.

Sections 302 and 906: Threatening management with a big stick

SOX seeks to prevent the kinds of failures of leadership that happened at companies such as Enron, and much of the law is aimed at corporate managers and directors. Section 302 places responsibility for the content of the financial reports firmly at the feet of the CEO and CFO by requiring that they certify them. Certification is nothing new, but with SOX, the conditions of certification have become much more rigorous. There is zero tolerance for misinformation.

SOX: A Layperson's Translation

We want to help you understand the most important things about SOX. This means we try to put something very technical — law — into plain English. There are professionals who both make the law clearer and sometimes make it more complicated: Those people are called lawyers. Just keep in mind that we make no guarantees about our explanations here; go talk to a lawyer if you want that kind of help. Also, we can recommend another book for more information: *SOX For Dummies* (Wiley Publishing), by Jill Gilbert Welytok, who *is* a lawyer.

302: The CEO and CFO are directly responsible for the accuracy, documentation, and submission of all financial reports, as well as the internal control structure to the SEC.

(Translation: The CEO and CFO are on the hook for making sure the company's financial reports sent to the US Securities and Exchange Commission are right. We talk more about Section 302 in a bit.)

401: Financial statements must be accurate, without any incorrect information, and include all off-balance sheet liabilities, obligations, or requirements.

(Translation: It is no longer possible for companies to hide any information that might affect their share price if it became common knowledge. They must present their true face to the world, warts and all.)

404: All annual financial reports must contain an Internal Control Report, stating that management is responsible for an "adequate" internal control structure. Management should provide an assessment of the internal control structure, and report any shortcomings.

(Section 404 is another biggie; we'll explain this one in detail later.)

406: Companies must disclose whether they have adopted a code of ethics for their top financial managers and if not, why not. The code must establish standards and provide for avoiding conflicts of interest. It must mandate personal and corporate compliance with SOX regulations.

(Translation: A code of ethics will guide financial managers on how to behave should they be tempted to stray from the path.)

409: Companies are required to disclose on an almost real-time basis information concerning material changes in its financial condition or operations.

(Translation: If there are big changes to the company's financial condition or its operations, the company has to tell the SEC.)

802: Imposes fines and/or sentences of up to 20 years imprisonment for altering or destroying records with the aim to disrupt a legal investigation.

(Translation: Destroying documents is bad.)

906: Requires that each periodic report filed with the SEC is certified by the CEO and CFO and that it complies fully with the statute and presents fairly the financial condition of the company.

(Translation: So that CEOs and CFOs can never again say, "I didn't know.")

Section 302 requires that when filing either an annual or quarterly report, both the CEO and the CFO must certify that they have

- ✔ Reviewed the report

- ✔ Found that the report does not contain any material untrue statements, any material omission, and is not misleading

- ✔ Found that the financial statements and related information present the financial condition and financial results fairly and accurately

In addition, the CEO and CFO must acknowledge that they

- ✔ Are responsible for internal controls, have reviewed these controls in the last 90 days, and have reported on these findings

- ✔ Have provided a list of all deficiencies in the internal controls and information on any fraud that involves employees who are involved with internal activities

- ✔ Have noted any significant changes in internal controls or related factors that could have a negative impact on the internal controls

This set of acknowledgements is changing the way CEOs and CFOs work. They are forced to actively monitor and assess controls to ensure that no fraud can take place. Senior management now has to spend time and money finding out precisely, and in detail, how their controls are working. They can no longer — as many of the Enron management team did — plead ignorance.

SOX considers this new level of commitment from executives in certifying what they know so essential that it appears twice in the legislation: once in Section 302 and again in Section 906. This is what is becoming known as the "Belt and Suspenders Theory" (the name comes from the fact that some people, just to be sure their pants won't fall down, wear both a belt and suspenders).

In Section 906, the big stick appears. Here lie the criminal penalties for failure to comply: a $1 million fine or a 10-year sentence for executives who claim ignorance of misinformation, and $5 million fine or a 20-year sentence for executives who willfully provide misinformation. Some stick, huh? (However, the jail sentences will only be used in extreme cases, where executives are shown to have willfully misrepresented the facts. For errors in their compliance framework, senior staff members are more likely to face fines and penalties.) Figure 4-3 shows a timeline of convictions under SOX during the regulation's first year.

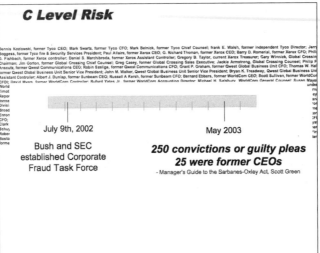

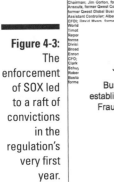

C Level Risk

Dennis Kozlowski, former Tyco CEO; Mark Swartz, former Tyco CFO; Mark Belnick, former Tyco Chief Counsel; frank E. Walsh, former independent Tyco Director; Jerry Boggess, former Tyco fire & Security Services President; Paul Allaire, former Xerox CEO; G. Richard Thoman, former Xerox CEO; Barry D. Romerial, former Xerox CFO; Phillip D. Fishbach, former Xerox controller; Daniel S. Marchibroda, former Xerox Assistant Controller; Gregory B. Taylor, current Xerox Treasurer; Gary Winnick, Global Crossing Chairman; Jim Gorton, former Global Crossing Chief Counsel; Greg Casey, former Global Crossing Sales Executive; Jackie Armstrong, Global Crossing Counsel; Philip F Anscutz, former Qwest Communications CEO; Robin Szeliga, former Qwest Communications CFO; Grant P. Graham, former Qwest Global Business Unit CFO; Thomas W. Hall, former Qwest Global Business Unit Senior Vice President; John M. Walker, Qwest Global Business Unit Senior Vice President; Bryan K. Treadway, Qwest Global Business Unit CFO; David Myers, former WorldCom Controller; Buford Yates Jr. former WorldCom Accounting Director; Michael H. Salsbury, WorldCom General Counsel; Susan Mayer

July 9th, 2002
Bush and SEC
established Corporate
Fraud Task Force

May 2003
***250 convictions or guilty pleas
25 were former CEOs***
- Manager's Guide to the Sarbanes-Oxley Act, Scott Green

Figure 4-3:
The enforcement of SOX led to a raft of convictions in the regulation's very first year.

Section 404: Ensuring a healthy immune system

The rules set out in Section 404 can be compared to the guidelines for a healthy lifestyle: Having a healthy immune system, for example, is not just a case of luck. We have to make good choices: eat lots of fruit and vegetables rather than junk food, drink lots of water, and take vitamins. Buying fresh produce and vitamins can be expensive, but we decide that being healthy is worth the extra expense. Lots of healthy individuals make a more healthy society. Section 404 is fresh food and vitamins for a company: It may cost you to implement the internal controls, but they ensure that your business runs wholesomely and that bugs like fraud are flushed out before they make the company sick. Lots of clean, healthy companies make for a clean and healthy investment culture.

The content of Section 404 is succinct, weighing in as it does at 168 words:

"(a) Rules Required. The Commission shall prescribe rules requiring each annual report required by section 13(a) or 15(d) of the Securities Exchange Act of 1934 to contain an internal control report, which shall

(1) state the responsibility of management for establishing and maintaining an adequate internal control structure and procedures for financial reporting; and

(2) contain an assessment, as of the end of the most recent fiscal year of the issuer, of the effectiveness of the internal control structure and procedures of the issuer for financial reporting.

(b) Internal Control Evaluation and Reporting. With respect to the internal control assessment required by subsection (a), each registered public accounting firm that prepares or issues the audit report for the issuer shall attest to, and report on, the assessment made by the management of the issuer. An attestation made under this subsection shall be made in accordance with standards for attestation engagements issued or adopted by the Board. Any such attestation shall not be the subject of a separate engagement."

What does Section 404 mean for business?

Section 404 requires that companies build up an internal control system that is checked by the CEO and CFO, and then by an external auditor. The control system should guarantee that the closing accounts are correct and should also have built-in checks to prevent fraud. A company's internal access controls and process controls must be able to spot inconsistencies. Many companies are choosing to automate their processes to help them monitor for fraud. The human element is, unfortunately, not a guarantee of consistently clean information.

Although Section 404 can be summed up in a few words, it is no lightweight. According to University of Austin, Texas business law professor Robert A. Prentice, in his forthcoming article, "Sarbanes-Oxley: The Evidence Regarding the Impact of Section 404," in the *Cardoza Law Review*, "whether SOX will ultimately be considered a success or not depends on the legacy of 404." Section 404 also has the loudest detractors and supporters. For more information, see the "The cases for and against Section 404" sidebar in this chapter.

The cases for and against Section 404

Supporters of 404 believe that to avoid fraud and improve investor confidence, companies must have good internal controls and independent audits. The reports produce clean information for the capital markets. Companies with poor internal controls tend to have more risk. The benefits of 404 — better gatekeeping, clean information, less risk — far outweigh the negatives. Since the implementation of SOX in 2002, no major domestic corporate scandals (except for backdated ones) have occurred. In other words, 404 and its SOX counterparts are doing the job they were meant to do.

Detractors believe the costs of 404 outweigh the benefits. Direct costs of 404 implementation have far exceeded expectations. A major factor has been the increased audit fees. These costs are especially burdensome for small companies. Companies are either choosing to list on the London and Frankfurt Stock Exchanges instead of in New York to avoid the regulations, or they are choosing to go private. Foreign firms are choosing not to go public in the U.S. All this is damaging New York's image as financial capital of the world. Detractors also say the law, with its emphasis on penalization, is too tough.

Information Technology: SOX in a Box

In any company, the Information Technology (IT) group — the computer geeks — plays a vital role in helping companies become compliant. When processes are defined, automated, monitored, and corrected, maintaining internal control and ensuring clean information is much easier. IT drives the financial reporting processes by managing data, documents, and key operational processes. Therefore, the role of the Chief Information Officer (CIO), who is responsible for the security, accuracy, and reliability of the systems that manage and report the financial data, now plays a vital role in the certification and compliance process. Far from being a dead-end job, the CIO is now a powerful political role in a company.

COSO's Five Main Elements of Internal Control

Control environment: The foundation for all other elements, influencing the control consciousness of the people within the organization and encompassing every aspect of how the organization is structured and works.

(Translation: This is the big picture. If your control environment is healthy and is already functioning well, then sowing the seeds of compliance will be straightforward. If your control environment is sick and needs help, you are probably looking at a big change management project.)

Risk assessment: The identification and analysis of risks to the achievement of the organization's business objectives.

(Translation: In order to know your business, you need to know your risks and know them well.)

Control activities: The policies and procedures that help the board and management ensure that their control decisions are carried out in relation to identified risks.

(Translation: You've identified your risks, your control environment is good, and now you need to set up the policies and procedures that will help senior executives make their decisions.)

Information and communication: This must occur at two levels: first, the board must communicate its control objectives to all employees; and second, the IT system must capture and report pertinent information in a time frame and format that enables the organization's board and management to carry out its responsibilities.

(Translation: Both the head and the body need to be working together. If the messages don't get to the brain, the body will die.)

Monitoring: The ongoing monitoring of internal control systems includes regular and ad hoc functional and management reviews. It should be based on risk assessment, with serious deficiencies being reported to the board.

(Translation: Procedures are not always perfect. They can have weaknesses or break down. You need to monitor them to ensure that you know when they are failing you. You are the master of your processes; they are there to serve you and not the other way around.)

As SOX regulations have enhanced the role of IT within a company, they have also created a boom in IT projects and solutions. Niche companies are providing SOX solutions, while large software vendors are also providing software to automate internal controls as part of a larger GRC project. SOX has created an internal controls industry that is run by an army of vendors and consultants.

IT frameworks: Your template for compliance

The SEC has mandated U.S. companies to use a recognized internal control framework. There are a number of these, including COBIT (Control Objectives for Information and Related Technology) and ITIL (Information Technology Infrastructure Library). Some companies may choose one framework to structure their controls, whereas others may cherry-pick sections from each, although that could be more time-consuming and lead to gaps. Sound like more rules? Maybe, but the IT frameworks are really skeletons on which companies flesh out their own unique set of business processes.

COBIT builds on the financial compliance framework provided by COSO. COBIT is widely recommended by analysts, auditors, and consultants. It is published by the Information Systems Audit and Control Association (ISACA) and the IT Governance Institute, which notes that the work that goes into meeting SOX requirements should not only be regarded as compliance but also as an opportunity to build strong governance models. ITIL is a best practice library developed in the U.K. from work done for Office of Government Commerce.

COSO's control framework

COSO was originally formed in 1985 as part of a private sector initiative by the National Commission on Fraudulent Financial Reporting. Since 2002, COSO has been extended and renamed. The COSO Enterprise Risk Framework emphasizes the importance of identifying and managing risks across the enterprise.

COSO defines *internal control* as "a process, effected by an entity's board of directors, management, and other personnel, designed to provide reasonable assurance regarding the achievement of objectives in the following categories:

✔ Effectiveness and efficiency of operations

✔ Reliability of financial reporting

✔ Compliance with applicable laws and regulations"

The SOX ripple effect

Implementing any of these frameworks has a huge impact on the IT and Finance functions within a company. Companies implementing COSO, COBIT, or ITIL should not underestimate the training and change management implications. People in Finance will have new processes to monitor, repair, and report on; IT employees will require new design and procedural skills; HR departments will have to hire or train people to make these shifts. Being SOX-compliant is not something only CEOs, CFOs, CIOs, board members, or auditors have to worry about. It changes the way everyone in a company works.

Paying Up: What's SOX Going to Cost You?

For most organizations, the first year of SOX compliance was not easy. It was costly and time consuming. Companies had to redesign and document their roles and processes. Usually managed as a project, SOX compliance caused significant disruption to business activities. Guidance from the authorities was limited, and the auditors themselves were often unsure of what was required. Because little SOX-compliant software was available, most initial projects were mainly manual or spreadsheet based and painstakingly slow. The basic goal of most companies was to get through the audit without material weaknesses, whatever the cost. Not surprisingly, costs were significant.

SOX Costs Then

KPMG, a global firm specializing in audit, tax, and advisory services, conducted a survey of 90 Fortune 1000 companies covering their first year compliance with SOX, which revealed that:

- ✔ Twelve percent of companies disclosed material weaknesses in their internal controls over financial reporting.
- ✔ On average, companies spent around $1 on SOX compliance for every $1000 of revenue.
- ✔ On average, companies remedied 271 control deficiencies in SOX during the first year. They still had another 77 deficiencies left to address at the end of that year.
- ✔ Two-thirds of the companies disclosing a material weakness in their internal controls over financial reporting changed their CFOs within three months of filing their SEC returns.

SOX Costs Now

In the early years, SOX cost. Now, SOX still costs, but a study commissioned by Financial Executives International (FEI) shows that the SOX-related costs are coming down. FEI surveyed 172 companies with a market capitalization above $75 million and found that in 2006, SOX-related costs came down 23 percent. Employee hours spent on compliance came down 10% from 2005 to 2006, while external hours (by auditors) decreased 14 percent. The survey also found that:

- ✔ Compliance costs were cheaper for companies with centralized operations than for those with decentralized.

- ✔ Twenty-two percent of respondents feel the benefits of compliance outweigh the costs (up from 15 percent in 2005).

- ✔ Sixty percent agree that compliance has improved investor confidence.

- ✔ Forty-six percent say financial reports are more accurate, while 48 percent say financial reports are more reliable.

- ✔ Thirty-four percent agree that compliance has helped prevent or detect fraud.

Chances are good that complying with SOX is going to cost you a lot, but not as much as it would have cost you if you were becoming SOX-compliant in 2003. The range of software vendors offering products to help you automate your internal controls has grown exponentially since then. Independent auditors have had a few years to absorb what they have to do. The SEC has clarified its requirements. A few years ago, the experts were all fumbling around in the dark, but they have seen the light. Their clarity will help you become SOX-compliant faster, better, and cheaper than your predecessors on the stock market in the prehistoric days of 2002.

Setting the Record Straight

Up to 5 percent of companies on the U.S. Stock Exchange have restated their financials since SOX. Auditors' thresholds for materiality are much lower, even when just looking at the numbers. If there are errors in previous years, or big mistakes such as the backdating of stock options, you will have to restate your previous financials. By facing the mistakes, you are saying to investors, "We did wrong, but we are willing to admit it and fix it."

Other Laws You Need to Know About

In 1988, prior to SOX, the U.S. government also reinforced the 1977 Foreign Corrupt Practices Act requirements, which define how you report your international trade to the government and outlaws bribery. According to the law, corrupt payments to foreign officials to obtain or keep business are illegal. Since 1988, the law also pertains to foreign firms or employees who act in the U.S. in furtherance of any illegal payments.

We're All In This Together: Convergence

SOX requires that US-listed companies have a system of internal controls and that directors monitor and report on operational risk. All companies must follow the U.S.-specific generally accepted accounting principles (GAAP). Similar standards are emerging elsewhere, and the spread of the International Financial Reporting Standard (IFRS) outside the US means that a convergence is taking place in financial reporting and requirements. Figure 4-4 shows you a map of SOX-like laws around the world.

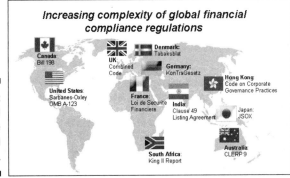

Figure 4-4: Financial compliance laws around the world.

Japan's J-SOX

In 2006, the Japanese Financial Instruments and Exchange Law was promulgated and it comes into being in 2008. This law has become affectionately known as J-SOX. Also inspired by corporate scandals, J-SOX requires that companies implement a management assessment of internal controls on financial reports. Like SOX, J-SOX is relevant to listed companies and their subsidiaries. It is expected that J-SOX will prompt mass audit automation, as it has in the U.S.

Australia's CLERP-9

The Corporate Law Economic Reform Program (CLERP) Law of 2004 aims to strengthen Australia's financial reporting framework. The details of CLERP are less prescriptive than SOX: They contain reforms to the existing corporate governance provisions, including changes to financial reporting and executive remuneration. Provisions are in place to ensure auditor and analyst independence.

Canada's C-11

Brought into law in 2005, C-11 has established a procedure for the disclosure of wrongdoings in the public sector and ensures protection for the person who discloses these. (Protecting the whistleblower is also a big part of SOX.)

Basel II

Basel II has created an international standard for banking that regulators can use when making regulations on how much capital banks must have to offset potential risk. The more risk a bank has, the more capital it should have in place to ensure that it stays solvent. This requirement proactively provides a big safety net should things go horribly wrong.

Sorting Out the Benefits of SOX

SOX is no longer in its infancy. The law has begun to mature and reveal its promise. According to the article "The Unexpected Benefits of Sarbanes-Oxley" by Stephen Wagner and Lee Dittmar, published in the *Harvard Business Review*, publicly held companies who have been through the SOX mill and come out the other end intact are seeing unexpected benefits. Some of these include

- ✔ A better control environment, where executives set the tone for ethical behavior and employees follow suit
- ✔ Facing the mountain of documentation required by SOX means making improvements to procedures and employees' understanding of these procedures
- ✔ The Audit Committee takes its role seriously

- ✔ Functions converge, processes become streamlined and standardized
- ✔ The reduction of needless complexity
- ✔ Strengthening weak links
- ✔ Reduction of human error by automating processes

SOX is not aimed at private companies. However, those that do choose to implement the SOX requirements will discover that this creates competitive advantage, as PriceWaterhouseCoopers stated in its 2006 white paper, "Finding the Silver Lining: How Private Companies Can Benefit from the New Governance and Disclosure Standards." SOX is the new gold standard for business management processes, and private companies may find that they ignore it at their peril, particularly if they are competing with listed companies for contracts. SOX rules will decrease the risks associated with consummating the deal for pre-IPO companies. For companies with sophisticated, widely distributed shareholders, the existence of well-documented internal controls and governance policies will attract investment capital at lower cost. And for closely held companies, a reliable control environment will help owners to protect and preserve their wealth.

Chapter 5

Fraud, Negligence, and Entropy: What Can Go Wrong and How to Prevent It

. . . .

In This Chapter

▶ Describing fraud

▶ Defining negligence

▶ Figuring out the consequences of bad management and inefficiency

▶ Getting clean

. . . .

Complying with regulations such as Sarbanes-Oxley (SOX) now means that companies and their senior executives have to get clean: certify that their financial reports are accurate, abide by a stated code of ethics, disclose changes to their material information, and refrain from shredding documents. Regulations also mean companies have to *stay* clean, and this process is called governance.

This chapter addresses how things got messy in the first place. We look at what the errors are — intentional or otherwise — that companies make on a day-to-day basis that open them up to fraud and bad governance.

In the U.S., the SEC prosecutes three levels of culpability: negligence, gross negligence, and fraud. In this chapter, we address these, as well as another quality that makes for financial unkemptness: entropy. *Entropy* means that things fall apart, not intentionally, but through bad management and bad systems.

The good news is that SOX's rigorous financial reporting requirements have led to fewer prosecutions for fraud and negligence. Research from Deloitte shows that the number of fraud actions has fallen since 2003, when SOX became law. Companies are getting clean and staying clean.

Defining Fraud

Fraud is a deliberate misrepresentation of events that causes another person to suffer damages, usually monetary ones. Fraud — or the opportunity to be fraudulent — is all around us. We are faced with the opportunity to commit fraud every day. We can walk out of grocery stores with items we haven't paid for, either by accident or on purpose. How we respond to a situation — either returning or concealing the items — depends on our situation, integrity, and character.

In companies, through lack of compliance and bad governance, employees are presented with opportunities for fraud all the time. The onus is on management to ensure that these opportunities are as rare as possible. Management must be proactive about fraud, removing the conditions from the workplace where fraud can occur.

Preventing the abuse of power by segregating duties

In the U.S. government, the well-known doctrine of separation of powers ensures that the executive, legislative, and judicial branches don't have undue control over their respective branches of government. In the world of business, this concept is called segregation of duties (SoD). The concept of segregation of duties has been in place in the business world for quite some time, but it is now being more fully implemented in the U.S. and around the world, due to laws like Sarbanes-Oxley and J-SOX.

Segregation of duties involves dividing up job functions so that the likelihood of fraud is greatly diminished and putting controls in place to ensure that key processes can be monitored. SoD helps ensure that no one party has too much power, much like in government, and that when two or more parties collude to commit fraud, it is detected before it is too late. Without such oversight, a single party or group could commit fraud, leading to damage of the institution and its shareholders, as was the case in the Barings Bank scandal (see the "The Barings Bank scandal — Operations risk extraordinaire" section for more information).

Segregating duties follows a pattern. This pattern helps keep key employees of a business in check. It starts with identifying a function that must be performed — a function that the company cannot afford to eliminate. This function, in order to be carried out, involves a power that could potentially be abused.

The functions to examine in this way generally fall within four categories of duties or responsibilities: authorization, custody, record keeping, and reconciliation. In a perfectly segregated system, different employees would perform each of these four major functions. One person should not control two or more of these responsibilities. Sometimes, a branch office is too small to assign these functions to different people and one person *must* take on more than one of these functions: In this case, a manager is assigned to oversee all of that person's transactions. This is an example of a *mitigating control.*

U.S. law states that fraud requires specific *intent* — you have to know that you are intentionally violating a law or regulation. That's why lying about your weight is not fraudulent, but lying about the capability of a product in order to entice someone to buy it is.

Motivations for fraud

One motivation for fraud is pretty obvious: garden-variety greed. However, there are others. When people are in a desperate situation — needing to pay for healthcare for their aging parents, for example — they might deliberately act in a fraudulent way at work to get the needed funds. This doesn't mean that they are greedy or bad, but that they are desperate and that the lack of controls in the work environment has created an opportunity for them to commit fraud.

The second situation is Cover Your, um, Assets (CYA) Syndrome. Someone makes mistakes at work, takes risks she shouldn't take, and then doesn't want to get caught, so she cooks the books and covers her trail. The basic motivation in this case is fear.

Sowing the seeds of fraud

Just like certain weather conditions promote hurricanes, certain corporate practices create just the right conditions for fraud to occur, including

- ✔ **Complexity:** Allowing the proliferation of unique roles. Roles are meant to simplify access control (and management) by standardizing the system access given to people in certain kinds of jobs. But pretty soon, Susan in accounts payable needs special privileges for year-end and Ralph in procurement needs some other permission and all the orderliness is gone. These "special" privileges are never revoked, opening the door for segregation of duties violation and — you guessed it — fraud

- ✔ **Letting users do too much:** Concentrating power in one employee so that an employee can commit fraud by, for example, creating a phony vendor and cutting a check to them

- ✔ **Unrealistic expectations:** Encouraging employees to meet unrealistic goals, especially when teamed with financial compensation that inadvertently places pressure on people to achieve these goals in any way possible

- ✔ **Lack of oversight:** Providing opportunities for employees to test the waters for fraud, resulting in weaknesses that go unnoticed by others

- ✔ **Shooting the messenger:** Demeaning or penalizing people who bring risks to management's attention

- ✔ **Brushing it off:** Rationalizing or trivializing bad behavior so that employees continue to exploit the situation and managers do not confront suspicious behavior

Some common examples of fraud

One type of fraud involves employees, who may be unaware of controls in place to prevent fraud, testing the waters to see if they can get away with something. For example, say a retail clerk discovers that customers pay for their catalog merchandise at the customer service desk. The clerk then finds a customer's order, gives it to him, receives the payment, and places it in the cash drawer. Payment comes in the form of check, credit card, or cash. The customer signs a receipt of merchandise and that record goes in the drawer with the payment copy. But the clerk is having difficulty making ends meet, so one day she decides to keep the cash and destroy the merchandise receipt for a $20 transaction. The clerk waits to see if there are any questions about the missing money. When no one questions her, she does it again; the next time, removing payment for two transactions. When the control (which matches the receipts to a shipment manifest) is eventually performed, it reveals missing merchandise. The controls that were invisible to the clerk gave her an opportunity to test the waters.

Another type of fraud involves savvy employees who know exactly how the controls work and can manipulate them to their own advantage. For example, a payables clerk who is responsible for managing payments knows that payments that don't reach the vendor are almost always questioned, and vendor reconciliations between payables and payments are done periodically. However, the payables clerk knows that reconciliations are sometimes four or five months behind. Every year, the company makes a charitable contribution in three installments. The amount is significant during good years and is usually reduced in bad years. The clerk changes the vendor name and address for one payment cycle to divert a payment to himself and, immediately after the payment cycle, reverts the name back to the charity. The charity never complains about not receiving the third installment because they assume the company has reduced its contribution because of a bad year. In this case, there was no segregation of duty between vendor changes and payments. This oversight allowed the clerk to divert the payment by using his own authorized capabilities for unauthorized purposes. The vendor reconciliation ignored the insignificant amount, among the millions in payments, and the clerk was able to pay his aging parents' healthcare bills: It's another case of desperation meeting bad controls.

Another type of fraud involves outright theft of goods from the company. Say that in the procurement process, an order is created and approved, goods or services are received, and then invoiced payments are made. A secretary places orders for stationery supplies and receives them, taking a large share of them home. She starts out with pens and then moves on to printer cartridges, creating an eBay store for printer supplies to supplement her salary. In this case, Segregation of Duties (SoD) would have prevented this problem by requiring that one person create the order, another person receive the goods or services, and a third person pay the invoices.

The Barings Bank scandal: Operations risk extraordinaire

Some dishonest people, of course, do a lot more damage than a clerk pocketing cash or a secretary filching office supplies. An extreme example of fraud is the Barings Bank case, where rogue trader Nick Leeson defrauded Barings Bank and its customers of billions of dollars, causing the bank to collapse. This was a case of CYA syndrome: Leeson made mistakes and had to employ a spiral of distraction techniques to cover his, er, tracks.

On Thursday, February 23, 1995, Nick Leeson, assistant director and general manager of Barings Futures Singapore (BFS), a branch of Barings Bank of England, left Singapore with his wife and flew to Kuala Lumpur, Malaysia. The next day, Leeson faxed his resignation to Barings, citing health reasons.

Taken as just a simple account of the activities of an ordinary person over the course of two days many years ago, this would seem to have no real significance. But Nick Leeson was no ordinary person. He was a rogue trader, and his activities in the few years just prior to 1995 caused the collapse of Barings Bank, a dramatic event that reverberated for years in the halls of banking worldwide.

In 1989, Leeson began his Barings employment with the settlements department of Barings Securities Limited, the trading division of Barings Bank. He was just 22 years old. Soon after arriving, he was sent to Hong Kong and Jakarta to sort out problems with Barings operations in both cities, and he was successful in doing so. These successes placed Leeson in a position of favor with his bosses, and in a few years' time, he was rewarded for his efforts.

In April 1992, Leeson was sent to Singapore to head the settlements and accounting departments of the newly formed Barings Futures (Singapore) Ltd. (BFS). This new position also included leading BFS's Singapore International Monetary Exchange (SIMEX) floor operation.

Both of these jobs effectively placed Leeson in the position of being in charge of both the front- and back-office workings of BFS. Because of this and also due to the complicated nature of Barings' regular management structural changes, it was unclear who Leeson was supposed to report to. In effect, he had no day-to-day boss, apart from supervision that he was supposed to receive from Barings in London.

Soon after arriving in Singapore, Leeson took the SIMEX traders' exam, which he passed. But he didn't tell SIMEX that he had been turned away by the Securities and Futures Authority in the UK when he applied to take the traders' exam there, due to his failure to report a judgment against him for a personal debt. Barings knew about Leeson's problem in the UK, but they too failed to inform SIMEX.

What followed was fairly complicated. Leeson set up a false BFS account and began making gambles in the SIMEX futures market (using monies from subsidiaries' accounts that were not supposed to be used) and racked up considerable losses. But instead of reporting those losses as losses, Leeson reported them as gains. This went on and eventually came to a head just after the Kobe earthquake in Japan, which caused the Japanese markets to tumble. Leeson had bet on a rapid recovery for the Nikkei, but this recovery didn't materialize. After it was over, Leeson's losses amounted to $1.4 billion, twice the amount of Barings' trading book.

The day Leeson and his wife fled Singapore, his superiors had arrived at the BFS offices and discovered the false account, but it was too late. The Bank of England attempted a bailout of Barings, but did not succeed. Barings was a 230-year-old institution, the personal bank to Her Majesty the Queen. About a week after Barings' collapse, the Dutch group ING purchased Barings for £1.

Here are some of the lessons that can be learned from the Barings Bank scandal:

- ✔ **Watch for warning signs.** Leeson's disqualification for the UK trader's exam should have raised an alert.

- ✔ **Don't play favorites.** Barings was impressed with Leeson's successes and thus didn't alert SIMEX that Leeson had been disqualified from taking the UK trader's exam.

- ✔ **Always segregate major responsibilities.** This case was a segregation of duties violation deluxe: Leeson was in charge of both back- and front-office operations. Not only could he create bogus accounts, but he could also move money into them and in turn report the losses as profits, all with no oversight.

- ✔ **Lack of supervision.** Management oversight is key. Leeson had no real supervision; it was unclear who his boss was. Given today's virtual workforce, this lesson cannot be overemphasized.

Negligence: More Likely Than Fraud

U.S. law defines *negligence* as acting with deliberate disregard of the consequences of the act. It defines *gross negligence* as acting with knowledge of the fact *and* with deliberate disregard of the consequences of the act. The difference between gross negligence and fraud is that fraud is considered as acting with intent. Fraud is so difficult to prove that the term is rarely invoked. Negligence is far easier to prove — and fits in quite well with human nature's tendency to drop the ball.

Lack of compliance with regulations such as SOX usually results in charges of negligence or gross negligence, which leads to fines. Therefore, a company may receive a SOX-related fine if management doesn't give a good reason why they haven't adopted a code of ethics, forgets to disclose material changes of information, or is slapdash about financial reporting and internal controls.

The classic example of segregation of duties failure is when an employee can set up a vendor *and* make a payment to a vendor. This scenario provides the employee with the opportunity to set up a fictitious vendor and pay himself. An auditor combing through a company's transactions will see this as a red alert.

Failure to segregate duties is known as setting the fox to guard the henhouse, because it provides employees with opportunities for fraud. Because fraud is hard to prosecute, SoD failures are more likely to lead to fines for negligence, gross or otherwise.

To mitigate the potential for charges of negligence, a company should segregate the duties, allowing one person to set up the vendor and another to pay the vendor. If, for practical reasons, the company can't segregate the duties, it needs to put in compensating controls, such as having a manager check all the transactions that the person who does too much enters into the accounting system.

Entropy: Errors, Omissions, and Inefficiencies

Entropy is the tendency for things in general to naturally fall into disorder. Think of the proliferation of papers on the top of your desk during a busy week. The same thing can happen in corporate accounting systems. The disorder is unintentional and it can happen because of bad management, inefficiency, and just plain not taking the time to rigorously follow an organizational system. No fraud or gross negligence occurs, but a company makes errors and omissions. This kind of lack of control is very expensive to companies in terms of loss of revenue, and it is often only recognized after it is too late.

When people work in large teams, assuming that someone else took care of a particular task can lead to work being neglected. Or, tasks might be done twice, because one worker doesn't realize that another worker already took care of a particular job. In this way, the work environment becomes inefficient, but no one recognizes it until it is too late.

As companies grow and start to become unwieldy, they also lose control of their system permissions. Some examples are

- ✔ **Roles:** A role contains a set of permissions in the system for an individual to complete their job in the organization. Roles need to be analyzed to ensure they don't contain any internal segregation of duty conflicts. For example, a role may contain the ability to set up a vendor and make a payment. And to make it worse, this role could be assigned to many people across a company, thereby increasing exponentially the chance of fraud.

- ✔ **Users:** Users are assigned roles to complete their assigned responsibilities. In most organizations, the assignment requires an approval to make sure that the roles are appropriate. However, many times, roles are not removed from individuals when they are transferred or take on additional responsibilities. An individual can acquire dangerous combinations of capabilities as additional roles are added and others are not taken away.

- ✔ **Superusers and temporary users:** *Superusers* are those people who have exceptional knowledge of the system and are given broad access. All organizations have these key individuals and an implied trust is given to these people that this broad access is only used when necessary. However, having too many superusers with access that is far broader than necessary can lead to trouble. Temporary users gain their privileges for special occasions, such as year end closing. In a pinch, it's easy to grant temporary users those privileges and forget to revoke them, turning temporary users into overly privileged characters.

Cleaning Up: The Mop-Up Operation

If you've taken a good hard look at your company, you may see that things aren't as clean and efficient as they could be. You want to get compliant and clean. How do you go about it? Since SOX was passed, companies and their senior management have had to learn to think like auditors.

Thinking like an auditor

SOX requires public companies to document every tiny step of each of their processes from beginning to end. The auditor's job is to follow each process (such as order to cash, for example) and ask the following questions:

- ✔ Who's involved throughout the process?
- ✔ What kind of access do they have? What other accesses do they have?
- ✔ Who has approved what?

This exercise is extremely time- and resource-intensive, especially when you consider that companies often have different systems (running their Human Resources on SAP and their Procurement on Oracle, for example), and within the various systems there are hundreds of different roles. The auditor is expected to understand both the business side and the IT side, and then pull all this data together to run reports. This monumental task is why auditors get paid so much. They are highly paid detectives, sniffing out SoD violations and the potential for fraud and negligence.

Making the computer your auditor

Managing all these interdependencies is like three-dimensional chess, and even massive spreadsheets with teams of analysts can't reveal all the possible combinations that could lead to problems, let alone monitor them in real time. The only way to handle all this kind of complexity is to automate it, making technology into a virtual auditor. Chapters 6 and 7 tell you how.

Chapter 6

Access Control and the Role of Roles

. . . .

. . . .

*I*n Chapter 5, we discuss how fraud can occur where duties are not clearly segregated. To minimize fraud, companies need to wisely segregate the duties of employees. And to segregate duties, companies rely on roles and access control.

The concepts behind these terms are simple. Everyone in the company should have a well-defined role that minimizes the opportunity for fraud. And when an employee needs to access a computer system, access controls need to be in place that allow the employee to access only what he needs to do to perform his job: nothing more, nothing less. In this chapter, we look at these concepts in-depth. We also discuss how roles can wind up being much more complicated and difficult to manage than you might expect. We also take a look at the SAP solutions for access control.

Understanding Access Control and Roles

Employees perform their duties once they are logged into the system, but it's also vital to monitor *how* they get there. Most companies have thousands of users. Each user has one or more role. Each role has access to a certain number of transactions in the system. Many companies have more than one system to which users have access. Each of these systems have hundreds of screens, with multiple transactions. All this adds up to a massive number of places where segregation of duties violations can occur — hundreds of thousands, in fact.

Access control is a gatekeeper function that patrols system access, ensuring that these myriad holes, these places where violations can take place, remain safely plugged. It's rather like the Immigration Department of a company's system: providing specific visas for specific stays in the country. Immigration carefully monitors who does what, separating the short-term holiday-makers from those who plan to do business in a country. Immigration checks passports, issues visas for those who need them and visa waivers for those who don't and occasionally, refuses entry to someone who they believe may pose a threat. In this way, they ensure that people enter the country for the right reasons and have the applicable amount of time in which to have their holiday or do their job. By cautiously giving the right people, the right kind of access, they ensure that no violations occur. So it is with access control.

Of course, employees aren't actually tourists or business travelers, and happily the vast majority are trustworthy. But good governance — and auditability — means that we need to carefully segregate duties. By not properly segregating duties, companies create opportunities for fraud as well as human error, each of which leads to revenue loss. This is why companies require a method to tighten up and organize access to financial systems. But before we take a look at where we stand today, let's take a look back and see how we got here.

Getting a Handle on Access Control

Access control refers to what a person can do in a computer system or application after she has signed on. The sign-on process is referred to as *authentication* — proving to the system that you are who you say you are. The most common form of authentication is password authentication. For the purposes of this chapter, we assume that authentication is already taken care of. To sign on, you might have had to do a fingerprint scan, a retinal scan, or simply type the password that is on a sticky note on your monitor (we hope not!). Now that you've signed on, what can you do? In this chapter, we talk about the access you and others have to applications, especially financial applications, after you have signed in or, in other words, after you have successfully authenticated yourself.

These days, we think of access control in terms of access to computer systems. But it wasn't always this way. Access once meant primarily physical access to buildings and rooms in buildings. You might have seen racks of keys on a wall (or a picture of such a key rack). Typically one person was in charge of all the keys and managed them from one office. If you needed access to a room you didn't have a key to, you would walk into the room where that key rack was, talk to the person behind the desk, sign out a key, and promise to bring it back. This was definitely primitive, but there was a record of who had what access and to where. And if a key was missing from that rack, the person in charge would come looking for it. Very few people had all the keys; for example, a janitor would have a jangling bunch of keys, with access to virtually every room because he or she had to clean them all or at least empty the trash every day. (The plot line of many films includes a scene of someone posing as a janitor to get to some secret information.)

Today companies have to control not only access to buildings, but also to computer systems. Both have become more sophisticated over time; rooms and buildings now have keyless entry and other fancy electronic entry systems. Access control to computers has also gone through some evolution.

Users and permissions

Way back in the mists of time, system administrators would give permissions to various users. Users would get a username and password and then would be given access to various applications. (Not all computer platforms allowed for this, though. PCs were meant to belong to a single person, so the whole concept of access control had to be added on later.)

The equation went like this: 1000 users equals 1000 sets of permissions. That's a lot of unique sets of permissions to keep changing or revoking as people changed jobs or took on additional responsibilities.

Your essential access control glossary

Lots of lingo gets thrown around in discussions about access control. Here are some of the terms you'll hear most often:

- ✔ **User:** An individual employee's technical access to the system

- ✔ **Superuser:** An individual with technical access to all system features and all transactions

- ✔ **Role:** Access to specific functions by virtue of the employee's job title or responsibilities.

Possible roles include salesperson, accounts payable clerk, and purchasing agent.

- ✔ **Access Control:** A means to control who does what in the system

- ✔ **Transaction:** A field or set of fields used to perform an action in the system (for example, Set Up Vendor Account)

- ✔ **Event:** An action performed by a user (for example, logging on, opening an application)

The roles revolution

As the number of users increased, it became harder for system administrators to manage their associated permissions. One day, someone had a bright idea. What if we give salespeople access to the system based on their job and not on their user name? It would be easier to manage access based on a limited number of roles instead of based on the number of users. Role-based access control was a major step forward, organizing and streamlining access to computer systems.

The equation changed. A thousand users have 50 jobs; 50 roles with associated permissions.

That looks pretty good, right? Much more manageable and auditable. And if a user changes jobs — or takes over someone else's duties — they could be assigned more than one role, but we still only need 50 roles.

How Access Control Got Messy

In theory, roles looked like a huge step forward, anyway. But like many good ideas, maintenance is tricky. And today, at many companies, there are once again almost as many roles as there are users.

How did access control get messy again? There are at least five contributing factors:

- Every user is different
- Virtual things are hard to track
- IT and business don't speak the same language
- Exceptional circumstances dictate exceptional access
- Large scale increases complexity

In the next few sections, we look at each of these factors in more detail.

Every user is different

Going from 1000 users to 50 roles sounded pretty good. But then, as life would have it, one salesperson needed a little more access than another one. And one accounts payable clerk needed slightly different access from another. Over time, the number of roles escalates to close to 900 roles for 1000 users, and a lot of those roles are similar, but not exactly the same. Now in walks the auditor, and the job of seeing whether duties are properly segregated just got a whole lot harder. If an auditor has 50 roles to check, that's pretty simple, though each one might be complex. But when almost every user has a unique role, checking 900 roles for segregation of duties violations is going to take a long time.

Virtual things are hard to track

Imagine you are sitting at your desk when suddenly, all the files and folders on your hard drive physically manifest in your workspace.

Okay, you can start breathing again; that can't happen. The fact is that virtual things are hard to keep track of. And so it is with access control.

The visual image of the keys on the rack made it easy to see when one was missing. The keeper of the keys would quickly find you if you had one out longer than you said you would.

Roles get messy in part because access is virtual. When someone needs access (a key, in this analogy) to get something temporarily (say someone's sick and they need access to their transactions), IT typically forgets to ask for the "key" back again; that is, to revoke the access. And when their colleague is back at work, the individual who got the exceptional access doesn't go back and ask to have it revoked.

Worse, sometimes (under pressure) IT hands out a "master key" so they don't have to keep track of five different keys late on Friday afternoon before the holiday weekend, but once again, they forget to ask for the keys back. Handing out a master key lets you open all the doors, or, on a computer system, access all the transactions. Such access must be carefully controlled.

Seeing a mess is difficult when that mess is on a hard drive or when it's a computer abstraction, such as roles. That's why unless a disciplined approach has been taken to controlling access, the mess is probably bigger than you know.

IT and business don't speak the same language

Sometimes, two groups simply don't speak the same language. Historically, access control has always been the preserve of the IT department, with no input from the business side. The IT department looks at access control from the perspective of technical roles, with application, transaction, screen, or field-level access. Businesspeople tend to think about job roles and would simply ask IT to set up access for a marketing manager, which seems very clear to the business person but offers no guidance about application, transaction, screen, and field access. This communication gap must be bridged.

When IT attempts to communicate problems to business, the same type of communication problem ensues. For example, if IT decides to check for segregation of duties violations and runs a report or a query, it may find a violation within the procurement department and notify them. However, procurement doesn't understand the report because it's too technical and not in their language. They hand it back to IT, telling them to fix it. Unless reports are written in language that business understands (we have made a payment to a vendor who shouldn't be paid, a duplicate check is going to go out), they won't take responsibility for access control problems.

Exceptional circumstances dictate exceptional access

IT departments do try to keep access control managed. However, at certain times, IT departments may be pressured by users. At year end, when people need to close the books, they want to run reports and get data into the system. Perhaps Mr. E, who has access to these transactions, has had to make an emergency visit to the doctor. His colleagues call IT and demand access to his transactions. Or perhaps someone in the payroll department is on vacation, and HR needs to run paychecks. Under pressure, IT hands out access. The problem arises when IT forgets to revoke the access, or when the users forget to remind IT to do so. In this way, you see users with roles that become more and more nonstandard over time, a kind of insidious accumulation of access, sort of like putting on weight over the holidays.

Large scale increases complexity

Small companies can get away with users having unique roles. When companies grow and develop a huge pool of roles, which they have created themselves or inherited through mergers and acquisitions, access becomes a nightmare to manage. Add to the mix multiple instances of different brands of software, and you find that managing users with unique roles becomes impossible. There are hundreds of roles. No one knows exactly what they all mean; they probably conflict with each other, and there are likely to be SoD violations within the roles themselves. This scenario leaves the company open to fraud.

If any or all of these situations prevail at your company, it's time to repair your access control. Poor access control is not only a security risk, but it's a mess for auditors to try and figure out, and you don't want unhappy auditors.

Getting Clean

So proliferation of roles, implementation of numerous software systems, and the passage of time have all contributed to a very complicated access control picture. Complexity is the enemy of security and good governance. So, how can you reduce this complexity?

Figuring out where you stand

Analysis is the first step toward righting the ship. Analysis entails bringing IT and businesspeople to the table and analyzing the roles that exist and their associated SoD violations. For example, duties are not properly segregated if a user can both

- ✔ Set up a vendor *and* make a payment
- ✔ Change an order *and* complete a goods receipt
- ✔ Change a receipt *and* make adjustments to inventory

Automating role analysis is a good idea if you have the tools to do so. This automation does not replace the meeting of the minds between IT and business, but can simplify the process and make it easier to untangle the mess.

Ten SoD violations you may not have thought of

Most people know that you shouldn't allow the same person to set up a vendor and cut a check. But some SoD violations are a little less obvious. Here are 10 more segregation of duties violations to get the wheels turning as you analyze your roles:

- ✔ Depositing cash and reconciling bank statements
- ✔ Approving time cards and distributing paychecks
- ✔ Preparing an order and changing a billing document
- ✔ Changing an order and creating a delivery

- ✔ Creating a journal entry and opening a closed accounting period
- ✔ Creating general ledger accounts and posting journal entries
- ✔ Maintaining accounts receivable master data and posting receipts
- ✔ Maintaining bank account information and posting payments
- ✔ Maintaining assets and creating a goods receipt
- ✔ Completing goods transfer and adjusting physical inventory counts

We once heard an anecdote of an access control consultant who would visit a company and talk to its IT department about roles. He would ask them to provide six roles that they thought were good and six roles that they thought were bad. After running a scan with an automated tool, he invariably found that almost all the "good" roles were bad, too. Consider the impact of these bad roles: If one role has three SoD violations, and 3,000 users have that role, that bad role creates 9,000 conflicts.

The sheer number of potential violations that most companies have shocks them into reality. Where they once believed they didn't have a problem, they now know it is time to be tactical, to fix their controls, and clean up their roles.

Starting the conversation

The first step is one of the hardest. You need to bring IT and businesspeople to the table together, along with internal auditors.

If the roles that exist are causing SoD violations, somewhere a breakdown of communications is occurring among these stakeholders.

Examining the org chart

Some of the problems may stem from the jobs themselves. Are employees given conflicting duties? Cleaning up their roles in the system won't change the problem if what is needed is a fundamental reorganization that segregates duties effectively among employees.

Defining auditable roles

Who owns and defines the roles? It's highly possible that businesspeople think this is the province of IT. But the people who define the jobs should define the roles that reflect those jobs. Therefore, ownership should belong to the business process owners. By taking responsibility for this area, line-of-business managers accept that good role management is part of their every-day business.

Mapping the business roles to technical roles

Here is where the IT department comes into play. Business roles need to be mapped to technical roles.

Business process owners can define which permissions make up a role, document role status, and keep change histories. They can redesign roles and analyze what would happen if a role changes. (For example, how many people would still be able to do their jobs, and would new SoD violations be created?). Business process owners can develop new roles. This kind of control consciousness will take the discomfort out of company audits. Companies learn to be proud of their good, clean roles.

If you think that it sounds like line of business managers should take the lead here, you're correct. They need consultation and communication with IT so that these two groups can develop a common language. But business process experts, not IT managers, should be ultimately responsible for defining roles in a way that achieves clean access control and avoids SoD violations.

By standardizing and centralizing role design, testing, and maintenance, technical experts and business process owners can speak a common language. Taking these steps increases consistency and lowers IT costs.

When you can't segregate duties

If only one person handles accounting in a small branch office, you can't segregate those duties. In these cases, SoD is not the ultimate answer. Sometimes duties can't be segregated properly because of a small or remote staff. Such cases require management oversight to ensure that SoD violations are not occurring. Instead of segregation of duties through access control, a compensating control needs to be put in place so that a manager reviews the transactions entered by such employees. Chapter 7 describes these types of controls in more detail.

Staying Clean

After the roles are tidy, a method to detect violations, prevent further violations, and fix violations that have occurred — across systems, across instances, and across applications — must be put into place.

Change is constant, and as employees are promoted, go on vacation, are transferred, or move to another company, the nice clean roles may get messed up again. Staying clean requires continued vigilance and review as these events take place to ensure that roles remain clean. Two things can help companies stay clean: identity management that makes it clear who did what (nice for auditing) and compliant user provisioning, which makes it easy to set up users the right way the first time.

In the online world, we have all grown used to needing different usernames and passwords for different Web sites. We all know the pain of forgetting a password. In the corporate world, it is much the same — employees need access to servers and applications, all with many different passwords and different schedules for changing them. However, the pain of forgetting a password in the corporate world is greater, and the cost of resetting a user password is high — estimated at between $50 and $500 per password.

Identity management solutions allow employees to sign on once and have their identities tracked throughout the system. This helps with auditability; all transactions are associated with that person's identity, no matter where they are executed across the system landscape. Compared with correlating multiple usernames and passwords from different systems, the audit trail with identity management systems is much improved.

Identity management helps keep track of who is doing what. Setting up users is known as user provisioning. Users are given an identity that gives them access to all the systems they need and assigns them the roles necessary to do their jobs in a way that is free of SoD violations (which is why you'll hear it called compliant user provisioning). Because all of this setup work can be complex without automation, it can take a long time — as much as a week — to give new employees access to all the systems they will need. Automating user provisioning accelerates this process to just a few hours — which means workers are happy with the access they need and auditors are happy because the access is clean from the start.

Part of user provisioning relates to assigning roles with their associated access. When a variance from an existing role is requested, a review process should be put into place to see if such variances are really needed or if the access can be handled in another way. The idea is, once again, to keep roles clean and standard, known quantities, free of SoD violations and without those "just for this user" variances that eventually create access control problems.

Managing Exceptional Access

What if you have a small branch office and just one accounting clerk? What if you have year-end closing and need to grant exceptional access to the system?

Remember the master key? The key supervisor hands it out to someone who needs it desperately, and never gets it back. The people who receive these special keys are called *superusers*. Just like Superman, superusers have super-powers and can do anything.

Superuser access is hard to manage and risky to control, and yet it is sometimes needed. Some users are given carte blanche access, giving them free access to all systems, all objects, all transactions. This is the worst case scenario, because it means that their company has no control over who does what.

Furthermore, one of the first questions external auditors ask is "How many users have superuser access?"

For all these reasons, exceptional access needs to be managed carefully. Rather than handing out such access freely, both IT and business need to coordinate their work so that privileges can be granted, monitored, and revoked in a timely fashion to prevent SoD violations.

The SAP Approach: SAP GRC Access Control

Like many of the dilemmas in GRC, automation can reduce the scope of the effort and make day-to-day enforcement of business rules easier and more cost effective. For example, a major retailer recently took its company public. Before going public, the retailer had six employees scouring Excel spreadsheets to validate that the company was not creating risks by giving one employee too much access to any of the systems. It chose to automate this process instead, saving considerable time and cost.

SAP GRC Access Control provides a comprehensive, cross-enterprise set of preventive and detective access controls that enables business managers, auditors, and the IT team to define and oversee proper SoD enforcement. It addresses risk analysis and remediation, enterprise role management, compliant user provisioning, and superuser access management.

Risk analysis thoroughly scans existing roles to check for violations. This analysis handles a heterogeneous system landscape, which means it encompasses not only SAP software but also enterprise applications from Oracle, PeopleSoft, and JD Edwards. The application delivers a comprehensive database of SoD rules that addresses all core processes (see Figure 6-1).

Figure 6-1: SAP GRC Access Control uncovers access control risks across diverse system landscapes.

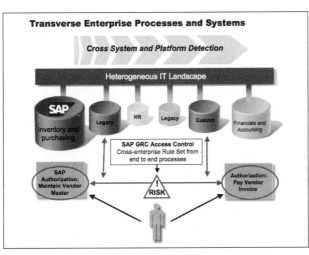

SAP GRC Access Control also offers oversight of exceptional access. When special privileges are needed, a temporary ID grants the user regulated access. Such a user may be given access to conflicting roles and be able to perform certain emergency transactions, but everything that user does in the system is logged in a report for scrutiny. The temporary ID is issued with an expiration time or date, so that after a certain point, the user is logged out of the system. The IDs are automatically revoked so that no follow-up is necessary.

Compliant user provisioning, another feature of SAP GRC Access Control, streamlines adding users and ensures that as new users are added, access control stays clean. The idea is to automate everything from one authoritative source, usually the HR system, where you define a new user account. SAP GRC Access Control detects the creation of a new account and interprets the business role attached to the user account into technical roles. Once it knows what this user does to perform his or her job, and what accesses are needed, it can create a user account, an identity with a username and password, and all the information necessary to give this person the appropriate access for his role.

SAP GRC Access Control also provides a documented log of events — who had access to what, who put what kind of information in and who approved access to what transaction. These are just the kind of things that warms an auditor's heart.

Where Do You Go from Here?

After a company has gotten clean and is staying clean, the idea is to stay in control. The sprint phase is over, the access control muscles are fit and well-trained, and it's time for the marathon. By staying healthy, keeping their roles clean and eyes open for SoD violations, a company will be prepared for the auditor's next visit.

Proper SoD and access control over sensitive transactions is one of the most effective safeguards against fraud. This is usually difficult to deploy and sustain given the thousands of users, roles, and processes that all require testing and remediation. Automating this process helps ensure that access control is handled cleanly and consistently.

In Chapter 7, we expand the discussion of controls from access control to controls placed in business processes to ensure that business processes are proceeding in an efficient and auditable fashion.

Chapter 7

Taking Steps toward Better Internal Controls

. . . .

In This Chapter

▶ Obtaining better internal controls

▶ Discovering the advantages of automated controls

▶ Putting automated controls into practice

. . . .

*A*lmost every problem that a company confronts can be traced back to a lack of good internal controls. Good internal controls mean that you know what is going on in the business, in every key business process. Strong internal controls can also help you monitor and reduce risks. Internal controls are really the essence of good governance, taking a policy and translating it into the details of day-to-day business practices.

In this chapter, we look at the importance of good internal controls and how automating those controls can streamline your business and help you catch the exceptions to the rule. Finally, we look at the SAP solution for automating internal controls: SAP GRC Process Control.

Understanding Internal Controls

Internal controls may mean different things to different people. To a clerk in the purchasing department, having an internal control may mean double-checking vendor invoices for inconsistencies; to a CEO, an internal control may mean evolving a control policy to ensure effective overall governance. Also, control owners and business process owners may find themselves at loggerheads. A *control owner* is in charge of designing controls and making sure they work properly to prevent problems. A *business process owner*, on the other hand, is mainly concerned about running his or her department, looking at the bottom line. If, for example, an employee is able to create a vendor and pay a vendor, the control owner recognizes that this situation urgently calls for a swift segregation of duties to mitigate risk. However, the business process owner may believe that there is a legitimate need for the dual responsibility. (Their concerns can be reconciled, as we'll see later in this chapter.)

Controls encompass all the actions, processes, or physical barriers that direct or guide a resource to achieve a desired result. Often they prevent, detect, or correct risks from becoming barriers to success. Here are some different types of controls:

- **Preventative controls:** These controls prevent a bad event from happening. For example, a company may use a private network to ensure that company data is not exposed to public networks.

- **Detective controls:** These controls determine whether a bad event has already happened. For example, when a bank statement is received, it is reconciled to the customer's records to detect processing errors by the bank or customer.

- **Corrective controls:** These controls come into play once a problem is discovered. An example would be removing access from users who have excessive privileges or executing a backup and recovery plan after a physical disaster has occurred.

The adoption of good internal controls in order to become SOX- (or regulation-) compliant is a top-down process that starts with management. Management recognizes that the regulations exist and cannot be ignored. They select a team to define how the regulations, including the attendant standards and practices, will be implemented as controls in the company. Control owners and business process owners work out how to incorporate these regulations into the business through automated controls.

After the controls become woven into the fabric of the company — sweeping strategically across processes, locations, and systems — they help close off avenues of risk. Companies may then enjoy such happy side-effects as preventing unintentional errors, improving efficiency, and keeping auditors smiling and building shareholder value in the process.

Exploring the Benefits of Better Controls

Companies have processes. These processes contain risks, which are barriers to success and avenues for fraud and negligence. Therefore, companies must have controls. Nowadays, with the compliance requirements of regulations such as SOX, companies are trying to be more proactive about their controls. Being more proactive about controls requires effort and input, but also has many benefits.

Benefit one: Business process improvement

One byproduct of implementing strong internal controls is business process improvement. When companies start to take a close look at their business processes and document, measure, and monitor them, they can make them more efficient and streamlined. It gives companies a chance to examine their processes closely and ask themselves probing questions such as, "Why does it take seven people for us to do something, when Company X only needs three people to do the same thing?"

Benefit two: Management by exception

By establishing a norm (such as "The process works this way and when it doesn't, a control will alert us"), companies learn to manage by exception. Controls start to function as a barometer of how things are operating in the company — and give an early warning of how things could go awry, or an indication of trends. Controls can also flag how companies need to change or improve their processes. If companies don't continue to assess their controls and respond to the changes that controls indicate are necessary, they could be considered negligent.

Benefit three: Real-time monitoring

Automated internal controls are like traffic cops. They prevent accidents (by directing the flow of traffic), detect accidents (by listening to the radio), and clean up after accidents (removing damaged cars and calling an ambulance to take the injured to hospital). (We cover automated controls in more detail in the section, "Seeing How Automated Controls Make Things Easier" later in this chapter.)

Like traffic cops, automated internal controls can be on duty 24 hours a day, seven days a week, monitoring both past activity and activity taking place in real time. In any automated process, key points in the process should serve as checkpoints to make sure that previous steps were completed and the next processing step is ready for execution. In most companies, the checks and balances used to monitor the automated processes rely on staff to review reports or transactions to make sure that the transaction is recorded accurately and in accordance with accepted accounting guidelines.

Before automation, auditors were the primary feedback loop to managers to ensure that processes were operating effectively and efficiently. Auditors played the role of traffic cop, but without automated internal controls, their methods were not adequate. Auditors used sampling techniques — selecting a sample of transactions and tracing them through a process, while giving special attention to the checkpoints, and looking for evidence that staff had reviewed reports.

Without automation, which covers so many more transactions in a shorter period, auditors are limited as to how many tests they can perform within their given review time. They take the results of their sample test and project them to the entire population of transactions processed by the system. Because of the gap between the testing methods and the processing methods, samples are not always representative of the total population.

As traffic cops, automated internal controls have the power to apply the same method of testing on an ongoing basis. *All* transactions can be tested and exceptions are more easily highlighted. Management can then address — and report on — any exceptions.

A lack of internal controls: The trading scandal at Societe Generale in Paris

A rogue trader at the French bank Societe Generale somehow lost close to $7.1 billion by engaging in secret, unauthorized derivatives trades. According to a January 29, 2008, article in the *New York Times,* the trader in question, 31-year-old Jérôme Kerviel, admitted to French officials that he had placed the unauthorized trades, which were actually worth around $70 billion — more than the worth of the bank itself — before many of them were reversed.

Apparently, according to the same *New York Times* article, once these trades were detected, the bank was able to move quickly to stop many of them, hence the loss of (just!) $7.1 billion.

And in a February, 6, 2008, *Washington Post* article, French Finance Minister Christine Lagarde was quoted as saying that the internal controls that Societe Generale had in place didn't function and that when they did they weren't properly followed up.

Kerviel, for his part, also admitted to officials that he had hacked his fellow employee's computers at the bank and penned fake emails to cover his tracks. In one press report, a colleague of Kerviel's described him as a "computer genius."

Kerviel had apparently taken only four vacation days in 2007, which he himself told police was an obvious sign that a trader doesn't want his actions reviewed by supervisors or fellow employees. If, for example, the human resources department at the bank had a control in place to warn them when an employee isn't taking his or her vacation days, a query to that person's supervisor could be sent asking them to check into the matter.

The case is far from settled as this book goes to press, but Lagarde has already issued an 11-page report, which suggests that banks generally focus more on internal fraud, involve managers and committees in supervising risk controls, reinforce internal controls over how much money traders can risk, and raise the fines that France's banking commission can levy on banks that violate regulations.

Benefit four: Mindset changes

Implementing automated controls requires more than changes to software. Doing so also requires a mindset change. Management commits to a code of ethics and to a new control consciousness, but they also have to ensure that this filters down throughout the company.

Here is an example of how automation and better internal controls required a mindset change. When companies implemented the automated procure-to-pay process, vendors often complained that their invoices weren't being paid. In the old manual process, the accounting clerk would call the ordering department and ask if the goods had been received or where the receiving documents were in the process. In the automated process, the goods were delivered to the ordering department but no paperwork was presented. Instead, the receiving personnel were expected to enter the goods receipt into the system. The quantity entered was then electronically compared to the *invoiced receipt* quantity. Under the manual process, before the receiver could use the goods, the delivery person would ask for a signature. However, if the goods were delivered and able to be used, there was no incentive for the recipient to enter their goods receipt into the system. So when companies looked at the invoice receipts, there were many items not covered by a goods receipt.

This imbalance held up many vendor payments — the system was not going to pay an invoice for goods that were not received. It became essential to report outstanding invoices without goods receipts as part of internal controls to motivate employees to make timely entries.

Seeing How Automating Controls Makes Things Easier

In the early 1990s, most companies had their own systems that they built to run their accounting, purchasing, and personnel functions. With these systems came the necessary controls — sometimes as many as 500 of them. In these home-grown systems, controls would be tested at various times, either quarterly or at month-end, or, for some controls (such as three-way match), perhaps only once a year. Typically, companies would manage their controls in an Excel spreadsheet, with an attached control plan outlining the 10 to 15 steps to take if a particular control broke. This process was an extremely intensive, laborious, and time-consuming.

Widespread adoption of enterprise resource planning (ERP) in the late 1990s enabled companies, among other things, to automate their common processes. ERP helped integrate each of the functional areas into an end-to-end process that could be automated. After processes were automated, companies needed to automate their checks too, and so automated internal controls were born.

To understand how this changed the business landscape, look at one example of a process before and after automation. Before automation, the procure-to-pay process involved lots of paperwork: the ordering department would send paperwork to the purchasing department, which would then select the vendor, negotiate the price, and inform the ordering department of the expected arrival. The purchasing department would send delivery information to the warehouse or mailroom staff who would match the order with the delivery manifests when the goods arrived. The goods would be delivered and the receipt signed and sent to the accounting department. When the vendor invoiced the company, the accounting department would compare the invoice quantity with the received amounts. They would then verify that the invoice price was equal to the order price, and schedule the payment based on the invoice terms. The procure-to-pay process involved multiple departments and a whole lot of paper.

Now, after procure-to-pay is automated, all the paperwork comparisons done by people in the accounting department are no longer necessary. Instead, when the order is entered, the received quantity is recorded and automatically compared and the invoice is paid on schedule according to the invoice terms. Also, the work of the purchasing department is minimized: A department can create orders and preselect vendors without having to involve the purchasing department in every transaction. When the goods arrive, the recipient records this event during the receiving process, where the quantities received are compared with the quantities ordered. When purchasing receives the vendor invoice, they can then compare the price and the quantity before making payment.

The arduous paperwork and continuous checking is removed when a process is automated. That's because the software is doing the checking for you.

The newsletter *Compliance Week*'s series, *GRC Illustrated,* points out these additional benefits of automated controls:

- ✓ **Cheaper, with fewer errors:** The average purchase-to-pay transaction can be reduced from $12.03 to $8.58 when moving from a low to a high level of automation. Automated transactions are between 10 and 25 percent less prone to error.

- ✓ **Better protection:** Preventative controls embedded in a system cannot be ignored and are not subject to interpretation.

- ✓ **Quicker to detect and fix:** There is little or no time lag between an event occurring and being detected, so management can be notified immediately of a problem.

✔ **Embedded into core systems:** When compliance is embedded rather than bolted on, it enforces policies at the point of access and the point of transaction.

✔ **Simultaneous control and monitoring:** A well-designed automated control offers both control and monitoring. In effect, testing is built in. Further, automated controls can produce reports that serve as their own documentation. All of this makes an auditor's job easier.

✔ **Automatic evidence:** Automated controls produce evidence on the fly, in audit trails and transaction logs.

✔ **Death of the sample:** Some processes benefit from having every transaction analyzed, instead of just a sampling. Some precarious patterns and trends only reveal themselves when *all* transactions of a particular type are scrutinized.

✔ **Ripple effect:** The operational benefits to implementing controls extend beyond financial compliance. Companies can use the principles of governance, risk, and compliance to improve all business processes by introducing transactional, master data, and configurable controls to help monitor processes, and then improve them.

Automated internal controls are like speed cameras; they catch every single violation of a control instead of the occasional scofflaw. And like speed cameras, they reduce effort — after you install speed cameras on a highway or residential street, police officers don't have to sit around with radar guns looking for cars going over the speed limit, pulling them over, and writing tickets. Figure 7-1 illustrates the reduced effort and increased efficiency of automated controls.

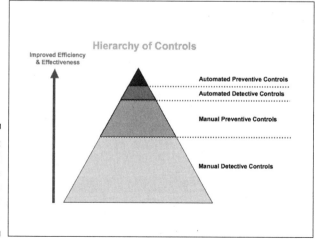

Figure 7-1:
Automated controls are far more efficient and effective.

Taking Five Steps to Better Internal Controls

The evolution and automation of internal controls have a number of advantages for companies — lowered costs, fewer errors, management by exception, and regulatory compliance. And, by improving internal controls in a particular area, companies can take the lessons learned and then scale those improved controls out to the whole organization.

There are five steps to a healthy internal control environment:

- ✔ Documentation
- ✔ Testing
- ✔ Remediation
- ✔ Analysis
- ✔ Optimization

In the next few sections, we look at each in more detail.

Documentation: The mapping exercise

A company looks at SOX and other regulations to see which areas of their business are going to be affected by the regulation's requirements. They then go through an intensive mapping process, identifying the business processes, subprocesses, and departments that are involved.

The next step is to highlight the risks and compliance issues. For example, when someone is taking orders from new customers, they need to make sure that a credit check is performed every time. The company should develop a control that will be done from outside its order-taking system that checks all transactions and reports back on whether the system is running credit checks for all new customers.

Then companies develop controls. Manual controls tend to be vulnerable to human error or fraud, so companies automate as many of their internal controls as they can. They write scripts or programs that will be kicked off on a preset basis to perform control checks and then report back. Some manual controls will still be needed, but automated controls can substantially reduce the amount of work needed to monitor controls.

Testing: Real-time and historical

After the documentation phase, companies then implement control checks, either preventative checks, such as those that seek out Segregation of Duties (SoD) violations, or detective checks, which are after-the-fact checks on what happened (historical) or what's happening right now (real-time). By automating both real-time and historical checks, a company can form a clearer idea of how their business is operating.

Remediation: Fixing the problem

When an internal control flags an issue — either a control violation or a control failure — someone must fix it. The control software should automatically create a case in the system that includes all the details of what happened, why the case has been created, what control has failed, and who is going to fix it. The system should ensure that cases are automatically assigned to the people who are responsible for that business area: the business process owners as well as the control owners.

When the system creates a case, it should notify the control owner that they are responsible for investigating the failure, and notify the business process owner that a problem has been found and that she is now responsible for fixing it.

Responsibilities for fixing the problem differ depending on what happened with the control. Investigation of the problem could show that there's a control failure instead of a control violation. In the case of a control failure, such as a control that raises false positives, only the control owner needs to adjust the control and run it again to make sure it's working.

In the case of a control violation, the work mainly falls to the business process owner, who must then fix the problem. When the business-process owner fixes the problem, she records all activities: what she did, how it's going to solve the problem, and why it will no longer be an issue. After she records all of that, she can close the case. She runs the control again and makes sure that it passes this time.

Analysis: Reports for management

In the analysis phase, managers report on the control environment. The senior management in charge of compliance (whether it's the compliance team, the Chief Financial Officer, Chief Risk Officer or the Compliance Vice

President) runs reports: what controls have run recently, how many failed, and which business processes are most at risk. The most important of these reports is always that which impacts a significant account, or anything that ends up on the income statement.

The reports are available so that companies can measure and analyze their regulatory compliance. At a board meeting, management will now ask, "How are we doing with regard to financial compliance?" and having this quick, up-to-the-minute status will enable them to ascertain how compliant the company is.

Optimization: Barring risk

Finally, the control software should optimize controls by preventing risks from entering enterprise applications. Companies that implement preventative measures such as compliant change control (see Chapter 13) and compliant user provisioning (see Chapter 6) will see a reduction in control violations because risk never enters the enterprise applications that they use to run their business.

Getting to Know the SAP Approach: SAP GRC Process Control

SAP GRC Process Control is a single solution for enterprise control management. It provides centralized control management for automated and manual controls. It enables management by exception: It prioritizes remediation activities and gives managers visibility into what is happening in the control environment. In the next few sections, we look at the highlights of the SAP GRC Process Control solution.

SAP GRC Process Control provides a single system for automated and manual controls. It manages financial controls, operational controls, and IT controls across multiple enterprise systems and aims to improve controls through regular assessments. Figure 7-2 provides an overview of the bottom-up structure of SAP GRC Process Control.

Single system of record

To ensure good governance, you need a single system of record. SAP GRC Process Control includes the SAP GRC Repository, which documents and stores records for all governance, risk, and compliance information across a company. SAP GRC Process Control leverages all this information and links it to security frameworks like COSO and COBIT and legislation like SOX, so that companies gain a clear understanding of their control matrix. It also helps you to avoid redundancies, take controls and reuse them in different contexts, and identify control gaps.

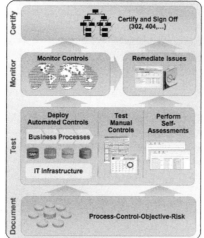

Figure 7-2:
SAP GRC
Process
Control.

Continuous monitoring

SAP GRC Process Control monitors business process controls for fraud, abuse, and inefficiencies. It continuously checks for weaknesses in master data and configuration set-ups and flags specific transactions that show heightened risks across your company's critical processes, such as procure-to-pay, order-to-cash, and reconcile-to-report. (See the next section for more details on the controls for these vital processes.)

SAP GRC Process Control helps eliminate false positives by integrating directly with enterprise applications and enables your company to drill down on supporting data for faster solutions to problems.

Out-of-the-box monitoring

SAP GRC Process Control has a predefined rule set for SAP and non-SAP software that companies can adjust with their own parameters to create a wide variety of custom controls. Companies can quickly ramp up and get controls in place because they don't have to create them from scratch. SAP GRC Process Control delivers automated controls monitoring for the following business processes:

- ✔ **Reconcile to Report:** The financial close process is extremely vulnerable to errors and miscalculation, particularly if a company has multiple locations and financial applications. SAP GRC Process Control guards against these risks by closely monitoring subledgers, general ledgers, and financial consolidations, while at the same time enabling companies to reduce manual controls, streamline the financial close, and ensure the accuracy of financial results.

- ✔ **Order to Cash:** The order to cash business process concludes with revenue recognition, making it vital that companies have the right controls in place to prevent human error or intentional fraud. With SAP GRC Process Control, companies can implement automated process control monitoring to identify revenue leakage, improper shipping cut-offs, and other potentially fraudulent activities. In doing so, companies ensure control effectiveness and efficiency for their order management, inventory, accounts receivable, and general ledger applications.

- ✔ **Procure to Pay:** SAP GRC Process Control controls the efficiency and efficacy of the purchasing, inventory, and accounts payable applications by helping companies to enforce corporate procurement policies and reduce spending on goods and services. Companies can monitor the real-time status of procure-to-pay activities as they are processed by multiple applications across the enterprise, giving them better visibility into how transactions are affecting working capital. It helps them eliminate duplicate vendor payments, lost discounts, and improperly valued inventory.

End-to-end internal controls

What are some of the other advantages of having end-to-end internal controls? For one thing, internal and external auditors will be relieved of the onerous task of sifting through hundreds of transactions. Instead, the system will provide them with reports.

SAP GRC Process Control helps companies monitor controls across their IT landscapes to ensure proper change management and to prevent risks from being introduced into production environments. These controls help ensure the integrity of enterprise system data, the reliability of application processing, and the proper development and implementation of software.

Of course, some controls require human intervention. SAP GRC Process Control supports manual control activities with smooth, workflow-driven procedures that automatically notify the appropriate people of tasks and action items and remove potential confusion. When control testers are unable to respond quickly, workflows escalate or reroute notifications. Testers are walked through guided procedures, and approved spreadsheet templates and policy documents help minimize data collection errors. Control testers can attach files and documents to serve as evidence of work done, while the software maintains a complete audit trail and change history of work done. SAP GRC Process Control also captures the monetary risk quantification for failed tests, letting you know not only what went wrong but how much that risk could cost you if it's not mitigated.

SAP GRC Process Control provides remediation case management. It detects global exceptions and prioritizes corrective action. The workflow-based notifications alert users to failed tests or assessments while documenting remediation activities and resolutions. Dashboards and reporting help provide insight into failed controls as well as allowing you to drill down for details about how to address the underlying problem being identified.

SAP GRC Process Control also helps companies prevent control exceptions from turning into material weaknesses by providing real-time visibility into all GRC activities. Companies can use a geographical heat-map that superimposes their business over a particular operating region, allowing them to identify trouble spots for control exceptions and drill down for answers. Companies can assign cases for fixing on the centralized remediation workbench, and actions are tracked, documented, and measured.

The product can normalize the certification process by providing a hierarchical bottom-up progression of sign-off activities from business process owners to location owners, corporate signers, and up to the CFO/CEO. Sign-off status is monitored through dashboards and reports to ensure that executives are kept informed of progress.

Chapter 8

It's a Small World: Effectively Managing Global Trade

*T*he world is growing smaller every day. Sure, it's a cliché, but when it comes to trade it's never been truer. More and more, we are buying goods from other countries, and we are sending our exports abroad. (Figure 8.1 illustrates the sharp growth in exports.) We live in an age of unprecedented globalization.

Today, a doctor in India might analyze X-rays from a patient in London, or a Japanese auto company might build cars with Brazilian parts in a factory in the United States. The pace of exchange is only speeding up as new free trade treaties are inked from Central America to East Asia. Companies are increasingly sourcing, manufacturing, and distributing goods on a global basis.

The open doors mean business opportunities, but they also mean new headaches. Managing global trade adds an extra layer of complexity to any business. It's one thing to source a widget from Walla Walla, but an entirely different experience to get it from a factory in Guangzhou, Bangalore, or Minsk. How do you ensure the widget arrives at the same time every month? What global trade treaties need to be complied with? How can you track all the documentation?

When it comes to exporting goods, how do you ensure that the thousands of orders you ship every day don't end up in an embargoed country or, worse yet, in the hands of terrorists? You're probably thinking "Wait . . . terrorists?!?" Before you reach for the antacid, read on.

By creating an organized system for dealing with global imports and exports, these challenges and others can be effectively managed. This chapter gives you an understanding of how global trade works and the best practices to put in place to ensure you meet the requirements of global trade regulations.

How does global trade relate to GRC?

For companies involved in importing or exporting any part of their value chain, the C in GRC is familiar. Global trade requires tremendous effort in the area of compliance. Companies that don't comply with global trade regulations face fines, penalties, or the possibility that their goods are stuck somewhere gathering dust because the proper paperwork hasn't been filed. You can easily translate these implications into risks, the R in GRC. For example, in addition to compliance issues, global trade presents risks because it is often difficult to forecast when goods will be delivered. Putting the proper policies and procedures in place ensures that a company has an effective governance structure for global trade.

Understanding Four Reasons Why Global Trade Is So Complex

Four major bottlenecks lead to problems in global trade. By understanding each of them, you can begin to understand how to put together a strategy to manage them. The four major reasons why global trade can be tricky are

- ✔ Long supply chains
- ✔ New regulations and security initiatives
- ✔ Modernization of government IT systems
- ✔ Increasingly complex regulations

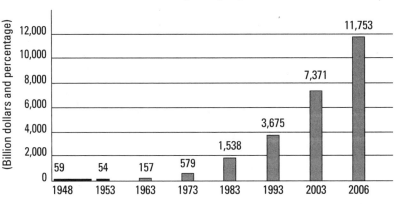

World Merchandise Exports by Region and Selected Economy

Figure 8-1: Growth in value of world merchandise trade (Source: World Trade Organization).

In the next few sections, we look at each in detail.

Long supply chains

Cross border transactions accounted for $10 trillion in trade in 2007. That figure is expected to grow to more than $70 trillion by 2025. The world is being knit into one giant marketplace. Companies are selling more goods overseas, manufacturers are sourcing parts and goods from overseas suppliers, and companies are outsourcing production to a number of foreign nations to save money. Figure 8-2 shows the leading importers while Figure 8-3 shows leading exporters.

Leading Importers in World Merchandise Trade, 2006

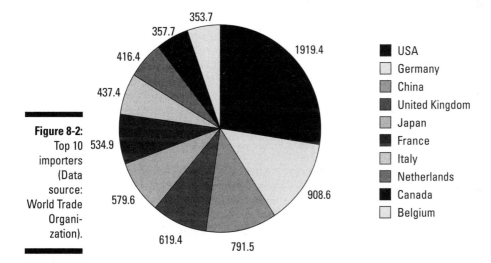

Figure 8-2: Top 10 importers (Data source: World Trade Organization).

- USA — 1919.4
- Germany — 908.6
- China — 791.5
- United Kingdom — 619.4
- Japan — 579.6
- France — 534.9
- Italy — 437.4
- Netherlands — 416.4
- Canada — 357.7
- Belgium — 353.7

The length of supply chains brings up new problems many companies aren't prepared for. How do you get the goods out of a foreign country? You may discover, for example, that it takes 50 days to import parts from China one month, but 55 days the next month. This uncertainty forces many companies to keep expensive safety stock on hand. These issues also feed into the decision about where to source goods from. For example, it may be more expensive to source goods from Vietnam than China, but the Vietnamese delivery is more predictable. In that case, it might actually be easier to just source the parts from Vietnam. Duties and tariffs also must be figured into the costs of global trade.

Leading Exporters in World Merchandise Trade, 2006

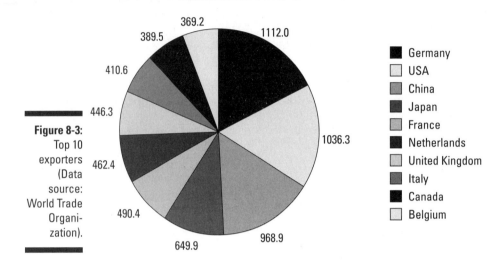

369.2
389.5
410.6
1112.0
446.3
1036.3
462.4
490.4
968.9
649.9

Germany
USA
China
Japan
France
Netherlands
United Kingdom
Italy
Canada
Belgium

Figure 8-3:
Top 10
exporters
(Data
source:
World Trade
Organi-
zation).

New regulations and security initiatives

Have you been hassled at airport security checkpoints recently? Taking off your shoes, getting rid of nail clippers, and having the contents of your luggage rifled through became common after September 11, 2001. But the terrorist attacks also meant increased inspections on the import and export of goods.

Governments around the world enacted new regulations and security initiatives in the wake of the attacks. The United States and other countries have tried to ensure dangerous materials that could be used to make bombs or other weapons aren't shipped to terrorists. Therefore, companies shipping abroad need special licenses from the government to ship certain products.

Governments also restrict certain goods, such as firearms, from being shipped to certain people or organizations. The act of managing the export or import of these controlled goods is known as "product-level compliance." Governments also issue outright bans on shipping anything to certain individuals or groups, such as terrorist-related organizations. The act of managing and monitoring all the people and entities in the supply chain is known as "party-level compliance." To make things more complicated, there are more than 50 different "restricted party" lists that various governments and government agencies have developed and update on a daily basis.

Violations of these regulations can result in large fines and even jail time for company executives (see the "$100 million export fine" sidebar elsewhere in this chapter for more information). President Bush recently signed into law an amended version of the International Emergency Economic Powers Act

(IEEPA) that increases the maximum fines for violating export control laws from $50,000 per violation to $250,000, or twice the amount of the transaction that is the basis of the violation with respect to which the penalty is imposed. The maximum criminal penalties for committing willful violations of IEEPA-based export control laws will increase to $1,000,000, with a maximum jail sentence of 20 years.

Finally, you also have to be aware of the additional layer of embargoes and sanctions. For example, shipping goods to Cuba, under most circumstances, is illegal for U.S. companies.

Modernization of government IT systems

Governments are notoriously slow adapters of new technology, so it may come as no surprise that many are just now automating systems for keeping track of import and export documentation. Nevertheless, companies must have systems in place to interface with various customs authorities electronically. Here are a few of the key international customs players and how they handle import and export documentation:

- ✔ **United States:** Exporters are required to electronically file the export declaration via the U.S. Census Bureau's Automated Export System (AES). U.S. Customs has also automated its import system, which is called the Automated Broker Interface (ABI). Certified licensed brokers usually handle the filing of import documents for most companies because the process is so highly complicated. However, a growing number of companies are self-filing these days because doing so is cheaper and they can control their own data. Another key development is the Automated Commercial Environment or ACE, which represents a business process transformation on the part of Customs that will help electronically speed legitimate trade while providing greater security. The frequently asked questions document on ACE is 113 pages long, indicating that there will be quite the learning curve when and if the Automated Commercial Environment becomes a reality.

- ✔ **European Union:** The E.U. embarked on a six-year program to modernize its customs systems in 2004. The European eCustoms Initiative will create a paperless environment for customs and trade documentation. All 25 E.U. member states will be on the common system by 2010. The initiative includes the New Computerized Transit System (NCTS), the Automated Export System (AES), and in 2008, the Automated Import System (AIS).

- ✔ **Australia:** Australia has put in place an electronic system for customs clearance called the Integrated Cargo System (ICS). Companies are able to access customs and other government agencies through a single electronic window.

Considering importing or exporting: Points to ponder

Here are some basic questions for you to keep in mind when setting up your importing and exporting system:

✔ Which laws and regulations do I have to consider?

✔ How do I classify products and calculate duties?

✔ How do I ensure electronic communications with customs authorities?

✔ How do I ensure I have the right import and export documents?

✔ How can I keep track of inventory at a customs warehouse?

✔ Can I take advantage of international trade agreements?

✔ Can I claim refunds on my exports?

✔ How can I mitigate the financial risks of importing and exporting?

Increasing complexity of regulations

The explosion in global trade has resulted in an equally large increase in trade regulations. A typical cross-border shipment can involve more than 25 parties and create 35 documents. It gets even more staggering: There are more than 600 trade laws and 500 trade agreements to be considered when shipping internationally. Keeping up with the document trail can be maddening.

According to a 2003 report from the Aberdeen Group, "Ensuring that shipments comply with international shipping regulations is one of the most time-consuming aspects of trade." The situation hasn't gotten any better since this statement was made. Additionally, importers and exporters must frequently deal with a variety of agencies in the same country to ensure that they are in compliance with, for example, the U.S. State Department as well as the Department of Commerce.

In addition, here are some terms that can help you through some of the alphabet soup of security initiatives and regulations created by government bureaucracy:

✔ **International Traffic in Arms Regulations (ITAR):** A set of government regulations that control the import and export of defense goods and services, such as guns and munitions (and this can include military technology, such as encryption or night vision goggles). It requires that defense-related items only be shared with U.S. citizens, unless special approval is given by the State Department.

- ✔ **Customs Trade Partnership Against Terrorism (C-TPAT):** A voluntary U.S. Customs regulatory program that aims to keep terrorists from infiltrating the supply chain in the United States. The program requires important import/export businesses such as importers, rail lines, airlines, cargo companies, and others to certify their supply chain security procedures and share their security guidelines with their business partners.

- ✔ **Export Administration Regulations (EAR):** Part of the US Commerce Department, the Bureau of Industry and Security (BIS) implements and enforces the EAR regulations. Commercial products as well as "dual use" items that have both commercial and military use fall under EAR regulations.

- ✔ **Sarbanes-Oxley Act:** It may not seem like an act that was passed to ensure greater corporate accountability in the wake of Enron and other scandals would impact global trade regulation, but it does. The act requires company officials to verify the accuracy of financial statements including the values of imports and exports. It is also important to maintain a paper trail in case of an audit.

- ✔ **Container Security Initiative (CSI):** No, it's not a TV show. CSI is a US Customs and Border Patrol initiative passed in 2002 and is focused on ensuring that terrorists are not able to deliver goods by ship.

- ✔ **REACH:** Passed in June 2007 and coming into effect in phases, the EU's Registration, Evaluation, Authorization and Restriction of Chemical substances (REACH) legislation will impact many companies who export products to the EU. For more information on REACH compliance, see Chapter 12.

- ✔ **Harmonized Tariff Schedules:** The HTS comprises a hierarchical structure for describing all goods in trade for duty, quota, and statistical purposes. This structure is based upon the international Harmonized Commodity Description and Coding System (HS), administered by the World Customs Organization in Brussels. Accurately classifying your goods according to the HTS is one of the most tedious and important steps when exporting or importing products.

Now that you have an idea of some of the challenges facing companies that want to trade internationally, let's look at some best practices for setting up a global trade process on both the import and the export side.

Figuring Out the Complexities of Importing

Importing and exporting are vastly different processes. Importing goods is mainly about figuring out how to speed your items through customs, whereas exporting is much more about making sure your company complies with regulations, such as embargoes and restricted party lists. In this chapter, we start by looking at importing, which is broken down into a number of steps.

Classifying an item: What is it?

One of the most difficult, expensive, and time-consuming elements of importing goods begins before the item even arrives at the border. The importer must classify the good, or assign it a 10-digit code called a Harmonized Tariff Schedule. Customs authorities use the number to determine the tariffs and duties an importer pays. Specifically, the first six numbers of the code are the same for a particular item in every country (that's the harmony in the Harmonized Tariff Schedule). The last four numbers vary from country to country, but describe the item more specifically and provide information for the statistical purposes of tracking trade.

 Classifying an item is difficult because the importer must take into consideration all of the things that make up the item. For example, a simple item such as a t-shirt can be classified in many ways depending on where it's manufactured, as well as its material, color, stitching, and packaging. For more complicated items, the complexity quickly escalates and, for the most part, can't be determined without the blueprints of the product itself.

Because the process is so complicated, most companies outsource the classification process to law firms that specialize in the area. Unfortunately, this option is expensive and slow.

Classifying a product is also important when determining where to source goods from. The import duties and taxes can have a major impact on the cost of a good. For example, it might cost $8 to manufacture a good in China, but $10 in Vietnam. The tariff on the item is $5 from China, but only $2 from Vietnam. Even though it is cheaper to manufacture the good in China, it would actually be cheaper to source it from Vietnam.

Making way for the goods: Pre-clearance

After a product is classified, the import process begins. An importer or buyer creates a purchase order inside an order management system. The importer sends the purchase order to the exporter, who arranges for the items to be transferred to a port to get shipped or flown out of the country. At the same time, the exporter sends an Advanced Shipping Notice (ASN) to the importer or to the broker the importer has hired to guide the import process. The ASN lists the items and their value so the importer can calculate the duty and prepare the proper import documents.

The whole idea is to finish all this paperwork before the goods arrive, so they can speed through customs to get to your store or factory.

Making it through: Clearing Customs

The next step is clearing goods through customs. Most companies outsource this task to a customs broker, but a few larger companies, such as Wal-Mart, handle it in house. Most companies rely on a broker because the process is complex and requires a special license to clear items through customs. For U.S. Customs, the two key documents that must be filed are forms 3461 and 7501, which tell Customs what the importer is bringing into the country. This is known as making an *entry*. As mentioned earlier, U.S. Customs now requires these items to be filed electronically. Most companies use the data from the purchase order to populate these forms, which are then sent to the customs broker. If the importer is a self-filer, the forms are filed directly with Customs' Automated Broker Interface. When the documentation is completed, the goods are trucked (also known as drayage) to a warehouse and then distributed to the importer's store or factory.

Reconciling value: The step most often missed

One of the most important steps in the importing process is one that many companies never take: reconciling the product values they declared in their backend systems with the actual value customs assigned to the items. This value is known as the Customs Declared Value and it can be very different from the value the importer originally listed. The difference between these values represents an unreconciled inconsistency in the accounting system. The issue of proper reconciliation has become especially important because the Sarbanes Oxley Act requires that company officials verify the accuracy of financial statements, of which import values are a critical part.

Getting the lead out: Brand protection

One theme that you'll see again and again in this book is that the buck essentially never stops. Companies are partnered in long and complex value chains around the world. And guess what? You can't say you're responsible just for your part because the marketplace, and increasingly, the government says otherwise. Mattel learned this lesson quite painfully in 2007 when its brand became synonymous with lead paint on toys. Laws like the Foreign Trade Corrupt Practices Act, which relates to bribery in other countries, mean that legally and in terms of your brand, you and your partners are one big family and as we all know, what one family member does affects all the rest.

Making Sure You're Complying with All 19,391 Exporting Restrictions

Exporting is generally less complex than importing, but there are a whole different set of challenges involved. Violating export laws and regulations can carry a much greater cost in terms of fines and damage to a company's reputation than similar violations on the import side. (And no, there probably aren't *really* 19,391 exporting restrictions, but sometimes it seems like it!)

Knowing who you're dealing with

An exporter *must* understand who he is dealing with at all times. There are two possible pitfalls:

✔ Shipping to someone on a restricted parties list

✔ Shipping to someone in an embargoed or sanctioned country

In the wake of Sept. 11, countries have put in place additional security measures to ensure that dangerous goods don't fall into the hands of terrorist groups. This has resulted in a profusion of restricted party lists, or individuals or groups that can't have goods shipped to them. The difficulty for businesses is that there are more than 50 restricted party lists around the world and some countries — such as the United States — have more than one list for different agencies. To make matters more confusing, these lists are regularly updated, so keeping on top of changes can be extremely hard. Third-party companies monitor and update these lists, which can be purchased and downloaded for use with global trade software.

The $100 million export fine

Just how serious are penalties for not complying with global trade regulations? Try $100 million serious. In March 2007, a prominent American company agreed to plead guilty and pay a fine of up to $100 million for failing to obtain the proper export license for shipping night vision goggles parts to China, Singapore, and Great Britain. The company also pled guilty to leaving information off of arms exports reports from 2000 to 2004. U.S. Justice Department officials said the company was willingly violating the export restrictions and didn't take action to stop the violations until the department found out what was going on. The company faced two major problems: it shipped the wrong items and it shipped them to the wrong destinations.

Companies must also make sure they do not ship goods to sanctioned or embargoed countries. This seems straightforward, but many companies fail to grasp how these regulations actually work. If a company is U.S. owned, it must comply with U.S. embargoes and sanctions. For example, that means that, with few exceptions, a U.S. company with operations in Canada can't ship goods to Cuba because the U.S. has an embargo on Cuba.

Checking restricted parties lists and embargoed countries might not sound so bad until you consider scale. Many companies are shipping thousands of orders a day to dozens of different countries, and there are more than 50 restricted parties lists around the world. Checking those orders against all those lists can quickly become a logistical nightmare. However, there are ways to smooth the process by automating it (see the last section in this chapter for details).

Obtaining the right export licenses

Exporters must also track whether a product needs an export license, which is required for certain classes of goods, such as firearms, advanced technology, and medical devices. These products are called *controlled goods*. How do you know whether you need an export license? In the U.S., you find out through the Commerce Department's Web site (www.bis.doc.gov/licensing/exportingbasics.htm). Using this site, you can find out whether the item you are trying to export has an Export Control Classification Number (ECCN), which means you need a license to export that item. Items that are not controlled fall under and are referred to as EAR99 or NLR (No License Required).

Sidebar: Helpful government links on global trade

Here are some links to trade-related government Web sites you may find helpful:

- ✔ U.S. Bureau of Industry and Security: www.bis.doc.gov/

- ✔ U.S. Customs and Border Protection: www.cbp.gov/

- ✔ U.S. International Trade Commission: www.usitc.gov/

- ✔ U.S. Department of Treasury: www.treas.gov

- ✔ U.S. Directorate of Defense Trade Controls: http://pmddtc.state.gov

- ✔ Office of U.S. Trade Representative: www.ustr.gov/

- ✔ Export.gov: www.export.gov/index.asp

- ✔ European Commission Tariff and Customs: http://ec.europa.eu/

- ✔ U.S. Office of Regional Security and Arms Control: www.state.gov/t/pm/rsat/

- ✔ Office of Foreign Asset Control: www.treasury.gov/offices/enforcement/ofac/

- ✔ Sarbanes-Oxley Act: www.sarbanes-oxley.com/search.php?q=404

Knowing how the product will be used

The first important question to ask when you're exporting is who you're exporting to. The second important question is what is the item and what will it be used for. The company with the $100 million export fine didn't violate the who — they violated the what. The company knowingly shipped a product with a military use out of the U.S. without the proper permission.

Here are some of the major compliance concepts governments use to determine if a company has followed global trade guidelines:

- ✔ **End use:** Before exporting an item, you have to think about what it is, who will get it, and what it might ultimately be used for. Under global trade compliance regulations, a company that ships an item overseas can be held responsible if the buyer uses it for an illegal purpose, or if the buyer turns around and sells it to someone else, who uses it illegally.

- ✔ **Dual use:** A company can also be held responsible if it ships a product to a buyer that uses it in an unintended way that is illegal or harmful. For example, a reputable medical supply company sold plasma filters to a medical organization in Europe. The filters ultimately ended up in the hands of a terrorist organization that found they could be used to filter anthrax just as effectively. This example raises the question of how a company could know all the ways its products could be used maliciously. The answer is that the company must take reasonable care and once such nefarious uses are brought to light, it must attempt to guard against them.

- **Reasonable care:** The Customs Modernization Act of 1993 has made it the responsibility of all importers and exporters to take affirmative steps to ensure compliance with the Customs laws. For organizations, a compliance program must be institutionalized, both to set up proper procedural safeguards and to ensure that all employees understand what is required. When the government audits a company, they want to see if the company has demonstrated "reasonable care" to comply with the law.

These regulations may be unsettling, especially for companies that ship sensitive materials, but there are ways to ensure you don't fall victim to one of these violations. The compliance regulations include a provision called *reasonable care*, which means if a company can demonstrate it did everything possible to avoid an illegal end use or dual use, it may not be held responsible for the misuse.

Taking Advantage of the System: Trade Preference Management

Trade agreements and most favored nation status can make doing business in certain countries much more attractive. For example, the North American Free Trade Agreement (NAFTA) eliminated trade tariffs on many goods traded between the United States, Canada, and Mexico including agriculture, cars, textiles, and computers.

Such agreements allow companies to qualify for duty-free exports as long as the goods meet certain criteria. Many companies leave millions of dollars on the table each year by not taking advantage of these agreements because it requires personnel or knowledge they don't have. Companies should think about taking advantage of global trade preferences.

Discovering the Different Ways to Manage Global Trade

As you have seen, managing global trade is only slightly less complicated than bringing about world peace or landing a man on the moon. So how do companies manage it? Historically, the answer has been not very well because there has not been a truly great way of tackling global trade tasks on both the importing and exporting sides.

Some companies have done little to comply with restricted parties lists. They have either been ignorant of restricted parties lists or have hoped they wouldn't get caught shipping items to banned individuals.

Other companies have managed to comply with the regulations in a limited way by using manual means, but at great expense of time and money. For example, an employee at a company might compare a handful of international sales orders against various restricted party lists. If it's a major company with hundreds or thousands of sales orders each day, the employee might only be able to ensure a fraction of the sales orders are not violating import and export regulations.

This is no way to run a global trade operation in today's security-charged environment. In fact, you might be a little freaked out at this point with all the talk of terrorists, restricted party lists, export licenses, and myriad regulations. Fortunately, there are applications that can take the heavy lifting out of global trade management. Global trade management software can automate nearly all of the tasks, including checking automatically to ensure that you don't ship goods without a license or to a restricted party.

Using the SAP Approach: SAP GRC Global Trade Services

SAP GRC Global Trade Services manages all the complexities of international trade including full regulatory compliance and management of risk while trading on a global basis. It consists of separate modules that enable companies to improve their supply chain and comply with international regulations.

SAP GRC Global Trade Services automates the key tasks needed to effectively trade with partners around the world. What's more, SAP GRC Global Trade Services is integrated with SAP's other GRC solutions, such as SAP GRC Risk Management (see Chapter 2).

The product requires minimal installation and ramp-up time; it is installed on a single server, and there is no client software to install. Authorized users around the world can access the application via their Web browsers.

Components of the solution include

✔ **Export management:** Automates and streamlines complex export processes to ensure faster delivery to customers by minimizing delays at national borders while ensuring compliance with relevant regulations and mitigating the financial risk of global transactions.

- ✔ **Import management:** Helps to expedite customs clearance for import shipments to reduce costly buffer stock and implement just-in-time inventory management. SAP GRC Global Trade Services allows you to easily classify products, calculate duties, streamline electronic communication with customs authorities, ensure import compliance, and efficiently manage letters of credit.

- ✔ **Trade preference management:** Helps you make the most of international trade agreements with capabilities to solicit vendor declarations, determine the eligibility of products for preferential treatment, and issue certificates of origin to customers.

- ✔ **Restitution management:** Enables you to manage and calculate the restitution for the export of common agricultural products (CAP) out of the European Union with capabilities to assign securities, manage export licenses, maintain recipes, and calculate and apply for refunds.

SAP GRC Global Trade Services automates, streamlines, and standardizes the global trade compliance tasks that many companies have ignored or struggled with in the past. Many companies have manual compliance systems, which are slow and require a large staff to carry out. SAP GRC Global Trade Services also saves money by keeping tasks in house — such as classifying products — that were once outsourced, and by helping companies take advantage of global trade preferences in international trade treaties. Most importantly, SAP GRC Global Trade Services helps companies avoid hefty fines or even jail time that can result from failing to comply with global trade regulations.

Part III
Going Green

The 5th Wave   By Rich Tennant

"I asked for software that would biodegrade after it was thrown out, not while it was running."

In this part . . .

You'll find out about the various issues your company needs to consider before taking the leap into the wild green yonder, from the benefits you stand to reap from voluntarily deepening your shade of green to the harm you risk by insisting that the color you are now — whatever it may be — is just fine and dandy. You'll explore the three components in your company's overall green routine: your people, processes, and products.

You'll find out about watching over people, as OSHA requires, to optimize your work areas, assess risks, develop the best standard operating procedures, manage and report incidents, inspect your various job sites, and, of course, educate employees about health and safety matters. You'll then turn to processes — the array of practices your company must engage in to successfully account for the effect its operations have on the environment, consumer health, and employee safety. And finally you'll look at products, where you'll find out about how keeping your product-handling green will prepare you to comply with existing and upcoming environmental legislation.

Chapter 9

Making Your Company Environmentally Friendly

● ●

In This Chapter

▶ Discovering the advantages of going green now

▶ Looking at companies that are environmentally friendly

▶ Complying with the bird's nest of environmental regulations

● ●

G *oing green.* Everyone has heard the phrase, but what exactly does it mean? It's rapidly becoming one of the day's trendiest catchphrases, but the idea behind going green conveys a deep truth about a way of living that individuals and businesses would do well to adopt. The focus? What is happening to the earth and how it affects our quality of life, not to mention the potential financial impacts.

When individuals go green, they demonstrate their concern for the preservation, restoration, and improvement of the natural environment in just about everything they do. They express consideration for conserving natural resources and preventing pollution, from how much water they use while taking a shower or washing the dishes, to the quantity and type of fuel their vehicles consume, to the products they use to clean and the sources of energy they tap to heat and cool their homes.

In particular, people are increasingly concerned about how energy production using fossil fuels such as coal, oil, and gas impacts the environment, and, in turn, our future quality of life. They are also making choices based on whether products and services are earth friendly, ethically produced and made, recyclable, and energy-efficient.

When a business goes green, whether it is a global leviathan, such as Shell Oil or a small but bourgeoning startup in the discrete manufacturing industry, that business demonstrates its commitment to these matters, which are increasingly becoming government mandates or regulations. In addition, however, green businesses are also obligated to enhance the health and safety programs for both their employees and the public, at times on a global level.

This is why, unlike today's consumers, most companies don't really have a great deal of leeway when it comes to going green. Of course, they have a hand in the *extent* to which they green themselves, but they must all comply to a minimum degree with an expanding battery of environmental directives and standards that are inextricably tied up with — yes, you guessed it — GRC.

This chapter introduces the various issues your company needs to consider before it takes the leap into the wild green yonder, from the benefits your company stands to reap from voluntarily going as green as possible to the harm you risk by insisting that the color you are now — whatever it may be — is just fine and dandy.

Whether you are committed to the principles of environmental stewardship or have given little thought to the ways your company's processes and products affect the world and its people, this chapter is designed to demystify what it means to go green and show you how to make choices that reduce your company's impact on the environment. You also find out that the sooner you start to build a more nature-friendly company, the happier, healthier, and safer you, your employees, your customers, your neighbors, and the rest of the planet will be.

Discovering the Three Ps of Going Green: People, Processes, and Products

The business world today is one of environmental plans that are as globalized as they are country-specific. It is a world of high-profile failures and successes that can make or break not simply a corporation's fiscal year but the corporation itself. It is a world, as well, of complex legislation ranging from laws that protect the tufted plover of Lower Tasmania to those that guarantee the rights of both a company's employees and the communities that are affected by the waste products of the company's production efforts.

It is a world, in short, of environmental governance, risk, and compliance management: a mix of legislation, common sense, and PR smarts that combine to form a policy expressive of a company's overall philosophy and worldview. For a business to maintain a balanced environmental, health, and safety policy, it must constantly juggle three vital factors: its people, processes, and products. Managed smartly, however, the rewards of compliance can be as big as they are surprising.

The next few chapters explore in detail each of the three components in your company's overall green routine: your people, processes, and products. Chapter 10 focuses on keeping employees safe; Chapter 11 covers making sure your processes are green; and Chapter 12 delves into the issue of making environmentally friendly products.

Going Green: It's Not Just for Tree-Huggers Anymore

No doubt about it, global warming is changing the earth and with it, the way companies conduct their business. Nicholas Stern, an adviser to the British government and the former head of the World Bank, has predicted that if greenhouse gas emissions continue to rise, the ensuing climate change could rip off 20 percent of the global GDP by 2050.

Every single business today, large or small, should be in the process of going green. A whole bunch of carrots are available for those who do: The payoffs can be very rewarding. On the other hand, there are plenty of big ugly sticks poised to smack those who remain stubbornly entrenched in their old, "brown" ways, and probably the biggest stick of all is the negative impact on a company's brand.

Ten green giants

The following companies have been named by *Fortune* magazine as world leaders in the current green rush for having gone above and beyond what's required by law:

Company	Revenue	Country	Employees
Honda	Japan	$84.2 billion	145,000
Continental Airlines	U.S.	13.1 billion	44,000
Suncor	Canada	$13.6 billion	5,500
Tesco	Britain	$71 billion	380,000
Alcan	Canada	$23.6 billion	68,000
PG&E	U.S.	$12.5 billion	20,000
SC Johnson	U.S.	$7 billion	12,000
Goldman Sachs	U.S.	$69.4 billion	24,000
Swiss Re	Switzerland	$24 billion	10,500
Hewlett-Packard	U.S.	$91.7 billion	156,000

Understanding Why Your Company Should Go Green

A 2006 Sierra Club poll showed that the proportion of Americans who worry about the environment "a great deal" or "a fair amount" has jumped from 62 to 77 percent. Environmentalism, in other words, is on everyone's radar. As such, the choice for today's companies doesn't simply lie between the extremes of the far-out tree hugger who chains himself to a redwood tree, on the one hand, or, on the other, to falling into a bottomless abyss of paranoid anxiety about impending lawsuits.

The speed with which information travels is another factor that is sobering companies into going green. By the time a company finds out about an environmental problem, the news about that problem may have already spread around the world. Pick up a magazine or newspaper, and on any given day you're likely to see reports about green successes or failures. Green is news, and news travels faster than ever.

Going green is literally everywhere. We could easily compare the current shift toward enhanced environmental awareness to the events that resulted from the dot.com boom of the early to mid-90s. Just as it was news then to have a Web site, or even brochureware, so, too, is it news to be green now. Of course, this won't always hold true. Trends become fads, and fads eventually become norms. For smart businesses, however — that is, for businesses that go green proactively now — some nice press for being an environmental pioneer is just one of the benefits.

The fact is, lots of companies used to go green because they had to, either by law or as a last-ditch effort to improve their public image. Now, however, those same companies have found that reducing pollutants and wasteful practices also contributes to the increased efficiency of internal processes. All of this — need we spell it out? — creates a positive impact on the bottom line. Companies can profit substantially from going green!

Just listen to Sir Richard Branson, the mogul king sitting at the top of the Virgin empire. "I believe we need to make a virtue out of investing in clean technology and renewable energy," he said in an interview for Saab's Web site (www.saabbiopower.co.uk/), "and not be ashamed to want to make profits out of it. For too long, environmentally friendly technology and issues about the environment have been seen as a corporate social responsibility issue and not an opportunity to create new wealth in the future. Governments alone cannot solve the problems we face unless the capitalist world invests in a sustainable future."

Profits aside, there are many, many reasons why your business needs to go green. Here are five that even your kids will agree make sense. To go green is to

- Differentiate yourself from the competition
- Create major customer satisfaction
- Improve your reputation
- Meet *and* create demands for green products
- Do the right thing

In addition, creating green environments and green buildings provides lots of benefits for lots of different groups of people. Here are just a few examples of how going green benefits multiple parties, beyond just employees and customers:

Local environments benefit from

- Greenhouse gas reduction
- Improved water quality
- Improved air quality
- Solid waste reduction

Organizations benefit from

- Lower waste disposal cost
- Safer and healthier working environments
- Reduced use of materials
- Unique marketing potential

Cities benefit from

- Enhancements to existing recycling programs for increased value
- Demonstrated environmental leadership
- Preservation of local quality of life

Owners and residents benefit from

- Lower utility bills
- Healthier/more productive living and working environments
- Reduced maintenance costs
- Increased resale value
- Preferential mortgages

Going Green Is Good Business

A fantastic way to motivate yourself to go green fast is to examine the long list of real-world benefits and rewards that your business is sure to reap the moment you begin. Going green is not simply the right thing to do; it makes good business sense too. In this section, you'll learn how going green can enhance your image, build trust with regulators, and influence the course of life on Planet Earth (pretty heady stuff, that).

Enhance your image

From making your customers happy to building trust with regulatory authorities, from reducing your risk exposures to nurturing the ecosystem, you can find numerous ways to do the right thing while simultaneously improving your company's image. The next few sections outline several companies who have gone green and detail some of the benefits they've reaped.

Consumers and shareholders alike never have been easily fooled, so they know who is genuine and who is simply *greenwashing* (that is, appropriating one or another environmental virtue for the sake of creating a false, pro-environmental image). The evidence is there. People who live and work in green environments are healthier and safer. Knowing as much, your customers only want more, which is why they are the ones who sit behind the wheel of the machine going green.

Hewlett Packard

As you can see from our list in the "Ten green giants" sidebar, HP isn't the only global manufacturer heeding the call to go green. It has experienced a 120 percent increase worldwide in the number of inquiries connected to the environment since the last half of 2006. In 2005, the company received $6 billion in requests for proposals that had some environmental element. Pat Tiernan, vice president for corporate social environmental responsibility, has said that that number continues to climb.

As such, the company has taken the full lifecycle of products into account when greening its supply chain. For example, they provide all of their partners up- and downstream with a list of substances that are either hard on the environment or entirely banned and then take measures to ensure that these partners are adhering to respective laws. Bonnie Nixon Gardiner, global program manager of supply chain social and environmental responsibility, says this policy is "non-negotiable."

Wal-Mart

Starting with toothpaste, milk, soap, soda, beer, DVDs, and vacuum cleaners, Wal-Mart has begun working with suppliers to gauge and reduce the energy it takes to manufacture, purchase, and distribute their products. In addition, the company has pledged to encourage the rest of its suppliers to respond to their new program. One means of doing this entails working more closely with them, as well as with organizations such as the Carbon Disclosure Program. The company's Chief Merchandising Officer said, "This is an opportunity to spur innovation and efficiency throughout our supply chain that will not only help protect the environment but save people money at the same time."

If other companies in the Consumer Packaged Goods (CPG) industry can implement likeminded energy-reduction policies, especially those businesses with supply networks on the scale of Wal-Mart's, proliferating efficiency standards and product innovation across multiple industries becomes an even greater possibility.

Sun Microsystems

One of the ways that Sun has responded to the public clamor for a deepened shade of green is to decrease the number of distribution centers in its supply chain. To do this, it has simply increased the amount of finished product that ships directly to customers. The resulting benefits are clear — less energy, less plastic and paper, and less manpower. Savings from these cuts go towards improving other green processes, such as, for example, the means by which they disperse information to partners and customers. By using the Internet to communicate, Sun has reduced paper costs from $10 million to $1 million and saved two million pounds of paper each year. That's nearly 6,000 trees still out there converting carbon dioxide to oxygen for the rest of us!

Timberland

According to Gary Smith, Timberland's senior vice president of global supply chain, the outdoor clothing and shoe company has implemented a sustainability agenda that accounts for the use of energy, materials, chemical, and systems across its supply chain. Recently, for example, it installed a wind tower at one of its sites. Elsewhere, it has implemented solar panels to heat the water used to steam materials in its hand-sewn shoes. About one-third of the company's product line (over 10 million pairs of shoes) now incorporates water-based adhesives. Just four years ago that number was nearly zero. It is also taking measures to replace its polyvinyl chloride (PVC), a plastic considered detrimental to public health and the environment, with greener materials by 2008.

DHL

DHL's director of environmental strategies and policies, Winfried Haeser, says the company sees reliance on fossil fuels and their damage to the environment as a challenge to be addressed on a global scale. One of the ways it has reduced its resource expenditure was to ensure the highest possible loading cycles are matched with the shortest possible distances traveled by its vehicles, using internal optimization software to map out the best delivery routes. Consequently, DHL has cut delivery mileage by 14 percent since 2001 and added more than 20,000 tons of airfreight capacity without the need for additional flights. The company is also searching out alternative fuel technology, including bio-fuels and natural gas. According to current calculations, such means could save several million euros per year by 2012 and cut greenhouse gas emissions from its road vehicles to 5 percent below 1990 levels, a target that is in line with provisions of the international Kyoto Protocol.

IBM

This techno monster has responded to customer demand by launching its "Project Big Green." The program commits $1 billion per year to increase the level of energy efficiency in the information technologies markets. Since the program's birth, IBM has been more heavily bombarded by customer requests than ever before.

Build trust with regulatory authorities

The maze of environmental regulations becomes more complex each day, which in turn places a burden on regulatory agencies. As a result, regulators place a high value on companies they can trust to do the right thing. Creating a transparent audit trail and the means by which to access the wide range of required documentation is a great way to build valuable goodwill with these guys. Plus, it has been shown time and again that people like doing business with companies they believe are on the up and up. When you comply with environmental, employee, and consumer protection regulations of all kinds, you are more likely to have a positive image in the public eye and in the media. Provide full evidence of your compliance to all regulatory authorities, and you can hardly lose.

Influence future events

If you don't already know, you may be surprised to learn that mega-corporations such as Xerox, Ford Motor Company, and Johnson & Johnson have joined ranks with a host of powerful NGOs (non-governmental organizations) like The Nature Conservancy and the National Wildlife Fund to become members of the U.S. Climate Action Partnership (USCAP). If that's not enough, they have also requested that the U.S. government "quickly enact strong national legislation to require significant reductions of greenhouse gas emissions." According to their promo, they believe that addressing the "climate change challenge will create more economic opportunities than risks for the U.S. economy."

Many businesses are also signing up for programs like the California Climate Registry Voluntary Program and the U.S. Voluntary Reporting of Greenhouse Gases Program. Companies in the former program voluntarily report their CO_2 emissions for the first year and then, after three years, their top six air polluters, as well. Those businesses in the latter program — including utilities such as Niagara Mohawk, Houston Lighting and Power, and New England Electric Systems, manufacturers like General Motors and Alcan Ingot, coal producers such as Consol and Peabody, chemical giants such as Dow and DuPont, and IT innovators like IBM — report any activity that reduces emissions of greenhouse gases or increases carbon fixation or sequestration.

Saving the planet, clearly, is not the only reason to take such a proactive stance in the overall move to go green. Nor is the prospect of making a few more fast bucks. What all these companies have in common is a vision of the possibility that they get to help draft the very regulations they will soon need to oblige. In other words, joining the go-green game early on can garner you a precious advantage: that of receiving advance notification of future changes in the regulatory industry. Staying ahead of the game can enable companies to forecast trends and influentially engage key people and agencies. Furthermore, they can also meet and, frequently, beat regulations before enforcement policies are set.

What can this mean for you? While your competitors are rushing to catch up, you will already be in the process of seeking out other ways to increase your competitive advantage. With prospects like these, is it any wonder that USCAP has pledged to "work with the President, the Congress, and all other stakeholders" to enact a climate change program at the earliest possible date?

Implementing Green Practices

Just by planting trees, switching light bulbs, and filtering your water, you can make a real difference in the environment. In the next few sections, we take a look at a few practices your company can adopt to make going green easier.

Trees matter

More than 20 percent of the world's oxygen is produced in the Amazon rainforest alone. And yet since 1992, the number of rainforest acres has dropped by 50 percent. Ponder this for about a millisecond and you can see why businesses everywhere have begun to engage in tree plantings. Accor North America, for example, is planting 20,000 trees throughout the United States and Canada — one for each of its employees. Another such philanthropic company is Milliken Contract; since launching Trees for All on Arbor Day 2006, Milliken customers have added about 8,000 trees of renewed forests through their online program.

Let there be (green) light!

If every American home replaced just one old light bulb with a compact fluorescent lamp (CFL) bulb, the country would save enough energy to light more than 3 million homes for a year, more than $600 million in annual energy costs, and prevent greenhouse gases equivalent to the emissions of more than 800,000 cars. Imagine what the numbers would be if businesses began to use these bulbs across their entire operations.

Here are some of the advantages of CFL (ENERGY STAR) bulbs:

- Use about 75 percent less energy than standard incandescent bulbs and last up to 10 times longer
- Save about $30 or more in electricity costs over each bulb's lifetime
- Produce about 75 percent less heat, so they're safer to operate and can cut energy costs associated with home cooling

Water: To bottle or not to bottle?

Some companies provide bottled water for their employees. This seemingly healthy choice is actually very negative for the environment. A 2001 report by the World Wide Fund for Nature estimates that approximately 1.5 million tons of plastic are wasted in the bottling of 89 billion liters of water each year. Notwithstanding the plastic itself, the energy needed to make and deliver these bottles to market depletes limited fossil fuels. Due to their unregulated use of resources and their production of billions of plastic bottles, bottled water companies are creating a real strain on the environment.

For individuals and businesses alike, the alternative to consuming bottled water is to use local water treated and purified with your own systems. The three most common methods of water purification are reverse osmosis, distillation, and water filtration. By offering employees filtered water instead of water bottles, you and the environment both win, again.

Reduce your risk

A vital part of going green involves continually tracking your key performance indicators and compliance with internal and external regulations to ensure that you are not breaking any laws. Such practices enable you to manage risk in a way that minimizes everyone's bad dream of costly fines or forced shutdowns. And the trend of adding C-suite jobs with titles like Chief Compliance Officer and Chief Sustainability Officer further reinforces the need for "owners" to be responsible for managing these risks. The company's success depends on it. Of course, your key stakeholders will love you all the more, too, when you are on top of your GRC because you'll have the reporting and collaborative capabilities that enable you to communicate with them on a regular, timely basis.

Going Green Is also the Law

No one goes into business these days jumping for joy at the idea of complying with the laws in highly regulated industries. But facts, as they say, are facts. Environmental compliance regulations are not merely here to stay: They are growing exponentially. The current list includes such gems as ISO 14001, EPA Clean Air Act Title V, EPA Clean Water Act, EU Emission Trading Scheme (ETS), US SARA 313 and Canadian NPRI Reporting, Health & Safety Management (OHSA 18001, COSHH), Social Accountability (SA 8000), Risk Management (AS/NZS 4360), and Information Security (BS/ ISO 17799). And these are the "minor" ones! For a clearer view of the whole regulatory picture, read on.

Compliance

Are you a manufacturer of lingerie? Do you produce house paint? Are golf balls the bread and butter in your company's refrigerator? How often does your motherboard factory send waste material off to the county landfill site? Each and every one of today's businesses, no matter whether you are the man on the corner selling hot dogs or the leading builder of jet fighter turbines, absolutely, positively, without a solitary doubt *must* comply with today's environmental regulations, standards, directives, and laws, of which there are many. They don't call it "the long arm of the law" for nothing.

For better or worse, your operations affect consumer health, employee safety, and, just as importantly, the environment, which is why our current environmental compliance requirements in all their massive scope and complexity make the Sarbanes-Oxley Act look like a legislative midget. The American Chemistry Council, for example, estimates in its "Guide to the Business of Chemistry, 2005" that 3.4 percent of the industry's total revenue is spent on environmental health and safety. The bulk is directed toward capital equipment and remediation, but substantial expenditures are also handed to the consultants needed to help you comply. This is to say nothing of the technology you must implement if you want to stay on top of the game.

To the uninitiated, the notion of compliance can seem as abstract as the theory of relativity. Fear not, however. It can be complicated, just not *that* complicated. Although the requirements themselves may be, their subjects are not. Simply put, they are the three Ps we mentioned earlier: your company's people, processes, and products. When your business is compliant, it is managing its plants and manufacturing processes in such a way that your equipment, personnel, storage and distribution facilities, and products are not creating any damage as defined by the environmental and exposure specifications associated with current law. Simple, huh?

Environmental health and safety in the modern world: Complexity and compliance

Managing environmental issues is complicated today and only becoming more so. Companies are paying more attention than ever to this area because of pressure from the following forces, both internal and external to the company:

- Advent of numerous rigid environmental regulations

- Registration, Evaluation, and Authorization of Chemicals (REACH)

- Waste Electrical and Electronic Equipment (WEEE)

- Reduction of Hazardous Substances (RoHS)

- National, state, and local laws for plant security regulations (e.g., Toxic Catastrophe Prevention Act on NJ)

- Department of Homeland Security (DHS) chemical plant security regulations

- Facilities permits (e.g., Title V)

- Toxic Substances Control Act (TSCA)

- Increasing worker's compensation cost and regulations: $87B in US alone

- Mounting resolve for intensified risk assessments

- Escalating pressure for greater social and environmental responsibility

---

Well, sort of. You've also got to manage the levels of emissions and waste created across the full lifecycle of your operations, from R&D through delivery to the marketplace. And then of course your product has a half-life, and a full one, too, at whose end it must be properly disposed of. You are frequently held accountable for managing these, as well. Love them or hate them, they are not going away. The sooner your business takes them into account, the better off you are likely to be.

Risks of noncompliance: Fines and public relations nightmares

The consequences of noncompliance range anywhere from token slaps on the wrist to prison sentences for top executives to the loss of a company's goodwill to the forced closure of your business and consequent financial collapse. Recently, the most notable examples of trouble that can befall erring companies concern the disastrous events surrounding the toy giant Mattel.

Here's what happened around the world when *The New York Times* began revealing that the Chinese manufactures to whom Mattel outsources much of its work used lead paint in their toys:

- ✔ **June 15, 2007:** 1 million piece recall of the toy Thomas & Friends begins.
- ✔ **June 19, 2007:** Eric S. Lipton and David Barboza begin a series of stories on lead paint hazards in Chinese-made toys.
- ✔ **August 2, 2007:** US Consumer Product Safety Commission begins recall of Fisher-Price character toys for lead paint hazard.
- ✔ **August 14, 2007:** Mattel's total recall approaches 18.7 million toys.

The aluminum maker Alcoa was hurt so badly in a recent scandal that it is close to selling both its packaging and consumer business, along with its automotive castings business, and has plans to restructure its electrical and electronic solutions business in the Americas and Europe. Kahoot Products Inc., the maker of the plastic totem badges used by the Boy Scouts of America, had to recall 1.6 million badges, which are made in China. Is it any wonder that environmentally attributable childhood diseases, including asthma, lead poisoning, and cancer, cost the U.S. as a whole nearly $55 billion annually?

Obviously this problem is huge. The resulting flak has given all these companies — and Chinese manufacturers on the whole — a considerable black eye. The problem, however, is not merely an environmental one. Employees are involved because the materials they are handling are potentially toxic and the consumers who purchased the faulty products stand to be victimized, as well. This is to say nothing of the incredible fall that the brand owner takes, which in turn can have possibly disastrous consequences on the world economy; if things go badly enough, ripples can be seen around the globe. And even if no one is hurt, the entire toy industry is itself now poisoned by one of the greatest bugaboos of all — bad faith. Ask Union Carbide about bad faith; after killing 3,000 in Bhopal, India, they are one of the most abhorred companies in the world. Ask Exxon, too, a company that has scarcely been able to clear its name nearly 20 years after the Valdez oil spill! No doubt many companies bounce back from bad press, but is this a risk that you, your PR team, and your stockholders want to take? It's definitely something to consider.

A Final Word About Going Green

By now it should be abundantly clear that environmental health and safety is here to stay. Your plans for going green, therefore, should be a line item on your budget this month, not a few years down the road. Do not underestimate the nature and extent of the changes, either: the solutions required to accomplish this transition are not mutually exclusive to one or two of your departments or processes. Rather, you should anticipate implementing green methodologies across the entirety of your corporate ecosystem, top to bottom and side to side.

To do so, you want to consider the following matters:

- Protecting your employees, customers, and neighbors
- Reducing risks of occupational incidents and unauthorized releases of substances
- Preserving and, whenever possible, enhancing the environment
- Developing and installing a single, integrated platform that enables you to effectively monitor your GRC and environmental health and safety processes
- Complying with a burgeoning complex of regulations
- Improving your company's overall flexibility and transparency
- Providing near real-time reporting to all regulatory agencies

With more than 250 new environmental directives and standards around the world in 2006 alone, it is critical that your business deploy more open standards, flexible communications, and compliance support. The more you do, and the faster you do it, the more easily you can reach across multiple environmental regulations and regional variations, and the more manufacturers, dealers, suppliers, customers, and regulatory authorities will want to work with you. At the end of the day, you will all be benefiting the environment and each other, and you will be doing it while speaking the same green language.

Chapter 10

Keeping Employees Healthy and Safe

. . . .

. . . .

*J*ust as your first priority is to maintain the soundness of your own mind and body, so too should your company's first order of business be to ensure that the people in it are always healthy and safe. After all, it stands to reason: Your people are the lifeblood of your business — literally. Injured or sick employees present the unwelcome specter of misery and loss; recent estimates put the costs associated with occupational injuries and illness near $170 billion: costs that are not receiving the support of government subsidies but are simply draining your company's coffers. Healthy people, on the other hand, are happy people, and happy people make productive, happy businesses. At the end of the day, it's as simple as understanding that the shin-bone is connected to the knee-bone.

The mere thought that your company could be a major contributor to the astronomical costs associated with yearly occupational injuries and illnesses — again, the number is quickly rising toward the $200 billion mark — should be enough to send you and your top team members running to the board room for an emergency summit on how to design and institute a health and safety program comprehensive enough to protect the well-being of your employees, vendors, contractors, and visitors.

Perhaps you have already begun. If so, our hats are off. If, however, you have not begun, but are about to or if you are faced with islands of nonintegrated information, it's important that you first consider a variety of critical factors. As you know, the success of your business ultimately depends on how happy you keep your employees. Your employees' happiness, on the other hand, is really dependent on the extent to which your health and safety agenda includes managing their commitment and involvement, and providing them with training that meets industry-wide certification standards. You also need to create structured methods to analyze your worksites in ways that enable you to accurately assess potential risks and then develop the means to prevent and control hazards.

In this chapter, we cover the basics of safety, including implementing a safety plan, minimizing accidents, and educating employees. We also look at some of the many benefits of improved safety, including lowered healthcare costs and better employee recruitment and hiring.

Keeping Your Employees Safe and Healthy: The Big Picture

The ramifications of a health and safety plan are as extensive as they are positive. When you take planned, verifiable measures to implement a health and safety program that manages employee commitment and involvement, worksite analysis, hazard prevention and control, and certified training for all employees — from your ground-level workers right on up to your C-level hotshots — you can create a virtually foolproof program for success.

Have a look at the potential benefits. In addition to increasing the morale and productivity of your people, your business's turnover will decrease even as the quality of your product improves. Plus, you can almost certainly count on enhanced labor and management relations, along with an overall improvement in the use of your human resources.

Happy, healthy, whole employees translate to lower workers' compensation insurance costs, reduced medical expenditures, smaller expenditures for return-to-work programs, and fewer faulty products. You spend less paying for job accommodations for injured workers, and you also spend less for the overtime benefits that are sure to accrue when your healthy people have to step in for those who are not.

Both your employees themselves and their families benefit from your health and safety program, too. Staying healthy guarantees that their incomes are protected and their family lives are free of the discontent that would be sure to result from the anxiety and stress brought on by injury or illness.

In short, caring for and protecting people in your workplace makes them feel a part of the whole, a part of the world around them, so that when at last you are ready to create a unified strategy committed to environmental responsibility in every sector of the company's ecosystem, your employees will waste no time jumping on board the GRC wagon. The well-being of employees is good for everyone and everything — our businesses, our fellow workers, our families, our communities, and our economy.

Enabling and maintaining good health

Unless your employees maintain optimum health, they cannot perform at the high levels required to create superior products. To ensure their good health, your business should consider initiating a healthcare management program that includes

- ✔ A health center with qualified staff able to access vital information on demand; such data ought to entail personal information, case histories, injury and illness records, medical measures, restrictions, vaccinations, and the like; staff should be able to quickly and easily evaluate medical parameters, review general health statistics, display personal exposure record information, and provide statistics needed by workers' compensation associations

- ✔ Health surveillance protocols appropriate to each employee's personal exposure situation. As a means of reducing lost work hours, maximizing health center facility operations, and cutting company costs; all unnecessary protocols should be eliminated

- ✔ Physicians armed with statistics that enable them to recognize potential sources of danger, avoid occupational diseases, conduct occupational epidemiology studies, and provide evidence to any concerned persons or agencies that specified treatments and services have been rendered

- ✔ First-aid training for specified individuals, along with an accurate, regularly updated list of who has received such training and where in the company they are located

Avoiding accidents

People make mistakes, disaster strikes, fires start, chemicals spill, and forklifts go out of control. What we call accidents are almost always preventable (well, except for the natural disasters), and sometimes despite our efforts at prevention, they do occur. Certainly some industries have more inherent risks to the safety of their employees than others, particularly those involving mining, chemicals, construction, lumber, maritime activities, and manufacturing. Regardless of how comparatively safe or dangerous your industry is, safety risks are a concern for every company doing business today.

Your organization can take its first steps toward building a strong health and safety agenda simply by engaging in some good old-fashioned common sense, and then by applying universally recognized prevention principles. Foremost among these principles is an employee-training program that addresses the specific needs and requirements of your industry and a comprehensive system to manage all of this.

Information goes a long way toward combating the sort of ignorance or lack of awareness that is responsible for the majority of occupational injuries. Moreover, educating your people constitutes the foundation of the culture change that needs to transpire in your organization if its employees are to successfully participate in the transformation from a business that is brown, or yellow, or even pale green to one that is decidedly emerald-colored in terms of its environmental friendliness (more on this in Chapter 11).

Here is a list of procedures we suggest you follow to begin a program structured to help minimize employee risks:

- **Establish safety committees.** Committee members may include facility managers or administrators, various department heads, and employee representatives. The main goal of the committee is to assess all employee safety risks at the facility, keeping an eye on the most common areas of employee exposure to harm. After risks are identified, the committee can determine how to reduce those risks.

- **Encourage employee involvement and safety awareness.** Safety committees ought to encourage employees to actively participate in making decisions that affect them. You can talk to them about what problems they encounter in performing their duties that could contribute to injury. You can also solicit their suggestions. To promote further employee awareness, you may consider introducing a safety education program.

- **Reward safe work practices.** Developing an incentive program can help to motivate employees to more effectively follow workplace safety practices. The program might reward teams whose efforts result in a reduction of on-the-job injuries, or better yet, zero-based injury periods. Pick a perk, any perk. You may be surprised at how far these sorts of things can go to make people happy. You can also establish an employee safety goal each year for your facility, which can be expressed, for instance, as a target number of workers' compensation claims that are benchmarked against the average number from prior years.

Healthy benefits equal employee recruitment retention

Employees are your most valuable assets. In addition to focusing on their health and safety, rewarding them with additional benefits demonstrates the depth of your commitment to their well-being. Needless to say, strong benefits also make it easier to recruit and retain talented employees.

Health care, paid time off, and retirement plans are the most common types of benefits employees receive, but some companies are increasingly offering more types of benefits intended both to improve the quality of life of their current employees while simultaneously attracting the best possible candidates for new positions. Of course, these efforts also translate to enhanced morale and improved job performance.

For example, your company might offer tuition reimbursement for those employees who want to further their education while working. Your company might also consider creating daycare facilities in the workplace. To compensate employees who don't have kids, you can initiate a cafeteria plan. Under this umbrella, each employee is given a set allowance that can be used toward any benefit they choose. This way, they can pick the options from which they will receive the most benefit.

Other benefits provided by some employers include gym facilities to allow employees to fit exercise into their busy schedules, onsite massage therapy, cafeterias that sell reduced price meals to working employees, and onsite laundry services — all using organic foods, beverages, products, and supplies.

Lastly, flexible work plans are another type of benefit that has a proven positive influence on employee productivity, attendance, and morale. Flexible work plans allow your employees to adjust their working conditions within constraints set by the company and may include such options as flex-time, compressed work weeks, job sharing, and home-based work.

Moving Down the Road to Zero Accidents

Many companies across a spectrum of industries and sectors are no longer content to keep their occupational accident count to a mere minimum. Instead, in a movement motivated by the goal of having zero accidents, they are taking aggressive steps to eliminate them altogether. The ultimate goal of such an agenda is zero accidents, injuries, or illnesses, and zero environmental harm.

Organizing and managing a comprehensive health and safety program

To build a health and safety program that is as successful as it is comprehensive, you first need to identify and activate a central point of focus around which the rest of the components in your program can revolve. Regardless of the industry you do business in, whether it is retail, oil and gas, or discrete manufacturing, the perfect place to start is the place where your employees execute their actual work. From the workplace, you can evaluate and manage your risk assessments, review your incidents, and evaluate your work procedures. (Risk assessments are invaluable, providing you with tools for detailed analysis and documentation of the risks in each workplace.) In addition, your workplace scenario provides a springboard from which to generate statistics and create accident and near-miss reports, and update the company accident record. Finally, the workplace is an optimal place from which to organize, perform, and evaluate both site inspections and health and safety briefings.

Yet another protocol that you can establish around the workplace to help meet your health and safety objectives pertains to exposure summaries. Creating a summary for each workplace enables you to see an overview of every employee and thus more easily assess their performance on the basis of predetermined timeframes. Later, when you compare individual summaries with your risk assessments, you'll be able to more clearly see the strengths and weaknesses of your agenda and make any needed adjustments. For example, having ascertained that one of your workplaces stands in jeopardy of an accident due to high levels of employee exposure to hazardous substances, you can now introduce the safety measures needed to establish or guarantee the safety of your people. The sorts of patterns that were once obscure now become discernible as a result of the regular documentation provided by your exposure summaries.

The next key step here is to figure out how you can use technology to help you manage incidents and stay organized. Automation can reap many benefits and can help you identify patterns of risk that may be undetectable using manual processes. Furthermore, in addition to implementing software that can help you track and ultimately greatly reduce incidents and accidents, your company should have an easy-to-use interface or e-mail-based form that makes it easy for all employees to enter near-misses. Tracking these near-misses closely can help you reduce accidents even further.

Assessing risks

Unless you have mechanisms in place to regularly assess the risks inherent to your operations, you stand little chance of developing improvements to your overall health and safety program. The processes involved in releasing hazardous substances and materials, taking control measurements, following accidents or near-misses, executing preventive monitoring are all classic opportunities to assess risks.

Any number of methods can be deployed to do this. You can begin with the oldest trick in the book; that is, by using observation. Actually watching how people work to pick up the little details that contribute to an overall pattern of behavior can produce amazing results. The more ways you can discover to prevent accidents — much less near misses — the better off you and your employees will be in the long run.

In addition to the various observation techniques you implement, you can also compare measured values and reference values, and you can evaluate questionnaires. When a risk cannot be quantified by measurements, you can contrast standardized criteria, such as laws or other sources. Protection goals and safety measures for a given risk can then be defined and assessed yet again to determine their level of success.

After you have measured your data, it is important that you process and effectively manage it. It is equally vital that all of the steps and tasks required to define, perform, evaluate, and document your measurements are taken into account, as well. Creating an exposure record is a great way to systematically record the risks in your work places, including hazardous substances, noise, climate, and lighting, all at the same time. You can also update the exposure record automatically to create a hazardous-substance inventory to meet legal requirements. As changes to your exposure record accrue, you will have a complete history available at any time.

By evaluating the relationships between employees and various assessed risks, you can propose accurate health-surveillance protocols for each employee, derived from his or her personal exposure. Such a measure will also result in reduced healthcare costs; unnecessary employee health-surveillance protocols are effectively eliminated, thus reducing visits to the doctor.

Standardizing your procedures

Critical to the success of your health and safety program is the establishment of clear standard operating procedures for handling and working with hazardous substances (more about this in Chapter 12), machines, and installations, or for performing tasks that are potentially dangerous. Two types of standard operation procedures ought to be in effect at all times. The first type guides individual procedures; the second provides boundaries for groups of employees.

Laws such as the Toxic Substances Control Act (TSCA) in the United States, the hazardous-substance directive in Germany, and other, similar EU legislation, require that standard operating procedures for handling hazardous substances contain certain information, including definitions and descriptions of

- Workplace and tasks
- Hazardous substances
- Dangers to humans and the environment
- Protective measures and rules of conduct
- Behavior in dangerous situations
- First aid
- Waste disposal measures

Managing accidents

Beyond your company's obligation to guarantee the well-being of your workers, you want to reduce your accident count to a minimum — preferably zero — if only because doing so reduces costs. As a result, your concern with accident statistics and their analysis is crucial. Not only do you need to record and report accidents that have happened, but you also must account for every near miss — episodes in which no one was harmed, but could have been. And when you analyze data for both accidents and near misses, you can produce more effective and informative accident reports.

OSHA

The goal of folks over at the Occupational Safety and Health Administration (OSHA) is to ensure the safety and health of employees in the United States by working with them and their employers to create better working environments.

According to their statistics, in 2005 there were 4.2 million occupational injuries and illnesses among U.S. employees. Breaking it down, approximately 4.6 of every 100 employees experienced a job-related injury or illness, and in 2006, 5,703 employees lost their lives on the job.

Clearly, it's a good thing we have these guys around: Believe it or not, they have made a difference! Over four million injuries and nearly 6,000 deaths may seem like a lot, but it could have been much, much worse. Since its inception in 1971, OSHA has helped to cut workplace fatalities by more than 60 percent and occupational injury and illness rates by 40 percent. At the same time, U.S. employment has increased from 56 million employees at 3.5 million worksites to more than 135 million employees at 8.9 million sites.

OSHA's top priority is getting reports of imminent dangers. Second on the list are fatalities or accidents serious enough to send three or more employees to the hospital. The third-level priority derives from employee complaints, while referrals from other government agencies come fourth. Fifth are targeted inspections, such as the Site Specific Targeting Program, which focuses on employers that report high injury and illness rates, along with special emphasis programs that zero in on hazardous work and equipment. Follow-up inspections are the final priority.

OSHA has the last word concerning health and safety laws of the land. From Dow Chemical, DHL, and UPS to AAA, Martinizing Dry Cleaning, and the local mom-and-pop news stand, all businesses great and small must comply with the legislation over which OSHA presides. If you don't play by the rules, you're liable to get hurt. OSHA cuffs violators with penalties ranging up to $70,000, depending on how likely the violation is to result in serious harm to employees.

One of these rules concerns employee rights. Every business owner must post a federal or state OSHA poster to provide their employees with information about their safety and health rights. To speak with a compliance assistance specialist about training and education in job safety and health issues, you can contact the OSHA office nearest you. OSHA also provides businesses with an interactive training application that "walks" users through specific OSHA standards and helps them to identify potential hazards throughout a given workplace. You can also find information on specific topics by visiting the OSHA Web site (www.osha.gov).

Managing your accidents and near misses and creating legally compliant reports for them begins with an accident record. Enter data about accidents and near misses and the people who experienced or witnessed them. In addition to the information that is legally required for your reports, you may also want to enter data for your own company-specific accident recording policies.

Inspecting your sites and creating new safety measures

Another key role in effective health and safety programs is filled by site inspections. Among the numerous rewards they bestow upon the smart people who execute them is the ability to ensure that their employees are adhering to established health and safety rules and regulations, both legal and private, and to maintain safety technology and health protection standards. Of course, inspections also serve to emphasize the importance of such standards to employees in every corner of your corporate landscape.

The data you need to plan and perform a site inspection should be available as a consequence of the activity in the areas where actual work is performed, and of your risk assessments, too. When a risk is noted during an inspection, you need to implement and track measures to reduce or eliminate it. Typically such measures fall into three categories:

- Technical measures, such as maintenance orders
- Organizational measures, such as physically separating persons and hazards or using timed access
- Person-related measures, such as holding safety briefings

Storing information about various safety measures is a good idea, including

- Responsible parties
- Priorities for mitigating risks
- Planned, execution, and check dates

You should be able to produce and review the safety measures implemented following a site inspection at any time.

OSHA, by any other name, around the world

Most first-world countries have a framework of health and safety law that is backed by a means of enforcement. In addition, people injured as a result of their work generally have the right to sue their employers in the civil courts for negligently causing such injury.

Almost all countries have their own legislation, frequently within widely differing court systems. The British, for example, have the Health and Safety at Work Act of 1974 (it is set, however, in the context of the European Union, whose laws take priority over those of the member states).

Here are a few of the Act's requirements (those in other countries are similar, give or take differences here and there). Under this Act, employers must:

- ✔ Provide a healthy and safe workplace
- ✔ Take reasonable precautions for the safety of themselves and of others (including, of course, contractors, visitors, and paying customers)
- ✔ Prevent onsite operators from emitting toxic substances into the general atmosphere
- ✔ Ensure that their products are reasonably safe, and provide information on safety precautions to be taken in their use
- ✔ Allow for the appointment of trade union or employee safety representatives and set up safety committees, if requested by representatives

Educating your employees

Laws and regulations in all sectors insist that companies train their employees in the basics of workplace safety. Depending on your industry, employees may need to learn how to handle hazardous substances or operate heavy machinery and dangerous electrical appliances. Whatever the case, health and safety briefings also teach them about the risks they encounter on the job and the measures that are required to avoid them. Typical briefings teach employees about current industrial hygiene and safety and accident-prevention regulations, too.

Accident prevention briefings nearly always take precedent, however, touching on technical and organizational safety measures, such as installing protective grids or establishing fully enclosed systems, may be included. Because many accidents result from people behaving in a way that isn't safe, safety education is a key to preventing them.

Making the Case for Automation and Integration

In all likelihood, your company's operations are vast. Your organization's footprint includes a supply chain that begins with human relations and runs out to cover the logistics inherent to all your plant operations, wherever they may be in the world, and the timely shipping of your product to a demanding market. If you haven't reached this stage yet, you are headed in that direction. Either way, you need to ensure the health and safety of every single one of your employees, vendors, contractors, and visitors. Moreover, the reports you produce must be directed not only to your C-suite, but also to various other employees, the public, the government, and a plethora of local agencies, all according to rigid schedules.

Called upon to create such accountability using stand-alone means and applications or, worse, manual techniques, you would quickly succumb to a quagmire of logistic complications and bureaucratic difficulties, thus obstructing your ability to function as a business. You must change your methods to meet the demands of the times, and you must do it in a way that enables you to continue growing.

To implement your occupational health and industrial hygiene and safety programs such that they are comprehensive, the means by which you activate and manage them should work in concert, focused to achieve a single, clearly articulated goal. In the end, any aspect of this program that is stand-alone is more likely to function as an obstacle to your ends than as a support. When you integrate, you can

- ✔ Access all existing data (human resource business processes, plant maintenance, and materials management, among others) from a single location to see a wider picture

- ✔ Improve cooperation among different departments and enhance the flow of information

- ✔ Update dependent data instantly. Changes to hazardous-substance data, for instance, can result in generation of new standard operating procedures

- ✔ Track and control safety measures automatically

- ✔ Expand your range of reporting options. Extract data from industrial hygiene and safety, occupational health, HR, and logistics

- ✔ Complete documentation of all processes. Accident management, health and safety briefings, and health-surveillance protocols can all be managed from one location

- ✔ Achieve global standardization of procedures and documentation

Remember, your aim is not simply to lower accident counts, but to achieve total prevention. By seamlessly integrating your data, your processes, and your people, you guarantee better safety for your workforce while simultaneously decreasing their stress. Just as importantly, because you can comply more easily with both current and forthcoming employee health and safety laws and policies, you create deeper public trust. You also save substantially on healthcare costs to boot.

Taking the SAP Approach to Employee Health and Safety

SAP offers enterprise-class software to help companies organize and control their efforts around employee health and safety through two modules of SAP EH&S: Occupational Health and Industrial Hygiene and Safety.

The Occupational Health module

The functionality included in the Occupational Health module streamlines and improves the standard processes required to manage the well-being of your company's employees. In addition, it helps forge the way for implementing a full-scale healthcare management program throughout your enterprise, all of whose processes protect data, uphold medical confidentiality, and consider current legal requirements.

The Occupational Health module offers the following advantages:

- ✔ Automatic assignment of protocols based on actual employee exposure and tasks

- ✔ Automatic monitoring of protocol frequencies

- ✔ Elimination of superfluous examinations, which saves time and money for your occupational health department, your employees, and your company as a whole

- ✔ Access to all relevant industrial hygiene and safety information

- ✔ Active participation of the occupational health department in risk assessments, site inspections, and decisions to release hazardous substances and materials for public and private use

- ✔ Minimization or elimination of the need to edit HR data

- ✔ Appointment scheduling based on current time management data

- ✔ Documentation of all processes in compliance with current law

✔ Standardization of data entry

✔ Flexible reporting based on validated data

✔ User-specific combining of necessary functions

✔ Worldwide deployment in a range of languages

Because Occupational Health integrates with the entire SAP landscape, all of your departments can benefit from its functionality. For example, the solution enables you to ensure that each employee receives the health surveillance protocols appropriate to his personal exposure situation. As a result, you eliminate those health surveillance protocols that are unnecessary, maximize use of your health center facility, and increase the time your employees spend on more productive activities. Because your company can actively pursue preventive health management with minimal staff and administrative effort, you gain the further advantage of reducing your company's overall costs.

A final integration benefit of deploying SAP Occupational Health lies in the way it uses information already entered in the industrial hygiene and safety function of SAP Environment, Health & Safety (SAP EH&S) as well as in the HR management function of SAP ERP Human Capital Management (SAP ERP HCM). Data pulled from these systems can be triangulated to provide a total view into protocols, employees, and associated risks. This automation provides new efficiencies for organizations and most definitely impacts the bottom line.

The Industrial Hygiene and Safety module

Just as the functionality included in Occupational Health streamlines and improves the standard processes required to manage the well-being of your company's employees, so too does the functionality in the Industrial Hygiene and Safety module of SAP EH&S. When your company deploys it, you can easily gather accumulated data from the processes you follow to manage your industrial hygiene and safety programs and receive optimal support in making critical decisions. The resulting foresight you gain takes you further down the path toward zero accidents and total prevention.

In the next few sections, we outline the critical concerns that the Industrial Hygiene and Safety addresses.

Risk assessment

Using Industrial Hygiene and Safety, you can

✔ Build process flows, track resources, and deploy automated questionnaires to consistently collect the right data, create follow-up actions, track corrective actions, and report statistical summaries and detailed data. Communicate emergency preparedness and crisis management processes with ease.

✔ Employ summated ratings for mixed substances based on hazardous substances found in your workplaces, or based on compositions specified in the SAP EH&S substance database and calculation of indexes.

✔ Create hazardous substance inventories to meet legal requirements by establishing exposure records and updating them automatically. Ensure that hazardous-substance information and agent-specific information is stored and edited at one place only in your enterprise.

✔ Implement multilevel release processes before introducing hazardous substances or materials. If the use of substances or materials are not approved for entire enterprises, specific plants, or individual workplaces, set according locks.

Standard operating procedures

Industrial Hygiene and Safety provides support for standard operating procedures:

✔ Establish the right procedures to avoid any hazard. The content of each standard operating procedure is created from existing data. If any data that is marked as relevant — such as reference values or protective measures — is changed in the hazardous-substance database, the software creates new standard operating procedures automatically.

✔ Integrate procedures into existing report-generation and report-management functions of SAP EH&S to receive full status management and versioning of documents, as well as to import external documents into the application.

✔ Create standard operating procedures in any language by working with phrases, for example reusable text modules that you can translate into all the languages installed with the software. Build standard operating procedures for each workplace in all languages spoken by your employees (as required by law).

Accident management

Accident management is of course a key feature and the following highlights some of the ways Industrial Hygiene and Safety supports accident management:

✔ Create accident records to enter data for any type of accident or near-miss, defining general and specific fields via the SAP classification system.

✔ Generate accident reports at the push of a button, and dispatch them via your choice of mail, fax, or e-mail.

✔ Record accident causes in standardized formats. Use root cause hierarchies proposed by workers' compensation associations, or enter your own causes.

The following options are available for the statistical evaluation of accident data and the analysis of areas where there is a high concentration of accidents:

✔ Evaluations directly in SAP software, such as the 1000-employee quota or the one-million-hour quota

✔ Transfer accident data to SAP NetWeaver Business Intelligence or external statistics programs, allowing flexible evaluations that take other information into account, for example, from SAP ERP Human Capital Management (HCM)

✔ Transfer data from injury and illness records to accident management records; first-aid centers and accident administration can work together more effectively; duplicate data entry is eliminated

Site inspections

Industrial Hygiene and Safety provides support for site inspections. You can

✔ Create a site inspection using data stored in your risk assessment tools and work-area related objects. Use the questionnaire function to create checklists for recording detailed results in detail.

✔ Use the full functionality of SAP ERP's Plant Maintenance, Quality Management, and Customer Service components to create and process notifications via the industrial hygiene and safety measure tool. For example, you can create a maintenance notification — complete with the safety measures to be carried out — and transfer these tasks to Plant Maintenance for further action, while tracking their progress in Plant Maintenance from Industrial Hygiene and Safety. When all tasks have been completed, you will be notified in your Business Workplace inbox. In the final step, simply assess the result.

✔ Extract all costs incurred for processing industrial hygiene and safety measures developed after site inspections from the software and use them to calculate total amounts. An overview of costs to implement safety measures is available at any time. If any of the cost details are missing, you can add it manually.

✔ Review safety measures implemented following site inspections, along with their results, at any time. Use these measures for documentation and evaluation purposes.

✔ Know what you must report and when. Manage reporting calculations and use predefined templates to transform composite data and generate agency-approved reports.

Safety briefing and worker qualification

With SAP Industrial Hygiene and Safety, you can access the training and event management functions in SAP ERP HCM to manage health and safety briefings. Account for those employees who have received new training as well as those who require a refreshment course. Detect shortcomings in employee health and safety knowledge by comparing their skills sets to those required to perform respective tasks. Determine where employees can safely work, along with the machinery they can operate without danger to themselves and others, by regularly assessing their qualifications. Store results of employee training in your employee master data. Because many health and safety briefings are valid only for a limited period of time, SAP Industrial Hygiene and Safety automatically proposes repeat sessions.

Chapter 11

Making Your Business Processes Environmentally Friendly

*A*ll businesses have processes, the day to day work that gets the job done. These processes can be proactive about protecting the environment, or they can keep up the status quo. Energy use, site selection, green building, and recycling are some of the issues that affect all companies. Some companies have more to consider in the area of making their processes environmentally friendly; in particular, those in the manufacturing industry. In addition to the green measures all companies take, manufacturers can hold all their processes up to a green light and see how benefiting the environment in the areas of emissions control, energy management, and waste management also makes good business sense.

The costs of abusing energy, working inappropriately with hazardous materials, and subjecting people to unsafe and unhealthy working environments have materialized in more ways than one. Beyond the financial outlays, a vital regulatory culture has emerged, creating an atmosphere in which it is now virtually impossible to conduct business as usual, carte blanche. Businesses of every type and size must now proactively seek and develop new ways to comprehensively examine, analyze, and govern their processes such that they are both profitable and compliant with existing laws and regulations.

This chapter suggests a variety of ways and means to achieve these ends including changing your company's culture by establishing new energy management programs and discovering ways to build your facilities in solid green. Integrating a GRC program that encompasses all of your business phases, including your emissions control and waste management, is a point of critical concern that we shed a bit more light on, too.

Essentially, your approach to GRC needs to shift from one of bits and pieces — what amounts to a fragmented approach — to one that delivers key functionality across all dimensions of your business processes — a holistic approach. Without a holistic GRC program, you will be hard pressed to achieve the sort of flexibility and transparency that is required of your business if it is to meet current environmental regulations. With it, not only will you be compliant, but also you will be productive, profitable, and progressing in your program of going green.

Discovering Ways in which All Companies Can Go Green

Everyone affects the environment. When you go green as a company, here are a few areas where you can make changes that both help the environment and often save money to boot

- ✔ Establish an energy management program
- ✔ Build, renovate, and clean with sustainable resources and materials
- ✔ Recycle
- ✔ Reduce travel

The thing about processes is that they are what we do and have been enshrined as "the way we've always done things." And as you know, if you keep doing what you're doing, you'll get what you've always got. In other words, greening your processes means change, including a cultural shift that affects every employee in the company.

When your company goes green, the entire corporate culture must undergo what is known as a *paradigm shift:* a major alteration in the way it sees, thinks, feels, and acts about where its resources come from, how much of them there are, what their consumption can and cannot achieve, and, importantly, how much it costs to use them.

Reducing Your Energy Use and Costs

The prime mover behind changing your corporation's general lack of awareness of its energy resources into an attitude of understanding and respect lies in your ability to show people the consequences of their actions, along with the work processes that motivate those actions. People must be able to visualize in concrete terms the ways and means by which their actions correspond to the energy resources that they consume.

For example, the trick to increasing the knowledge of the employees at Kodak lay in giving them the means by which they could visualize in concrete ways the relationship between their actions and the energy resources they were consuming. The management team at Kodak understood that people usually don't fully comprehend the effect of leaving the lights on at night. For example, we get a bill at the end of the month, and we see that it is perhaps higher than the month before. Maybe we complain a bit about it, too. Ordinarily, though, that's the end of it. A significant shift in thinking and acting has not come about because of what is essentially a minor statistic.

However, Kodak's management also saw that people feel bad when they see carbon dioxide in the air. But they needed a way to create a link between that feeling and the fact that the longer we leave the lights on, the greater our carbon footprint.

To make it concrete, Kodak made polar bears their mascot to help employees connect their energy use with carbon emissions. News at the time showed a polar bear that was about to drown because the greenhouse effect is melting the polar icecaps; the hunting grounds this bear had once been able to swim to were no longer there, so he just kept on swimming, waiting for them to appear. Team Kodak made the effective connection between leaving the lights on and a drowning polar bear to help their people visualize the consequences of their actions.

In consequence of such presentations, Kodak's energy management program began to demonstrate quantitative and qualitative shifts. Of course it didn't hurt that Kodak leveraged the shift still more by displaying the facility's resource consumption right next to the My HR display, which is where everyone goes to see the bonuses they receive for contributing to enhanced energy conservation!

Data centers are a little too hot these days

The green issues developing from the increase in computing power have emerged as a preeminent concern for companies from Nashville to Hong Kong. And it's no wonder: Data centers consumed about 60 billion kilowatt-hours (kWh) in 2006, roughly 1.5 percent of the total U.S. electricity consumption. The energy consumption of servers and data centers has doubled in the past five years, too, and that number is projected to double again over the next five years, to more than 100 billion kWh. The result is $7.4 billion in annual costs. A recently issued EPA report ("Report to Congress on Server and Data Center Energy Efficiency"), however, showed that data centers in the United States can save up to $4 billion in annual electricity costs alone by developing and using more efficient equipment and operations.[0]

Building, Renovating, and Cleaning with Sustainable Resources and Materials

Green building principles are changing how we construct and use our workplaces. Provided you take the ten following suggestions for green building, you will have tools that are proven to lower overhead costs, improve productivity, and strengthen the bottom line.

Begin at the beginning with green design

Integrating green principles into a building's design can save 40 percent in costs and create 40 percent better performance than merely adding green gizmos to a building put together the old way. To gain maximum advantage, you must think green from the start. Here are just a few ways that better design can deepen your green ways: long, narrow building shapes maximize natural lighting and ventilation for workers; fixed elements, such as stairs, mechanical systems, and restrooms at a building's core create flexible and open perimeters, which also enable more daylight to reach work areas; operable windows and skylights allow natural ventilation in temperate weather; and windows with low emission glazing minimize interior heat and glare.

The best way to execute green design is to hire the right project team members, for example, from your architects and engineers to your contractors and consultants — people who have expertise with green design tools and technologies across the gamut. In all likelihood, these experts understand the principals and characteristics of certification systems such as that established by the U.S. Green Building Council's Leadership in Energy and Environmental Design (LEED), which has become a universal means of evaluating how green a building is. Figure 11-1 shows the web site for LEED. (For more on LEED certification, flip ahead to the section, "Getting LEED Certified" later in this chapter.)

Pick the right spot

To make your facility really green, you can't build it on the habitat of an endangered species or on farmland, parkland, or historic or prehistoric sites. Nor can you build it within 100 feet of wetlands. In-fill properties such as parking lots and vacant lots make for great places to set up sustainable developments, as do redevelopment sites such as rail yards and remediated brown fields. When you pick spots such as these, you do two things: First, you avoid adding to urban sprawl, and second, you avoid risking damage to other environmentally significant areas.

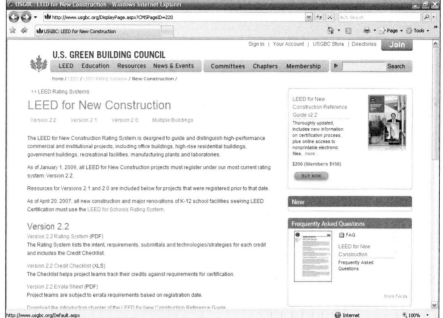

Figure 11-1:
The U.S.
Green
Building
Council
developed
the LEED
Green
Building
Rating
System.

Crunch your numbers

If your project team wants to build green on a standard budget, it first has to apply a cost/benefit analysis to each of the project's components. A green roof costs more to install than a standard roof, for example, but in the end, it brings a larger return on investment. It lasts longer and provides greater benefits. Standard roofs don't lower energy costs, either, nor do they enable you to manage your storm water.

Make friends with your site plan

Your business campus profits greatly when you minimize roads and parking lots, reduce grading and earth work in general, maximize sediment control, and create easy access to public transportation — construction costs will be lower and your overall footprint smaller. Taking these steps also earns you points with LEED (one of the three major rating systems currently in use by green builders worldwide, the other two being the U.K.'s Bream and Australia's Green Star.)

Reduce unnecessary strains on your HVAC

Until now, many people haven't considered just how much landscaping — or the lack thereof — can impact heating and cooling costs. The energy from heat islands — places where sunlight pours onto dark, non-reflective surfaces — transfers to building interiors, which in turn requires cooling systems to work that much harder. Covering west- and south-facing building walls with green screens (metal lattices planted with vines or climbing flowers) can substantially reduce this effect. Mature trees, too, can do the same by shading parking areas, roads, building walls, and roofs on low-rise buildings, roads, and parking areas. Finally, green roofs landscaped with drought-tolerant grasses and plants can also reduce the heat island effect.

Exploit the advantages of technology

Taking advantage of technology has always been a great way to get ahead. If you want to conserve energy, and sometimes even generate it, your company can install individual climate controls and motion-sensitive lighting sensors. Highly efficient HVAC systems are now on the market, too. These heating and cooling units don't deplete the ozone or require more energy than green (for example, chlorine free) refrigerants because they don't use refrigerants that are based on chlorofluorocarbon, hydrochlorofluorocarbon, or halon.

Command the water

Conservative irrigation systems, waterless urinals (believe it or not, these are more sanitary than standard urinals), and drought-tolerant landscape foliage (native plants preferred) that are just as happy with recycled or nonpotable water. These are just a few ideas to help make you master of your "hydro-verse." Water conservation should be a top item on your green building agenda.

Use green and recycled building materials

Building materials that are both sustainable and nontoxic can now be had on the cheap, including low and zero-VOC paints, strawboard made from wheat (as opposed to formaldehyde-laced particle board), and linoleum flooring made from jute and linseed oil (as opposed to toxin-packed standard vinyl). Not only are these materials comparable to or less than standard materials in price, but also they create a more positive impact on the environment. Other green materials include 100 percent recycled carpeting and heavy steel, acoustic ceiling tiles and furniture with significant recycled content, and soybean-based insulation.

Green on the scene: How SAP practices environmental awareness

Innovating new technology to optimize business processes is not the only thing on the SAP radar: This is one company that is highly concerned with how its practices impact the environment, as well. To that end, SAP has established a firm protocol of green procedures that begin inside the company itself. For example, to reduce CO_2 emissions at its Palo Alto campus, SAP uses electric vehicles and shuttles, and purchases as many local goods as possible. Moreover, its urinals are waterless, its lighting system has been revamped to considerably decrease energy consumption, and all paper products are recycled.

On a larger scale, SAP has a clearly defined global environmental policy that will be fully implemented by the end of 2009. To ensure this, a global head of Social Responsibility who reports directly to the SAP C-suite and board of directors has been appointed.

As a further reflection of this commitment to the environment, SAP has begun construction on a brand new complex in Philadelphia, PA to house its American headquarters (shown in the figure), the entirety of which will be LEED certified. Among the many features to be included in the campus structures are

✔ The ability to harvest natural daylight via sensors in the lighting system, which automatically dims lights as required (for example, rooms will go dark as soon as they are unoccupied)

✔ A geo-thermal cooling system that cools water underground before transporting it into buildings

✔ Green roofing

Toyota's emerald city

The South Campus expansion of Toyota Motor Sales' headquarters in Torrance, California, was as affordable to build as any basic low-rise business campus. Architects from LPA in Irvine, California designed 624,000 square feet of space in two three-story buildings on a budget of $90 per square foot. The buildings are long and narrow with north-south orientations to maximize interior daylight — more than 90 percent of the building's occupants enjoy natural light and outdoor views. Rooftop photovoltaic panels and highly efficient air-handling units and a gas-powered chiller enable the facility to achieve 31 percent more energy efficiency than the company's other, traditionally constructed buildings. As if that is not impressive, the business campus's 40-acre, drought-tolerant landscaped site consumes 60 percent less water than a campus planted with sprinkler-dependent turf. To save a whopping 20.7 million gallons of potable water a year, it uses recycled water for landscape irrigation, building cooling, and toilet flushing.

Build smart, build green

If you think that where and what you build is more important than how you build, think again. For example, providing your people with clean, healthy air in your buildings has got to be at the top of your list of priorities, right? To create it, you've got to consider your construction processes from the start. Ensure that your building crews coordinate their wet and dry activities; that way, you can prevent making dry materials breeding grounds for mold or bacteria by contaminating them with moisture. If your mechanical ductwork is sealed in the factory before shipment and then kept that way until you install it, there is less chance that it will be exposed to ambient toxins.

Renovate green

Not everyone is building, but renovation and upkeep are a constant process. If you are not building a new facility from scratch, green renovation is the way to go. Your green revamp can include everything from a new green roof to more efficient HVAC and lighting systems, enlarged existing windows, and low-VOC paints and flooring, to name just a few.

Clean green

Green cleaning is something all companies can do to help the environment and the health of their employees. Microfiber and green cleaning solutions can decrease environmental pollutants.

Solvents and cleaners run off through your drainage system and pollute the environment. If you haven't done it already, your organization can deepen its green by switching to nonpolluting cleaning products. Furthermore, the link between traditional cleaning products and asthma indicates that greening this area of the company may also help employee health as well as being safer for the environment. Some materials, such as microfiber, offer effective cleaning without chemicals.

Recycle

There's no question that recycling saves money and is good for the environment. The California Integrated Waste Management Board, estimates that over the next seven years, $2 billion will be added to California's economy and over 45,000 new jobs will be created by meeting the state's 50 percent recycling goal. Recycling just one ton of paper per year saves 17 trees and 7,000 gallons of water. The numbers are just as impressive when you recycle steel and glass, too. Salvaging a ton of steel saves 2,500 pounds of iron ore, 1,400 pounds of coal, and 120 pounds of limestone. When you recycle a single ton of glass, roughly ten gallons of oil are saved. These are real numbers, reflecting deeply meaningful benefits.

Recycling construction waste

Taking steps to recycle your construction waste saves you money while being kind to the planet. You'll find many online resources on this topic, but here are a few ideas to get you started:

✔ Ask subcontractors to include waste removal in their bids. This gives them an incentive to reduce waste as much as possible.

✔ Instead of hauling off the concrete and asphalt from demolished facilities, you can crush and use it as structural fill for the new building, saving major dollars. With such an option, why would you cart the rubble away and then actually pay for gravel you need to make structural fill?

✔ Ask suppliers to remove all unnecessary packaging to minimize construction waste.

✔ Process scrap lumber or wood into wood chips, compost, animal bedding, or boiler fuel.

✔ Sell metals such as aluminum, steel, brass, and copper to scrap metal yards.

✔ Keep cardboard only dumpsters on the job site so that a local recycling firm can pick up cardboard.

✔ Find out what recycling facilities exist in your area. You may be able to donate glass to be recycled into fiberglass or used instead of sand in paving materials. Asphalt shingles can be recycled for asphalt paving and street repairs in some areas.

You'll find more bright ideas online. Check out *Construction & Demolition Recycling*, an online magazine (www.cdrecycler.com/) as a starting point.

Sick building syndrome

Approximately 23 percent of office workers in the United States experience two or more sick building syndrome (SBS) symptoms a year, including dizziness, nausea, and eye, nose, and throat irritation. Since 2002, when the Indoor Environment Department at the Lawrence Berkeley National Laboratory in California conducted the study, that percentage can only have risen. On a positive note, however, the study also showed that the improved air quality that comes from designing, cleaning, and building green lowers SBS symptoms by 20 percent to 50 percent! Working in green facilities can also reduce allergies and asthma by as much as 25 percent, and employees can be spared outbreaks of the cold and flu by 9 percent to 20 percent. Healthy productive employees, lowered healthcare costs: The benefits just keep accruing. It's something to think about before that dreaded congestion in your head makes clear thinking a distant memory.

Of course, the solutions needed to achieve these ends require extra work, but in the end, considering their importance, they are well worth the effort. Providing convenient recycling bins near trash cans makes it easier for employees to recycle rather than simply trash their waste. Special recycling areas for office recyclables, such as printer cartridges can also be put in place.

Reducing travel

One way for CIOs to help green their companies is to reduce corporate travel by investing in state-of-the-art teleconference solutions, such as Cisco's Tele-Presence. Teleconferencing may not replace all meetings, but if new technologies can eliminate employee travel by just ten percent, the reduction in your company's budget, not to mention its carbon footprint, could be substantial. Various CIOs have confirmed that the performance of their company's sales teams have risen after they deployed videoconferencing. Less travel equals happier employees — another benefit.

Getting LEED Certified

If you're really serious about building green, you may want to consider pursuing LEED certification. To achieve LEED certification, your construction project must satisfy specific green criteria, which varies according to one of six credit categories. These include Sustainable Sites, Water Efficiency, Energy and Atmosphere, Materials and Resources, Indoor Environmental Quality, and Innovation in Design. Your project can also earn additional points when it incorporates green-building innovations. The level of certification your project is awarded depends on points earned, and ranges progressively from Certified, Silver, Gold, and Platinum. Figure 11-2 shows the Molecular Foundry at Lawrence Berkley National Laboratory, which achieved a LEED Gold certification. Compared with conventional building methods, this facility emits 85 percent less greenhouse gases, as shown in Figure 11-3.

Currently, 2,000 buildings are registered for new construction that adheres to LEED. Since 2000, 45 million square feet of structured property has been LEED certified.

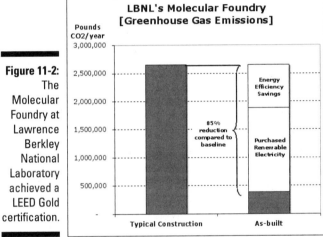

Figure 11-2: The Molecular Foundry at Lawrence Berkley National Laboratory achieved a LEED Gold certification.

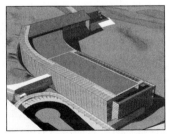

Figure 11-3: The CO_2 emissions for the Molecular Foundry are a fraction of those in typical construction.

By attaining LEED certification, your company's buildings are virtually guaranteed to reduce their impact on the environment, increase their occupancy rates, lower their operational costs, and, in all likelihood, increase in value. As if that's not enough, there's a good chance that they will promote improved employee productivity even as absenteeism is reduced. An overall surge toward greater corporate social responsibility should also be among the list of benefits you'll begin to accrue:

- The LEED standard has been adopted nationwide by federal agencies, and by state and local governments; LEED's ratings system and reference guide is the defining standard for building performance.

- Many private companies are now acknowledging LEED as the industry standard by which to measure how green their buildings are.

- LEED provides a clearly defined methodology for creating green practices and structures.

- Following LEED enables companies to avoid the need to establish local certification bodies.

- It makes good sense.

- It's the right thing to do!

Here are some companies who own buildings that are now LEED certified:

Pfizer	Toyota	MTV Networks Latin America	Comcast
Bank of America	Frito Lay	GM	PNC Bank
3M	Bank of America	Kimberly Clark	Ford Motor Company
Sun Microsystems	Comcast	Liberty Property Trust	The New York Times
FX Fowle	Adobe	Cisco	SAP

The following list includes examples of tax credits with which organizations have been rewarded for attaining LEED certification:

- Baltimore County, MD: ten year tax credit.

- Chatham County, GA: property tax abatement for first five years, which then tapers off by 20 percent each year for the next five years thereafter.

- Cincinnati, OH: 100 percent tax exception of assessed property value.

- In Maryland, all capital projects greater than $5,000 must earn LEED certification; commercial developers receive tax credit for building green.

- In Nevada, owners of LEED Silver Buildings receive tax abatements and tax exemptions for products or materials used in their construction.

> ✔ In New York, the State Green Building Tax Credit program provides a tax
> incentive to commercial developments incorporating specific green
> strategies informed by LEED.

Overall, an increasing number of states are pushing LEED certification, particularly for public buildings, as shown in Figure 11-4.

Figure 11-4:
LEED
Certification
Growing
(World Inc).

Assessing Your Environmental Risks

At the top of your priorities list should be the means by which you address
the level of environmental risk to which your business is exposed. In general,
risk assessment is the scientific process of evaluating the adverse effects
caused by a substance, activity, lifestyle, or natural phenomenon. When your
business assesses its risk, you specifically estimate the type and magnitude
of harm to which you may expose those who come into contact with hazardous substances and dangerous goods that you produce or use in your
processes and products.

Failing to assess your risks, or worse, failing to comply with current laws and
regulations carries penalties, frequently quite severe. Noncompliance could
in fact cost your business millions of dollars. It could even cost you your
business.

After you have endowed your business with the enterprise-wide vision that
results from a comprehensive risk assessment, management at all levels can
avail themselves of the data they need to successfully put effective governance in place, including setting policies and procedures to ensure compliance. This assessment will also lead toward improved decisions and superior

risk intelligence. You will be able to avoid those missed opportunities of the past, where efficiency could have been improved and risk/return portfolios optimized, where your ultimate business predictability and shareholder value could have skyrocketed but did not, all because you simply did not have the tools needed to do the job.

Greening Manufacturing

Every company in business today needs to implement a program of culture change, energy management, and green practices. However, if you conduct business in the automotive, electronic, high tech, oil and gas, life sciences, pharmaceutical, textile, food, consumer packaged goods, or cement industry sectors, among others, complying with environmental regulations is a long-standing practice (though of course, nearly all businesses can keep working to deepen their shade of green). This section talks about the challenges faced by these industries, starting with the C in GRC: compliance.

Green legislation

So far we've talked about how all companies can go green. However, for many industries, going green is not a choice; the C in GRC kicks in, and companies face compliance with a variety of regulations related to their processes. Here's an overview of green legislation applicable to processes. (Note that some green legislation, such as REACH, relates to products and is discussed in Chapter 12.)

Although federal governments have taken steps to address climate change in the wake of startling new revelations about the potential dangers we face should we continue to ignore the warning signs, it is the states or countries themselves that have largely motivated the enactment of more green legislation. The moves have assumed a myriad of forms, from energy efficiency rebate programs, renewable portfolio standards, and clean energy fund creations, to high-occupancy vehicle lane adoptions, reforestation, and low-carbon technology tax incentives. But the last few years in particular have seen increased public pressures on governments to step up engagement with all climate matters.

The Northeastern, Mid-Atlantic, and Western states account for nearly 35 percent of the U.S. population and just about a quarter of all consumed power. No wonder they have exercised the greatest efforts toward creating such regulations as the Regional Greenhouse Gas Initiative (RGGI) and the Western Governor's Association (WGA), both of which seek to implement cap-and-trade systems that create compliance carbon markets. Other green plans include low-carbon automotive and fuel standards and greenhouse gas emissions generator performance standards applied to power purchase contracts.

Power to the states!

The legal ramifications of climate change were finally acknowledged in the Supreme Court decision for Massachusetts, et al. v. EPA, et al. At long last, the state of Massachusetts was granted the right to sue the United States because of the injury it sustained from rising sea levels and other climate-related impacts. This granting of standing to sue rivals the importance of the Court's proclamation that the EPA has the authority to monitor greenhouse gases as an "air pollutant" under Title II of the Clean Air Act.

Beyond any new and impending regulations, there are two that have been in place for years and another that has just come into effect — the Environmental Protection Agency's (EPA) Clean Air and Water Acts, and Waste Electrical and Electronic Equipment (WEEE) — by whose laws your business must abide, regardless of whether you intend to go green.

EPA Clean Air Act

The federal 1990 Clean Air Act (CAA) was created by the EPA to help control and reduce smog and air pollution in the United States. It derives from the Clean Air Act in 1963, the Clean Air Act Amendment in 1966, the Clean Air Act Extension in 1970, and the Clean Air Act Amendments in 1977. Although the whole of America is accountable to CAA legislation, the states nevertheless contribute to ensuring that its requirements are met. State air pollution agencies, for example, conduct hearings on permit applications from power or chemical plants and fine companies for violating air pollution limits.

Corollaries to the CAA in other countries include the Clean Air Act 1956 in the U.K. and a similar Clean Air Act in Canada. In European Union, it is called Clean Air for Europe (CAFÉ).

The EPA wields the CAA to limit the amount of pollutants that can be in the air in the United States at any given time. According to CAA stipulations, states are not allowed to create weaker pollution controls than those the Act has set for the country.

Because pollution control problems often require special knowledge of local industries, geography, housing patterns, and the like, the EPA relies on states to create state implementation plans that outline the regulations they will use to reduce their pollution. All states must conduct hearings wherein the public can comment on and contribute to the development of implementation plans. Should the EPA disapprove of a state's plan, it can take steps to enforce portions of the CAA that they deem the state to have neglected.

To achieve new air quality goals and regulatory reform, the EPA has recently added new amendments to the CAA. Specifically, the new laws

- Encourage the use of market-based principles and other innovative approaches such as performance-based standards and emissions trading. In emissions trading, a system used in the European Union, companies are issued permits and if they don't use them, can sell them to other companies who need them at a profit, with the overall effect of reducing emissions

- Provide a framework from which alternative clean fuels can be used by setting standards in the fleet and California pilot program; these can be met by the most cost-effective combination of fuels and technology

- Advance the use of clean low sulfur coal and natural gas, as well as innovative technologies to clean high sulfur coal through the acid rain program

- Reduce enough energy waste and create enough of a market for clean fuels derived from grain and natural gas to cut dependency on oil imports by one million barrels/day

- Promote energy conservation through an acid rain program that gives utilities flexibility to obtain needed emission reductions through programs that encourage customers to conserve energy

Through provisions in the EPA, the United States government provides individual states with funding to conduct scientific research, engage expert studies, and engineer new, environmentally oriented designs.

EPA Clean Water Act

Until changes were made to the Clean Water Act (CWA) in 1977, it was known as the Federal Water Pollution Control Amendments of 1972. It is the main federal law governing water pollution throughout America. There is also a Clean Water Act of Ontario, Canada.

When the CWA was originally implemented, efforts focused on regulating discharges from traditional "point source" facilities, such as municipal sewage plants and industrial facilities, with little attention paid to runoff from construction sites, farms, streets, and other "wet-weather" sources. Greater attention is now being given to physical and biological integrity of the country's waters, as well.

Over the last decade, programs endorsed by the CWA have shifted from approaches focused on specific sources and pollutants to strategies that are holistic and watershed-based. This new methodology emphasizes protecting healthy waters as much as it does restoring damaged ones and addresses a complete spectrum of concerns, as opposed to the simply looking at those that are bound by the Act's regulations. Another characteristic of the new

It cost big bucks to pollute!

Together with the Environmental Protection Agency, nine states and 13 environmental groups filed a suit in 1999 against American Electric Power, one of the nation's biggest coal-fired electricity producers, contending that the company had violated limits set by the Clean Air Act at 30 of 46 coal-fired units. The company recently settled, agreeing to spend as much as $4.6 billion to reduce emissions of sulfur dioxide and nitrogen oxides. It is also forking out $60 million to clean up and repair damage it is accused of having caused to nearby parks and waterways.

Yet another recent case involves a group of residents and businesses that is suing IBM Corp. for more than $100 million. According to the 94 plaintiffs, one of IBM's former plants in upstate New York has placed an entire community and ecosystem at harm's risk by exposing it to toxic doses of trichloroethylene (TCE), a metal cleaning solvent associated with ailments, such as kidney cancer and brain damage.

approach pertains to the involvement of stakeholder groups in the development and implementation of strategies for achieving and maintaining state water quality and other environmental goals.

The CWA is the foundation of surface water quality protection in the United States today. Although it does not address the regulation of ground water or water quantity issues, it does ensure the reduction of pollutant discharges directly into waterways. In addition, the Act helps finance municipal waste-water treatment facilities and manages polluted runoff. It also hopes to achieve the broader goal of restoring and maintaining the chemical, physical, and biological integrity of the nation's waters so as to guarantee the protection of fish, shellfish, wildlife, and people who participate in water-related recreational activities.

The Act enabled the establishment of a system for granting and regulating discharge permits called the National Pollutant Discharge Elimination System (NPDES). This system regulates point sources that discharge pollutants into waters of the United States. Permits are issued by state environmental agencies and EPA regional offices. There is also a system of regulating the discharge of dredged and fill material into jurisdictional waters of the United States, handled by the Army Corps of Engineers under Section 404.

The creation of the Act further precipitated the EPA to institute guidelines that regulate water pollution from industry categories. These regulations have been published for 56 categories and apply to between 35,000 and 45,000 facilities that discharge directly to the nation's waters, as well as another 12,000 facilities that discharge into publicly-owned treatment works. They are responsible for preventing the discharge of almost 700 billion pounds of pollutants each year. The EPA has updated some categories since their initial creation, and has also added new categories.

Unfortunately, as of 2007, approximately half of the rivers, lakes, and bays under EPA protection are still not safe enough for fishing and swimming. Technology-based standards have been relatively successful because they apply to specific sources and are enforceable. The health-based and water-quality-based standards, which focus on specific toxins and the quality of specific bodies of water, respectively, leave much to be desired and are difficult to enforce. Non-point source pollution — usually diffused runoff from farms, streets, and yards — is the most important remaining cause of these problems; oversights prevented it from being addressed in the original Clean Water Act.

To help municipalities create wastewater treatment plants capable of meeting its standards, the Act provides for federal financial assistance in the form of construction grants. The Act also established pretreatment requirements for industrial users contributing wastes to Publicly Owned Treatment Works.

Waste Electrical and Electronic Equipment (WEEE)

Waste Electrical and Electronic Equipment (WEEE, European Community directive 2002/96/EC) was created to contend with the rapidly swelling mounds of electrical and electronic equipment in states of all members of the European Union (EU). The directive complements EU measures on landfill and the incineration of waste. Together with Reduction of Hazardous Substances (RoHS, Directive 2002/95/EC), WEEE became European law in February 2003, establishing collection, recycling, and recovery targets for all types of electrical goods. If your company is working with one or more members of the EU, it will affect your business.

This directive holds manufacturers of waste electrical and electronic equipment responsible for disposing of it in an environmentally conscientious manner, either by ecological disposal or by reuse/refurbishment of the collected WEEE. All such companies should plan to establish infrastructures for collecting WEEE such that users of electrical and electronic equipment from private households should have the possibility of returning WEEE free of charge. The directive requires the substitution of safe materials in place of various heavy metals (lead, mercury, cadmium, and hexavalent chromium) and brominated flame retardants (polybrominated biphenyls (PBB) or polybrominated diphenyl ethers (PBDE)) in new electrical and electronic equipment put on the market from July 2006.

WEEE man

Together with Canon, the Royal Society of Arts in the U.K. unveiled a 22-foot tall sculpture entitled 'WEEE Man' on London's South Bank in April 2005. Made from 3.3 tons of electrical goods — the average amount of electrical waste one U.K. individual creates in a lifetime — the sculpture, shown in the figure, was created as a means to stress the importance of the Waste Electrical and Electronic Equipment directive that became law in February 2003. Of the 25 EU member states directed by WEEE to transpose its provisions into national law by August 2004, only Cyprus complied. Since its creation, the sculpture has traveled throughout the United Kingdom.

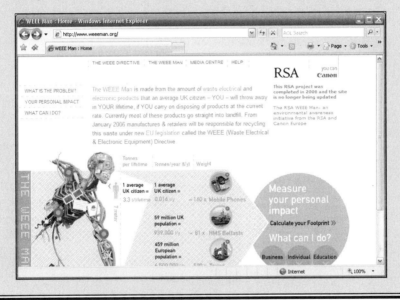

According to WEEE, the following items are defined as electronic waste:

- ✔ Small household appliances such as microwaves and vacuum cleaners
- ✔ Large household appliances such as refrigerators and washing machines
- ✔ Entertainment electronics such as televisions, stereos, and DVD players
- ✔ Office and communication such as computers, printers, phones, and faxes
- ✔ Lighting equipment such as fluorescent light tubes
- ✔ Surveillance equipment such as video cameras
- ✔ Sports and leisure equipment such as treadmills and Stairmasters
- ✔ Automatic issuing systems such as vending machines
- ✔ Electronic tools such as drills, saws, chainsaws, and lawnmowers
- ✔ Medical appliances and instruments

Adopting Green Practices for Manufacturing

With a view toward your risks and what you want to achieve, you can continue to pursue green practices, both where they are mandated and done proactively before mandates become an issue.

Establish an energy management program

Energy management is the discipline of conserving resources to lower costs to the greatest possible degree. All businesses need such a program to match the health and safety measures and emissions controls they have in effect.

The goal of all businesses, of course, is to get the best throughput at the lowest cost. For example, the last thing you want to do is make your lowest contribution products during the highest peak hours. What you do want, on the other hand, is to make your most profitable products using the assets that are at once the most productive and least costly.

After your company has established a corporate culture in such a way that everyone is on board and understands what is best for both themselves and the planet, you can begin to create a bill of materials for your energy resources. An energy bill of material, or BOM, is the same as any other BOM. It is a detailed list of the types and amounts of energy that are used to create a given product. Creating an energy BOM enables you to attach costs to your energies in specific ways. If you can't see how much it costs to use a given resource, you don't have the information that is required for revolutionary innovations. Nothing can be done to make improvements! It is important for you to see the exact impact that consuming a specific type and amount of energy has in the overall scheme of things.

To create your energy bill of materials, however, you need metrics — a means by which to accurately measure your energy usage in near real time. Therefore, you must first remove the archaic allocation of costs to resources from the equation. If you allocate your periodic energy bill across all your costs — when in effect that bill may include multiple stretches of time in a given period, one that includes various rates for the energy components that go into the bill — your view of the impact is bound to be skewed.

You cannot see a clear picture of your usage and costs until you first juxtapose your costs against the energy conditions of any given time. You need to shift from making decisions around your costs later in the day or week or month to making those decisions right now, at this very instant. This change is something that cannot be accomplished by enhanced awareness and nifty slogans. For example, you can attach metrics software to a specific heat exchanger to find out how much water is going through it at specific times in the day. Merely to introduce a kilogram of water to the process system requires energy. And if it leaves the system with more heat in it than when it was introduced, then that is wasted energy that results in unnecessarily higher costs.

Reduce emissions

Another way to guarantee the strength of your environmental compliance while simultaneously creating a distinction between you and your competition is to implement a superior emissions management program.

The first steps toward realizing this goal include building a structured representation of your plants and processes, defining and applying all forecast scenarios, analyzing your complex emissions data, and establishing performance goals based on your key performance indicators (KPIs).

Next, to ensure that you can gather the data required for you to surpass all compliance requirements, you have to track, analyze, and record emissions measurement data. You have got to build and deploy forecasting tools to assess the effects of operational modifications, as well, and create alerts to automatically detect excessive emissions output. Additionally, you need to measure the environmental impact of the excessive emissions you do create, employ tools to indirectly measure greenhouse gas emissions, and then calibrate and maintain that measurement equipment.

After you've gathered your data, you will be ready to document and create reports with it. Doing so means that you must analyze and present data in real-world scenarios, automatically generate and distribute detailed emissions records, maintain contact data for all pertinent authorities, and document your communications for shareholders, investors, and the public.

Finally, your organization will want to consider the best ways to participate in all potential emissions trading and collaborative scenarios. You can project certain success in this endeavor once you connect to trading platforms and emissions markets via integrated interfaces, generate all documentation and data required for trading approval, employ forecasting tools to estimate credits, and manage trading process with integrated transaction support.

At the end of the day, instead of interrupting operations just to meet regulatory requirements, you will have met them in a way that harmonizes with your existing manufacturing processes. And rather than searching for emissions credits to meet prescribed targets, you will have generated significant revenue by selling those credits on emissions trading markets.

Reduce waste

Unless your environmental health and safety risk assessment process has accounted for the ways your business treats and manages waste, you still have work to do. An optimum program centralizes waste management such that the master data for the by-products of your business processes are clearly visible, ready to answer any logistics, service management, reporting, and compliance concerns that may arise. This master data includes details on waste approval and disposal sites as well as all waste tracking documents, including waste manifests, consignment notes, transport notes, and data from any biohazard detection systems (BDSs) that may be in place.

Are your storage, disposal, and treatment facilities on- or offsite? Do you know exactly how much waste you generate, along with when and where it comes from? Have you reckoned your costs according to areas and types of waste? If you have satisfactorily asked and answered questions like these, it is probable that your waste management program is in good hands. If not, it's important you consider making some changes.

Deal with hazardous substances

Managing the hazardous waste bugaboo so that these substances don't sneak into places where they aren't wanted should be one of your greatest concerns. Establishing an efficient hazardous substances management system entails targeting the ways and means by which your company uses hazardous substances in its daily business. This, in turn, requires instituting documented ways to handle, store, transport, and dispose of them safely, and to track them systematically. For a more complete discussion of this subject, please see Chapter 12.

Like hazardous substances, your dangerous goods must be kept under strict observation at all times. This subject, too, will be thoroughly discussed in Chapter 12.

Optimize occupational health

A program that enables you to successfully prevent occupational illness and injury includes creating a health center with qualified staff able to access vital information on demand, health surveillance protocols appropriate to each employee's personal exposure situation, available physicians, and quality first-aid training. For a complete discussion of the subject, please see Chapter 10.

Promote industrial hygiene and safety

Every one of your company's processes needs to consider the well-being of your employees, vendors, contractors, and visitors. Included in these considerations are your standard operating procedures, work areas, employee training, benefits, incident/accident logs, exposure profiles, and compliance reporting. For a complete discussion of the subject, please see Chapter 10.

Ensure product safety

This uber-critical facet of your business lives at the core of Chapter 12. For now, suffice it to say that an appropriate product safety agenda can enable your company to control specification management, automate product composition calculations, initiate rule-based material safety data sheet (MSDS) authoring, automatically generate and ship MSDSs, receive support for global hazardous substance management GHS and REACH compliance, implement global label management, and deploy interfaces for data exchange with content providers.

Taking the SAP Approach to Making Your Processes Environmentally Friendly

To ensure both thorough compliance and progress toward environmental goals, you need a unified, enterprise-wide framework to correlate and align all current and forthcoming GRC initiatives. Without this single system of record, it's not likely your organization will be able to achieve a comprehensive view of your GRC activities. In turn, the chance that you will be able to assume a risk-based approach that satisfies multiple, interrelated company initiatives and regulatory mandates is equally doubtful.

Initiating a successful, unified GRC strategy entails two fronts. First, you need to implement a company-wide design for your environmental health and safety processes. Second, you must holistically integrate all of your systems to create a standard technology platform that provides collaboration and communication capabilities and allows you to adapt to new or forthcoming compliance regulations.

By implementing a central data repository that is reusable, transparent, and flexible — effactually embedding GRC strategies into the core of all your business methodologies — your company will minimize duplicated efforts, optimize effectiveness, and enhance simplicity over the long run. Along the way, you will also have established clear systems to manage inefficiencies in every aspect of your operational phases, from your product safety (which includes hazardous substances and dangerous goods) and waste management to your industrial hygiene and safety and your occupational health. If by then your business has not progressed beyond merely complying and reached that place where it is actually excelling, rest assured that it won't be long until you do.

This is SAP's approach to GRC — integrated so that your environmental risk assessment feeds into the SAP Enterprise Risk Management (see Chapter 2 for details).

Without customized software integrated into your organizational processes, your company will have great difficulty meeting industry demands to comply with the regulatory standards that seem to be growing up around you faster than luxury condos in every city center. SAP GRC environmental solutions include SAP Environmental Compliance for emissions control, energy management, and other regulatory mandates, as well as the Waste Management module in SAP Environment, Health, & Safety (SAP EH&S) for tracking the by-products of your processes. Both solutions are fully integrated into the SAP Business Suite family of business solutions.

SAP Environmental Compliance

The most difficult obstacle to surmount when attempting to comply with today's stringent emissions standards and engage in successful emissions trading is the inability to easily access and use the multitude of systems that are required to run a typical manufacturing plant. SAP Environmental Compliance enables you to overcome these barriers. Because it is a composite application with sophisticated cross-functionality, it provides you with access to emissions-related applications, functionality, and data that are trapped in assorted systems spread throughout your company. And not only can you fully access and exploit these wide-ranging data sources, but SAP Environmental Compliance also enables you to extract and integrate relevant emissions-related data from them, which is then used as the basis for on-going emissions calculations.

As you can imagine, the resulting benefits are legion. When you deploy this application to its full capacity, you can conquer access barriers, align your business processes, and enhance the flow of information throughout your business. The system can monitor, document, and control plant emissions output, maintain compliance status, and track, document, and create reports for performance benchmarks. You can also use it to engage in trading, energy management, and collaboration management to communicate with key stakeholders, both in and out of the company.

To perform these tasks, SAP Environmental Compliance uses

- ✔ Master data from SAP Human Resources

- ✔ Material consumption data from SAP Supply Chain Management

- ✔ Emissions-relevant substance data provided by the SAP EH&S capabilities in SAP Product Lifecycle Management

- ✔ Equipment data and functional hierarchies produced by the asset life-cycle management capabilities of SAP Product Lifecycle Management

- ✔ Plant maintenance cost information from SAP Financials

- ✔ Third-party data historians or other plant floor operational systems via SAP xApp Manufacturing Integration and Intelligence (SAP xMII)

- ✔ Emission-certificate pricing data from third-party emissions trading platforms

  By participating in emissions trading, companies that meet prescribed targets receive credits; they can then trade these credits like stocks to companies that haven't met their targets (the potential revenue from such trading is well into the hundreds of millions of dollars)

In addition, SAP Environmental Compliance works with SAP Product Lifecycle Management to create plant maintenance orders that optimize workflow for compliance tracking. It updates SAP Financial, too, so that emissions below the permitted levels are treated as financial assets, and it submits buy or sell emissions-certificate orders through trading platforms. All required data is regularly and systematically delivered to SAP Business Intelligence for reporting purposes.

Building emissions models and analyzing emissions

With SAP Environmental Compliance, your business can build structured representations of facilities and processes. You can also generate records that detail emissions types, source amounts, and environmental effects, and automatically estimate complex emissions data. Forecast scenarios can be defined and applied, and performance goals estimated based on environmental key performance indicators. When you need to document your communications as required by industry regulations, this application does it for you, automatically and on demand.

Managing compliance

Use SAP Environmental Compliance to track, analyze, and record emissions measurement data, control interactive processes, and exercise risk management responsibilities. This application evaluates existing emissions data, as well, and generates forecast scenarios to assess the effects of operational modifications. While your asset management teams can deploy it to calibrate and maintain measurement equipment, your operational teams can lighten their load by letting its functionality manage workflow and role-based tasks. Triggers that automatically generate alerts when emission values exceed plant limitations can be built within this application. It also enables you to measure the impact of excess emissions and determine corrective actions, and employ sophisticated scenarios and tools to indirectly measure emissions, such as greenhouse gas emissions (these are estimated using electricity consumption data).

Creating reports and documentation

With SAP Environmental Compliance's data warehousing capabilities, you have the power to analyze and present data and scenarios, generate and distribute data and reports, and maintain accurate, current information regarding all authorities involved. Moreover, you can deploy the application to manage role-based employee access to plant- and process-specific permits.

Controlling trading and collaboration

Gaining access to emissions trading markets requires your company to collect, document, and verify the data that is called for by various regulatory agencies. False or inaccurate data can result in the appearance of counterfeit credits on the open emissions markets. It goes without saying that those parties who are responsible can suffer punishments ranging in severity from fines to forced closure.

SAP Environmental Compliance gives you data management capabilities and reporting functions that adhere to formats required by regulators, plus integrated interfaces that connect to market places and trading platforms. You can comply with strict regulations and data provision requirements while taking advantage of all of the benefits of trading emissions and none of the risk.

SAP Environmental Compliance at E.ON Energie

One of the world's largest private energy services providers, E.ON Energie employs a workforce of 66,000 around the world, with 40 plants and buildings across Europe. Its subsidiary, E.ON Benelux, provides energy to the Netherlands, Belgium, and Luxembourg.

E.ON Energie needed to implement a low-cost solution that would ensure total regulatory compliance while increasing compliance efficiency and reducing costs for exception and incident management. At the same time, they wanted to reduce their risk of noncompliance and simplify their reporting processes.

SAP Environmental Compliance gave the company the tools it needed to meet these goals. It enabled them to automate their emissions, compliance, and permit management processes. The solution also provided them with the means to generate transparency and flexibility in the evaluation and analysis of their emissions data. The company was given an emissions data-auditing solution that meets modern accounting requirements, as well, along with support for automatic data uploading via SAP ERP and other systems.

SAP Waste Management: A core component of SAP Environment, Health, and Safety

The Waste Management module in SAP Environment, Health, and Safety centralizes functionality and tasks to improve the comprehensive visibility, logistics, service management, reporting, and compliance in all of your business's waste-related concerns.

SAP Environment, Health, and Safety is fully integrated with SAP ERP, so Waste Management enables you to access and use data from a host of related but disparate SAP applications, including SAP Materials Management, SAP Quality Management, SAP Production Planning, SAP Sales and Distribution, and SAP Controlling and Finance. Consequently, the business processes that are enabled by this sophisticated integration run enterprise-wide.

You can organize and manage data for approval manifests and waste disposal sites, to say nothing of all of your waste master data, including waste types, amounts, and locations. Procedural processing, invoicing, and cost control, too, can all be executed under the auspices of this module, as can any task related to producing reports and documentation.

The ability to automatically produce documents and reports on demand via pre-established templates and rules is a real boon, since the amount and types of documents and reports that regulators demand you use to track waste and comply with standards are astronomical. Your material master data, for example, must provide a detailed description of your waste, including its physical and chemical properties, any other specific properties, toxicological data, safety data, and associated dangerous goods data. Your waste manifests must be equally detailed. They need to specify the type and quantity of your waste, statistical analyses of it, consignment notes, transportation notes and transport emergency cards (tremcards), MSDSs, and BDSs. As well, you must list the name and location of your disposal partner, and the costs associated with the disposal. Invoices must also be produced. The list goes on. In short, the complications related to managing your organization's waste are enough to merit a business in its own right.

Before you can build any of the aforementioned documents and reports, you must first have clearly classified your waste. Depending on the concentration of hazardous substances in it, waste can be hazardous or non-hazardous. The Waste Management module of SAP EH&S simplifies and automates this classification with a tool designed for the automated derivation of data-using rules.

At the end of the day, compliance will not be the only thing you have achieved using this module. You will also have established credibility, both with the public and with the regulatory agencies that monitor you. This credibility has great value. When it comes to your brand, the benefits can hardly be estimated — the public loves businesses it believes are trustworthy. Your regulators are overwhelmed; companies that lighten their workload are not forgotten and receive such important benefits as early notification of forthcoming laws and regulations. News like this may enable you to implement changes faster and sooner and thus gain that extra edge against the competition.

Chapter 12

Making Your Products Environmentally Friendly

. . . .

In This Chapter

▶ Defining hazardous materials and dangerous goods

▶ Staying current on materials legislation

▶ Managing customer and supplier compliance

. . . .

*A*t the beginning of this Part, we discuss in general terms what it means to "go green," along with some of the main characteristics of "green people." The chief concern of any green person or company lies in whether their actions and the products they make or use are friendly to the earth, safe, ethically produced and made, recyclable, and energy-efficient. In short, both green people and green businesses are careful to consider the effect of their decisions not only on their own quality of life, but also on the quality of life of everyone around them. Going green is about considering our impact in all that we do, from cooking with organic food using energy efficient appliances to manufacturing pesticides in Vapi, India.

As our many examples in this chapter demonstrate, it's extremely unwise for any company in business today to shirk its regulatory obligations; noncompliance carries the potential of stiff penalties and lost good faith, either of which can prove fatal. The way to ensure that you stay on top of the compliance game in all your dealings, and hence profit in the process, is to implement a comprehensive GRC program that embeds environmental and sustainability initiatives in every aspect of your operations. The sooner you do, the happier you, your customers, and your suppliers will be. If that is not enough of an incentive for change, consider that after you take just a few basic steps, you'll have joined the ranks of many others who are doing their share to protect and preserve the environment. In this chapter, we show you how to put the focus on making your products green (and no, we're not talking about green beer and shamrock cookies for St. Patrick's Day).

Discovering What It Takes to Make Products Environmentally Friendly

Given the current social and environmental climate, it should come as no surprise to be asked pointblank whether your products are green. Regardless of the type of product you make, your ability to answer that question suitably will depend on a number of factors. Inasmuch as it is possible, for example, can you affirm that your products are organic and biodegradable? Are all of the materials and substances in your products GRAS — that is, generally recognized as safe, non-hazardous, and non-corrosive? Do your products limit the consumer's exposure to health hazards and use minimal amounts of resources to make? Do they minimize the overall impact on the environment? These are just a few of the considerations your company should be entertaining, if it hasn't already done so.

Your company has other matters to consider, too, however. The realm of environmental, health, and safety compliance — where your products must pass muster if you want to continue selling them on the open market — is no longer the exclusive province of companies in the chemical or pharmaceutical industries. The regulatory and brand expenses for failing — or, worse, refusing — to conform have ensured that compliance is now a central concern for the high tech and oil and gas industries, to say nothing of the food and beverage, utilities, consumer product, discrete manufacturing, and retail and service industries. Most municipalities, towns and cities, are now even bound to comply.

What this means to your business is that you must document to a T every material that goes into the products you make, sell, and distribute. In addition, adhering to these regulations means that you've got to maintain an up-to-date bill of materials, and document the structure, price, weight, and dimensions of the goods you produce.

Earlier we also pointed out that if you understand your processes, it's very probable that you understand and control your products, too. If this is the case, then you collect, organize, evaluate, and analyze data pertaining to your factories and suppliers, as well as to the countries they are located in or come from. It may be, on the other hand, that you don't know any more about going green than that everyone says it's a good thing. If this is the case, here are some further questions that your company will need to answer before you can determine how far you are from achieving truly green practices, and thus, from making environmentally friendly products:

✔ To begin with, what materials or harmful substances, if any, do you use in your processes?

✔ Can your suppliers provide immediate feedback about the compliance of the materials they use?

✔ Do you have an overview of environmental regulations in different countries and the ability to account for variations in compliance requirements?

Whether it's REACH, Restriction of Hazardous Substances (RoHS), China RoHS, Waste Electrical and Electronic Equipment (WEEE), or others in an expanding list of regulations and standards, the compliance challenges and risks you face are substantial.

Noncompliance can result in costly fines, legal ramifications for top executives, revocation of operating permits, and loss of brand value or important customers. If your company doesn't have a comprehensive GRC program — whereby environmental and sustainability initiatives are embedded in every aspect of its operations such that they are consistent across your enterprise and reflected in the communities where you do business — it's high time you figure out what you need to do to make it happen.

Figuring Out What Your Materials Are and What They Do

If you think that materials are the only things a product is made of, think again. Materials may indeed be the heart and soul of your products, but they are a heart and soul made of very, very important — to say nothing of tricky — things that regulatory agencies and watchdogs call "substances."

From man-made synthetics such as gasoline, concrete, and plastics to natural matter such as cotton, gold, and wood, every material in every product is comprised of substances. Some of them are pure, and some impure. Moreover, substances can be made of compounds or elements. Compounds are mixtures of two or more elements, such as water — a pure substance, by the way. An element, on the other hand, is a single substance, such as hydrogen or oxygen, that can't be broken down into constituent substances.

The question that is no doubt bouncing around in your brain right now like a stray kernel of popcorn is probably, "Why the basic chemistry lesson?" Don't worry. This is where the chemistry ends and the product compliance begins. The lesson is this: material or substance, pure or impure, everything with which you make your products must be certifiably documented, right down to their tiniest constituents. More importantly, you need to know the nature of every substance in your products, insofar as it is clean or hazardous. Why?

This is how today's laws demand that products be classified: either they are made of clean materials and substances — meaning they pose no threat to people or the environment — or they are made of materials that are hazardous, in which case they do pose a potential threat, however minor. Regarding environmental, health, and safety compliance, such materials constitute two separate categories: hazardous materials and dangerous goods.

As a business owner, investor, or consumer, after you recognize the far-reaching impact of these conditions, the way you see and engage the world will be substantially altered. Dow Chemical has recently acknowledged this in its efforts to help people understand that because chemistry is literally everywhere, there is scarcely anything more important in our lives. When consumers comprehend the full scope and impact of chemicals in their lives, they will be sure to insist that the companies with which they do business comprehend it, too — and then act appropriately. As a result, the way you do business can't help but to change.

Defining hazardous materials

In the United States, hazardous materials are defined and regulated according to laws and regulations administered by the U.S. Environmental Protection Agency (EPA), the U.S. Occupational Safety and Health Administration (OSHA), the U.S. Department of Transportation (DOT), and the U.S. Nuclear Regulatory Commission (NRC). Although each agency has its own definition, taken as a whole, these definitions provide a comprehensive picture of the nature of hazardous materials.

As we just mentioned, a hazardous material is any item or agent that has the potential to cause harm to humans, animals, or the environment, alone or through other factors or agents.

OSHA defines as hazardous any substance that is a health or physical hazard. This includes

Carcinogens

Irritants

Sensitizers

Toxic agents

Corrosives

Other agents considered hazardous include those that act on the hematopoietic system (the system that makes blood) or damage the lungs, skin, eyes, or mucous membranes.

Many chemicals are considered to be hazardous materials. Among them are

Combustibles	Explosives
Flammables	Oxidizers
Pyrophorics	Unstable-reactives or water-reactives

Chemicals that when normally handled, used, or stored may produce or release gases, dusts, vapors, fumes, mists, or smoke that have any of the previously mentioned characteristics are also considered hazardous materials.

The EPA piggybacks on the OSHA definition of a hazardous material and adds to it any item or chemical that can cause harm to people, plants, or animals when released into the environment by:

Spilling	Leaking
Pumping	Pouring
Emitting	Emptying
Discharging	Injecting
Escaping	Leaching
Dumping	Disposing

The DOT defines a hazardous material as any item or chemical that is a risk to public safety or the environment when being transported and monitors it as such under the following regulations and codes:

- Hazardous Materials Regulations (HMR)
- International Maritime Dangerous Goods (IMDG) Code
- Dangerous Goods Regulations of the International Air Transport Association (IATA)
- Technical Instructions of the International Civil Aviation Organization (ICAO)
- U.S. Air Force Joint Manual, Preparing Hazardous Materials for Military Air Shipments

In Europe, transportation by road is regulated according to ADR legislation (International Carriage Of Dangerous Goods By Road — "Accord européen relatif au transport international des marchandises dangereuses par route"), while transportation by rail is regulated according to RID ("Reglement International concernant le transport des marchandises Dangereuses par chemin de fer").

The NRC regulates items or chemicals that are "special nuclear source" or by-product materials or radioactive substances.

Defining dangerous goods

The same agencies that regulate hazardous materials in the United States (OSHA, EPA, DOT) regulate dangerous goods, as well. Many hazardous materials are also considered dangerous goods. They may be radioactive, flammable, explosive, toxic, corrosive, and biohazardous. Among them are oxidizers, asphyxiates, pathogens, and allergenics. In short, like a hazardous material, a dangerous good is any solid, liquid, or gas that has the potential to cause harm to humans, animals, or the environment, alone or through other factors or agents.

Dangerous goods are divided into nine classes, some of which include subclasses according to the nature of the harm they can cause.

- Class 1: Explosives
- Class 2: Gases
- Class 3: Flammable liquids
- Class 4: Flammable solids; substances liable to spontaneous combustion; substances that in contact with water emit flammable gases
- Class 5: Oxidizing substances and organic peroxides
- Class 6: Toxic and infectious substances
- Class 7: Radioactive material
- Class 8: Corrosive substances
- Class 9: Miscellaneous dangerous substances and articles

You might wonder why hazardous materials and dangerous goods are categorized and regulated by different laws if they are mostly the same? Well, actually, so do we. But the real point is that at the end of the day, all of these substances, chemicals, articles, and items must be managed, tracked, and reported on.

Realizing the Benefits of Compliance

The current global market presents more challenges than ever to today's businesses, especially those that are working in the design and manufacturing industries. The total product output of some companies can consist of literally hundreds of thousands of materials and substances. To guarantee their environmental, health, and safety compliance demands massive effort, to say nothing of money. Ad hoc and manual approaches no longer present viable solutions, because they are largely as expensive as they are inefficient, with a high percentage of them increasing the risk of non-compliance. Instead, companies must build infrastructures to ensure environmental and product compliance whose foundations lie in collaborative supplier and customer relationships. These solutions must be adaptive, as well; as products change, so, too, do market demands, and with them related environmental legislation.

The benefits of complying

Think about what the world is saying about product compliance:

- If you are to be fully compliant, your legislators demand that you fulfill all existing regulations.

- Your customers demand, as well, that you meet their compliance guidelines, which are frequently more rigid than those of legislators.

- The analyses performed by your sales and marketing department shows that your competitors are all compliant. Consequently, you must be at least as compliant as they are, if you want to survive.

- Negative messages regarding your inability to comply will not be tolerated by your shareholders. The good faith of your consumer base is dependent upon whether you can continue to enhance your brand's reputation.

Given these pressures, it makes perfect sense that so many companies are investing in environmental, health, and safety compliance solutions. According to AMR Research's 2007 IT spending projections, environmental, health, and safety compliance-related initiatives are the third most important areas impacting future IT investments. It only takes a quick glance at the evidence to see that the advantages of such investments far outweigh the liabilities.

The sort of comprehensive solution your business needs to step in line with green directives — one that is integrated into core business processes — will retrieve required compliance data from sources that are dispersed throughout your enterprise, automatically determine which data is missing to ensure strict compliance and minimize risk, and store it in structured form.

Centralizing the data ensures not only that it will be visible and available to all relevant parties across global operations, but also that the data accessed is current and accurate. Open standards and flexible communications enable manufacturers, dealers, suppliers, customers, and regulatory authorities to speak the same green language. Your IT costs will drop, too, because the same master data will be used for all materials and products. On the whole, compliance will be significantly streamlined, thus reducing the time and effort you spend on compliance efforts while freeing up resources to focus on other fundamental concerns. This in turn lowers the total cost of ownership.

There are still more benefits to implementing an enterprise-wide solution, each following from one to the next. For example, when auditors call, you'll be able to give them any documentation or reports that they request. As a result of your tip-top compliance record, the specter of legal fines and other consequences will vanish. And as soon as the public learns of this, your image in their eyes and in the media's will be all the shinier.

Finally, the barriers that lead to quality problems will largely disappear; your company's cross-departmental business processes will have been integrated. Your sales capabilities will skyrocket, too, because obstacles to the market will also have been eradicated. Come the end of the day, your competition will be hard pressed to keep up when your products are reaching the market faster, greener, and at far less cost.

The risks of failing to comply

Today's active laws and directives, Registration, Evaluation, Authorization of Chemicals (REACH) and Reduction of Hazardous Substances (RoHS) among them, are government-sanctioned. If your company should fail or refuse to comply with them, the penalties will be immediate. Frequently, they will be extremely harsh, too, as the record shows.

For example, when a number of Apple's products did not comply with environmental regulations, many countries in the EU were forced to stop purchasing them, resulting in heavy losses of revenue on both sides of the value chain. The same thing happened when Palm, Inc. failed to comply. One of their major products is no longer available to the European market.

If you are a company doing business in or with the United Kingdom, it can cost up to £5,000 per instance for failing to comply with RoHS. The same goes for failing to submit compliance documentation to any authority that requests it. The retailer Boots, for example, was penalized for not having informed its customers that a percentage of its profits are put into a product recycling fund.

In Germany, regulators fine noncompliant businesses 50,000 and ban their products from the market. In France, companies can be fined 7,500 for an infraction. Spain and Ireland, on the other hand, are off the charts when it comes to fines: In these countries, you can suffer penalties of upwards of 1.2 million and have your products removed from your customers' shelves!

A penalty was issued against a Dutch producer that refused to comply with the Waste Electrical and Electronics Equipment (WEEE) directive; another was levied against municipal authorities for failing to create a municipal recycling location. Sony used more cadmium in their PlayStations than is allowed for by RoHS in the Netherlands and paid for the mistake dearly: When the country refused to sell the product in 2001, Sony lost an estimated $110 million in revenue.

The moral to the story is clear: failure to comply with product safety regulations results in lost revenue and fines, delayed or restricted access to the market in the short term, and lost market share in the long term, all of which can result in still more costs that are precipitated by the emergency measures you will likely have to implement when confronted with these unwanted outcomes. As we noted in Chapter 9, the events that resulted from the failure of toy giant Mattel to produce environmentally friendly products were both disastrous and globally infamous. In 2007 alone, the company had to recall 18 million toys around the world. Because of this mistake, Mattel continues to face declining market share.

Using Hazardous Materials Responsibly

Whether you are producing and selling hazardous substances and dangerous goods or purchasing them for use in your own processes, managing them so that they don't sneak into places where they aren't wanted should be one of your greatest concerns. Establishing an efficient EH&S management system entails targeting the ways and means by which your company uses hazardous substances and dangerous goods in its daily business. This, in turn, requires instituting documented ways to handle and store them safely, and to track them systematically.

Specifically, you will need to

- ✔ Register your materials
- ✔ Store materials safely
- ✔ Classify and identify the hazardous substance
- ✔ Create an inventory that details all hazardous substances and dangerous goods in your possession
- ✔ Monitoring hazardous substance concentrations in the workplace
- ✔ Determine and assess risks to employees, vendors, contractors, and visitors
- ✔ Arrange, undertake, and monitor the success of protection measures
- ✔ Create standard operating procedures for work areas and substances
- ✔ Conduct employee health and safety briefings about hazardous substance handling
- ✔ Implement standard protocol to handle and report accidents
- ✔ Report safety records
- ✔ Package and identify hazardous substances and dangerous goods in accordance with regulations
- ✔ Create and manage labels, transportation emergency cards (tremcards), and current, accurate material safety data sheets (MSDSs)
- ✔ Ship material safety data sheets before delivery or when the hazardous substance is delivered, as well as after they have been changed

These tasks fall into four main categories: customer compliance management, supplier compliance management, compliance reporting, and comprehensive task management. In the next few sections, we look at each in a little more detail.

Customer compliance management

Your solution should enable you to respond to customer compliance requests quickly and accurately. It should also allow you to record all replies to customer queries about any given product and automatically tell you which customers require new documents in the event of changes or new environmental conditions. Such functionality will lower your costs across the board, especially if you're making large quantities of product in conjunction with multiple global suppliers.

Supplier compliance management

It is as important to exchange product data with suppliers as it is to do so with customers. Your solution to supplier compliance management should include a current, accurate database and be able to automatically request missing data about contents, substances, or compositions that you can receive from suppliers in standard formats. After you have the data, you'll need to document it for subsequent inspection. If details or regulations relevant to your product change, you should be able to send a request to your suppliers for updates.

Compliance reporting

Yet another functionality you need is the ability to generate and distribute reports that meet the requirements of all parties in the compliance chain — from regulatory authorities and product developers to environmental officers and customers. You also want to track both the creation date of particular reports and the recipients, so that you can generate and sending new reports in the event of detected changes. With strong document and data management capabilities, duplications will be a thing of the past, and you'll be able to circumvent the difficulties of conflicting data formats, multiple languages, and change management.

Comprehensive task management

Suppliers, customers, regulatory authorities, internal departments, factories, sites, and overseas subsidiaries — these are all participants in the compliance process, and you must be able to cooperate with each of them together and in groups. For example, when you want to see whether a product is RoHS compliant, you need to verify all information, such as the lead content of a part that you purchased from a supplier. If data is omitted, the ideal solution would automatically request that the supplier provide you with the exact lead-weight percentage of the product and confirm when the data arrives.

Working with Hazardous Materials

 It should go without saying that there are serious consequences associated with producing, handling, and shipping hazardous materials and dangerous goods, particularly if improper procedures are involved. Accidents while transporting these materials are of special concern, which is why a well-structured rubric of standardized procedures, methods, and regulations has been established to help ensure public and environmental safety.

Hazardous materials and dangerous goods work their way up and down the supply chain, from outside, on your vendor side, and from within, to your customers. Along the way, extreme care must be taken to store these bugaboos when and where needed. Meantime, you must know exactly where they are, and you must know how much there are, as well. To guarantee maximum control and subsequent adherence to applicable industry regulations, you need to establish a system whose functionality enables your operational teams to transparently maintain all dangerous goods master data, including their automatic classification using expert rules.

The laws that regulate the transportation of hazardous materials and dangerous goods are those we mentioned earlier in this chapter in the section called "Defining hazardous materials."

Packing

In the United States, the Hazardous Materials Regulation (HMR), created by the Department of Transportation (DOT) Pipeline and Hazardous Materials Safety Administration (PHMSA), outlines the rules for packing all hazardous materials and dangerous goods so that they can be safely transported. The HMR stipulates how to

- Classify and package hazardous materials
- Mark and label packages
- Complete shipping papers
- Provide required emergency response information

In addition, the HMR specifies whether the vehicle transporting hazardous materials must be placarded and the specific placards required, along with the amount and type of training required to handle and ship hazardous materials.

Not all countries use the same graphics (label, placard, and/or text information) in their national regulations. Some use graphic symbols, but without English wording or with similar wording in their national language.

Materials communications

Communicating information pertaining to the hazardous materials or dangerous goods you are transporting and the potential hazards associated with them requires that you produce and manage detailed documents about them, including multilingual material safety data sheets (MSDSs) and transportation emergency cards (tremcards), as well as the appropriate placards and labels on the goods themselves.

A sophisticated material safety data sheet (MSDS) system plays a key role in these areas. Its database constitutes the central storage location for all information about the materials your company uses or produces. And should someone be harmed by a hazardous substance or dangerous good, your current, accurate database enables you to record the incident in your exposure log and then create the subsequent required reports.

You'll need to be able to answer questions about your use of hazardous materials, so you'll need to have all your information in good order. Check whether the data in your vendor MSDS is up-to-date; organize your vendor MSDS for audits and other official checks; link vendor MSDSs to material masters; prepare safety operating procedures such that they are readily available in appropriate work areas; and, lastly, ensure that labels on incoming materials reflect hazardous information in respective vendor MSDSs.

Transporting materials

The transportation of hazardous materials and dangerous goods is subject to the most widely regulated practices in the world, which are standardized on the whole by Model Regulations on the Transportation of Dangerous Goods. This set of directives is issued by the Committee of Experts on the Transport of Dangerous Goods of the United Nations Economic and Social Council. The International Civil Aviation Organization's regulations for air transport of hazardous materials are a modified version of this model, for example. Many other individual airline and governmental requirements are incorporated with the ICAO's regulations, as well, per the universally abided International Air Transport Association Dangerous Goods Regulations.

Transportation by sea requires compliance with similar legislation, as well, and is overseen by the International Maritime Organization. To be certain that their national regulatory schemes accord with international law, individual nations around the globe have built the transportation regulations for their dangerous goods to meet the requirements of the UN's Model Regulations.

 No matter what mode you use to transport your goods, your company must ensure that the drivers of road vehicles and stewards (for those goods moving by rail, air, or sea) have instructions in writing that detail the exact type, quantity, and nature of those goods. Those companies that move goods by road in Europe, for example, must comply with ADR legislation. It demands that all drivers be in possession of a tremcard, composed in a language that he can read and understand. These instructions must also include a version in the language of the country of origin, of the recipient country, and of all countries through which the dangerous goods are being transported.

Keeping Up with Materials Legislation

The myriad laws, regulations, and directives that have been enacted since the mid-twentieth century to protect both humanity and the environment are the number one reason why today's companies need a substantial GRC solution for all matters related to environmental, health, and safety compliance. Among the ones that stand to most influence businesses and society alike are Registration, Evaluation and Authorization of Chemicals (REACH) and Reduction of Hazardous Substances (RoHS). The following sections detail those regulations that your company must comply with if you want to stay in business.

Toxic Substances Control Act (TSCA)

Congress created this Act in 1976 so that the EPA could track the 75,000 industrial chemicals currently produced or imported into the United States. Whereas the EPA can screen these chemicals, require reporting or testing of those that may pose a danger to environmental or human health, and ban the manufacture and import of those chemicals that pose an unreasonable risk, it nonetheless grandfathered most existing chemicals. This is significant, and stands in direct contrast to the European Union's newly enacted Registration, Evaluation and Authorization of Chemicals (REACH), which we cover in the next section. The primary subjects of TSCA regulation are polychlorinated biphenyl (PCB) products, including PCB disposal and limits for PCB contamination of the environment. The TSCA is found in United States law at 15 USC (C. 53) 2601-2692.

The TSCA has several subchapters, the second of which authorizes the EPA to impose laws for asbestos abatement in schools and requires accreditation of persons who inspect for asbestos-containing materials (the first subchapter treats the regulation of the aforementioned PCB products). The other subchapters require the EPA to publish a guide to radon health risks, perform studies of radon levels in schools and federal buildings, identify sources of lead contamination in the environment, regulate amounts of lead allowed in products, including paint and toys, and establish state programs to monitor and reduce lead exposures.

The TSCA supplements other Federal statutes, too, including the Clean Air Act and the Toxic Release Inventory under the Emergency Planning and Community Right-to-Know Act (EPCRA). As a result of the TSCA, the EPA has been negotiating with firms such as General Electric for the remediation of areas such as the upper Hudson River, which is contaminated with PCBs.

Registration, Evaluation, Authorization of Chemicals (REACH)

Until its final enactment on June 1, 2007, REACH (EC 1907/2006) was a matter not only of serious legislative debate, but also on the receiving end of bitter condemnation. And though it may still be grounds for all sorts of feelings, good and bad, the fact is that its regulations will force businesses around the world to make some excruciating decisions about tens of thousands of substances by June 2008, because that is the date of the first regulatory deadline set to affect existing chemical products. REACH, whose provisions will be phased-in over 11 years, now replaces 40 existing pieces of legislation in the European Union (EU). Companies can find explanations of REACH in the guidance documents, on the EU's REACH web site (see Figure 12-1) and a number of help desks are available for consultation. The European Commission is slated to conduct a series of reviews of REACH Annexes until December 2008 (Annexes I, IV, V, XI, XIII).

What REACH says

The TSCA (which hasn't been amended since its enactment over 30 years ago) is to REACH what a speck of dust is to the sun. The difference between them — to say nothing of both the immediate and long-term consequences of the latter — is enormous. Remember our discussion on the difference between substances and materials? Well, this is where those differences come into play even as they are obliterated. Forget materials. REACH forces companies to comply on the level of substances — an enormous task compared to complying with the TSCA.

Figure 12-1:
The EU's
REACH site
provides
compliance
information.

The current registration process, in which you must register every product you make with the European Chemicals Agency (ECA), covers nearly 30,000 substances. Of these, 2,500 are likely to be hazardous to human health or the environment and will have to undergo continued testing to show that they can be used safely. Over the next dozen years, however, as many as 100,000 existing substances will be subject to REACH evaluation, authorization, and, in many cases, restriction. Ultimately, the ECA estimates that a total of 150,000 to 200,000 substances will be registered, though some authorities put that number much higher, going so far as to suggest that there will be half a million applications for approval.

Who REACH affects

American companies under the impression that they will not be affected by this law because it derives from EU legislation are sorely mistaken. If you are one of them, you would do well to adjust your attitude immediately. In fact, REACH should assume the status of a critical business matter that will affect the operations of your company, your vendors, and your customers across whole enterprises.

REACH is so important that Robert Matthews, a REACH authority and partner in the Washington-based law firm McKenna, Long & Aldridge, has recommended that industry executives "elevate REACH compliance from the environment, health, and safety departments in [their] firms to the level of a business development-unit reporting directly to the company president." Recently, Dupont assigned top-level executives to manage REACH compliance and processes — an indication of how serious and important this issue is to businesses today.

Supervision from the top is necessary, Matthews says, because compliance with REACH by U.S. businesses will require executives to make decisions that will significantly affect their "product selection, exports, suppliers and customers and use of products by customers." Those businesses that fail to pre-register their products with the ECA in the six-month window between June and December of 2008 risk losing their phase-in status during the subsequent authorization period. If that happens, their products cannot be brought to market, because continued production or import of chemicals and substances that are not preregistered will be illegal. The ramifications don't end there, however. Your substance only needs to be *listed* as a candidate for blacklisting under REACH for it to lose status as a marketable product on a global level. In such cases, companies need to have alternative products ready to go.

One good thing about the preregistration process is that you are not required to provide every piece of data about your substances for long-term registration. To begin, you only need the name of the substance, its chemical abstract and European inventory numbers, and range of production volume. Each chemical product or substance will be given one registration number under REACH.

Registration is not the only process involved in complying with REACH, however. For example, those companies that produce or deal in common bleach, which is used in products as diverse as paper, makeup, and cleaning supplies, must also provide their customers with appropriate compliance documentation, conduct testing based on foreseeable use-case scenarios, and share resulting information with others in the industry so that they, too, can conduct testing.

The process by which multiple producers of the same substances share data is both facilitated and formalized when they gather together in substance information exchange forums (SIEFs). This collaboration will enable them to facilitate registration by compiling existing information (such as health risks, toxicity, test data, controls, and so forth), conducting studies and exposure scenarios, and resolving chemical classifications. Collaboration on this level requires some serious cooperation. And also merits extreme caution: Participating companies must avoid antitrust complications pertaining to the exchange of information or the making of agreements that may prevent, restrict, or distort competition. Beyond participation in SIEFs, two or more manufacturers or importers can choose to band together in consortia and handle their registrations jointly. Although such arrangements may facilitate compliance, they should also be reviewed carefully for potential antitrust issues.

The phenomenal effort required to participate in SIEFs, in conjunction with the sustained costs and effort required for REACH registration and evaluation, may push some companies to sacrifice pre-registration for some of their products, especially if those products are not among their top sellers. This, actually, is one of the goals of REACH. Over the long-term, it will force companies to withdraw what regulators have termed "substances of very high concern" (SVHC).

By forcing changes in the market strategies, research and development, product selection and substitutions of companies, REACH is sure to affect companies everywhere, even those that do not do business in Europe. In this sense, the law presents much more than just a matter of product stewardship and environmental concern.

As for the estimated costs of REACH, they are astronomical. According to the European Commission, the chemical industry alone is set to fork out $3.1 billion in direct expenses. The indirect numbers that will result from laboratory test work, managerial and administrative labor, new software implementation, safety-data gathering, and legal fees — to say nothing of the costs associated with merely using affected chemicals — are estimated to skyrocket as high as $2.9 billion.

According to a survey of 62 multinational companies by the Dutch company KPMG, 92 percent expect REACH to affect the availability or price of raw materials and products. Nearly 30 percent expect REACH to affect more than a quarter of all materials and products, and approximately 10 percent do not think they'll be able to manufacture certain products once REACH takes full effect.

Given the supply-chain issues that will result from the enormous scale of REACH, it is the small to mid-size companies that are likely to suffer the greatest losses, along with companies that produce specialty chemicals. For example, distributors will have to pass information up and down the supply chain, in which case breaches of confidentiality are sure to result. After customers learn who the major suppliers are, it is only a matter of time before the middleman is cut from the chain.

The following list includes some steps suggested to help prepare for and mitigate REACH's impact:

- ✔ Ascertain which REACH requirements will affect your products, customers, and suppliers

- ✔ Implement structures to guarantee executive responsibility and accountability

- ✔ Create a fund to handle your compliance response

- ✔ Decide which products you intend to pre-register well before the June 2008 deadline

- ✔ Define your research and development efforts to accord with REACH so that you can transition to alternate substances should any products be threatened by blacklisting

One approach to REACH: Dow Corning

Dow Corning, a manufacturer of silicones and polycrystalline silicon, is one of numerous companies in the chemical industry that sees the full scope of implications posed by REACH and is taking active steps to address them all on every front, including those to ensure sustainable development and improve the levels of protection to human health and the environment.

Preparing internally for SIEF and consortia participation, as well as for the registration of nearly 100 Silicon-based substances and other raw materials, filling gaps in data needed for registration dossiers, updating compliance documentation, and managing an extensive IT portfolio are only a few of the things Dow Corning is doing to ensure that their company is still viable under REACH.

Their business-centric approach also entails conducting product-line REACH workshops, educating professionals about REACH, highlighting issues specific to products lines, mining data, evaluating entire product portfolios, determining the volumes of substances manufactured and imported into Europe, and assessing the impact of REACH on sales and profits. In addition, to guarantee communication requirements both up and down the supply chain, the company is engaging in comprehensive dialogues with its suppliers, customers, and distributors. The immediate effort includes identifying a REACH contact person at each company and establishing solid REACH messaging.

Finally, the company's concern with future directions is manifested in their ongoing examination of the various business and investment decisions that will be driven by REACH to reformulate and requalify their product lines.

Reduction of Hazardous Substances (RoHS)

Reduction of Hazardous Substances (RoHS), an EU directive that is part of a global push toward more environmentally sound manufacturing practices and policies, restricts the use of six substances in new electrical and electronic equipment placed on the market after July 1, 2006. By making it illegal for companies to manufacture products with more than 0.1 percent of lead, mercury, cadmium, hexavalent chromium, polybrominated biphenyls (PBB), and polybrominated diphenyl ether (PBDE), RoHS aims to reduce pollution and prevent human health problems. China, Japan, and all EU countries are bound by RoHS.

Evidence of compliance with RoHS needs to be provided only if an enforcement authority asks for it. Failure of an organization to comply with RoHS can result in serious penalties (including heavy fines and jail time), not to mention a black eye for your reputation. When requested, you must provide documentation of compliance to the governing bodies through materials declarations or analysis. Some medical devices and military equipment that contain lead are exempt from RoHS regulation.

EU manufacturers must obtain a declaration of RoHS compliance for every part, component, and material they use. To prevent undue complications, however, they may obtain just one certificate of declaration for parts that belong to the same class or type with the same RoHS-compliant composition. Importers, however, must request equipment suppliers to declare compliance for their equipment.

In China and Japan, electronic information products (EIPs) must be labeled as 100 percent compliant or partially compliant (having one or more substances) with the Environmental Protection Use Period (EPUP), which states the number of years that the consumer will be safe from product leakage. Mandatory product testing is being considered in both countries.

The products affected by RoHS include

Household appliances	IT and telecommunications equipment
Consumer equipment	Lighting products/systems
Electrical and electronic tools	Toys, leisure and sports equipment
Automatic dispensers	

Business affected by RoHS include

- ✔ Manufacturers and sellers of electrical and electronic equipment
- ✔ Resellers of electrical and electronic equipment
- ✔ Companies that import or export electrical and electronic equipment from and to countries in the EU

The following list includes some steps suggested to help ensure that your products comply with RoHS:

- ✔ Test your materials
- ✔ Monitor your supply chain partners for compliance
- ✔ Searching for and switching to RoHS-compliant suppliers
- ✔ Produce, organize, and maintain proper documentation of compliance

Exploring the SAP Approach to Product Compliance

By now, you've seen that no matter what your business today, you must comply with a growing host of environmental regulations and customer requirements — a minimum of 15 environmental regulations in over 15 countries — by collecting, organizing, analyzing, evaluating, and documenting data about the precise makeup of your products. To do so requires software solutions that run enterprise-wide even as they streamline your processes. In short, you've got to automatically monitor the compliance status of your products, facilitate communication with suppliers and customers, and enable users to generate and manage reports quickly and efficiently. The SAP solution for environmental product compliance can help to meet all of these challenges. Developed on the SAP NetWeaver platform, the solution is part of the mySAP Product Lifecycle Management application, which seamlessly integrates with SAP Product Safety, SAP Materials Management, and SAP Sales and Distribution, among others. Specifically, it includes the SAP Environment, Health & Safety application (which contains SAP Hazardous Substance Management and SAP Dangerous Goods Management) and the TechniData Compliance for Products application.

Compliance for Products by TechniData (CfP)

Until now, the dominant means of gathering data across multiple disconnected sources has been the spreadsheet, which, in addition to being error-prone and expensive to maintain, generally impedes efficient analysis. The other shortcoming of spreadsheets is that you can't integrate them into your core processes to streamline compliance tasks. If you have been trying to meet compliance regulations using spreadsheets in conjunction with other stand-alone solutions, you've probably struggled, besieged from beginning to end by an overwhelming mass of disjunctive documents and data.

Technidata's CfP can integrate into your ERP ecosystem without any additional interfaces, providing you with a business solution that is both transparent and adaptive on a single standardized, platform. Armed as such, your company can ensure the successful attention to environmental requirements for product development, sourcing, procurement, and manufacturing — today and tomorrow.

The solution retrieves compliance data from widely dispersed sources throughout the enterprise and automatically determines which information is missing. After data is received, not only does CfP store it in structured form, but also it renders it to meet a diverse spectrum of data formats, including the International Material Data System (IMDS), Automotive Industry Action Group (AIAG), Institute of Electrical and Electronics Engineers (IEEE), IPC 1752, or Microsoft Excel. Consequently, all pertinent compliance data is available on demand to participants anywhere along the value chain.

The CfP solution offers a number of key functional areas for compliance management, all of which are accessible from the compliance manager cockpit, which serves as the central user interface. From the cockpit, you can import, export, and store all compliance data, because it is integrated with either the internal bill of materials in your SAP software or another external product-data management application. It also enables you to enter data manually, query supplier data, and check if products meet particular conditions. With CfP, all data is centralized, so you can reuse it at any time to fill requests for reports and declarations. You can run future assessment scenarios to determine the impact of alternative product parts or suppliers on your ability to maintain compliance, and you can generate, manage, and distribute customer documentation. The compliance manager cockpit interface supports version management, change pointers, and customer-specific standard formats, as well.

The scope and depth of businesses and products for regulatory agencies to monitor make it impractical or impossible to guarantee compliance under all circumstances. Consequently, they expect your company and your supply chain partners to maintain reliable due diligence processes. To determine that reasonable steps to comply have been taken, authorities will request compliance documentation and inspect the processes that you use to collect data and evaluate your product, as well as any number of other analyses. With CfP, you can rest assured that your business will easily pass these tests.

The key functional areas in CfP include

✔ General Compliance Management

- Manage activities such as to-do lists, where-used lists, and change requirements and communicate with all supply-chain partners.

- Control lists of materials and substances prohibited by WEEE and RoHS, among many others.

- Maintain product structure required to comply automatically.

- Calculate product data required to comply automatically.

- Retrieve comprehensive product status using traffic light functionality.

- Track work list tasks pertaining to new and updated regulations, BOM structure modifications, and customer requests.

✔ Compliance Reporting

- Generate flexible reports that fulfill all declaration requirements and define report release strategies.

- Analyze compliance issues according to supplier, part number, and regulatory-list criteria.

✔ Supplier Compliance Management

- Use latest communication standards (for example, Nemi, IPC, RossettaNet, AIAG) to exchange compliance request data with suppliers about all products.

- Define due dates and send reminders for compliance requests to all suppliers.

- Upload supplier compliance status and parts information using open data exchange capabilities.

- Enable all suppliers to retrieve compliance request information from your system.

✔ Customer Compliance Management

- Retrieve and manage customer compliance requests and statuses.

- Confirm compliance by declaring all customer compliance requests.

- Track all relevant data exchange with customers using flexible methods (e-mail, portal, and so on).

SAP EH&S

Like CfP, SAP Environment, Health & Safety offers a fully integrated solution for all of your product compliance issues on a single, standardized platform. The material master — the central data object in this system — is a product of this integration, reaching across the enterprise to centralize your core business data and enable you to access, examine, organize, modify, and document information pertaining to sectors as diverse as accounting, operations scheduling, distribution, warehouse management (including available stock), and purchasing — all toward the goal of quickly and efficiently managing your product safety, hazardous material, and dangerous goods needs. It is also used to represent raw and auxiliary materials, utilities, semi-finished products, production resources, and tools.

Here are the most important hazardous substance and dangerous goods management functions in SAP EH&S:

✔ **Substance specification management:** Flexible, central storage of all dangerous goods and hazardous substance and agent data.

✔ **Specification workbench:** Enter and edit all specification data from a central interface.

✔ **Phrase management:** Maintain language-independent information in text form.

✔ **EH&S Native Language:** Store, display, and print compliance reports correctly.

✔ **EH&S Expert and EH&S Easy Expert:** Automatically execute variety of work steps such as the rating of hazardous substances.

✔ **Material-to-specification assignment:** Assign one or more materials to a specification, or one or more specifications to a material (links to logistics processes are provided).

- ✔ **Bill of materials transfer:** Automatically generate hazardous substance composition from the bill of material.

- ✔ **Work area management:** Enterprise structuring from the point of view of hazardous substance management.

- ✔ **Risk assessment:** Introduce and track safety measures after determining and evaluating hazards.

- ✔ **Health and safety briefing:** Present organized health and safety information to employees who work with hazardous substances.

- ✔ **Document templates:** Use templates to facilitate the flexible creation of EH&S reports.

- ✔ **Report generation:** Create of EH&S reports.

- ✔ **Generation variant:** Link document templates with a validity area and one or more ratings to precisely control how reports are generated.

- ✔ **Report management:** Access, check, release, and manage all existing, inbound, and outbound EH&S reports.

- ✔ **Report shipping:** Manually and automatically distribute EH&S reports to employees, customers, and suppliers.

- ✔ **Material safety datasheets:** Define dangerous goods and hazardous material transport papers and generate them automatically or manually.

- ✔ **Sales and distribution processing:** Define dangerous goods and hazardous material checks and process them through SAP Sales and Distribution.

- ✔ **Global label management:** Determine and print correct labels for hazardous substances and dangerous goods.

- ✔ **Specification information:** Access and output all dangerous goods and hazardous system substance data.

- ✔ **Industrial hygiene and safety information system:** Access and evaluate work areas, exposures, risk assessments, and safety measures and create hazardous substance inventories.

- ✔ **Data import and export:** Transfer dangerous goods and hazardous material data to and from legacy systems, suppliers, and data providers.

- ✔ **Portal:** Provides access to all internal and external functions and information via a tailored interface.

- ✔ **Workflow:** Control the flow of tasks through process chains.

Among the features in SAP EH&S for managing hazardous materials and dangerous goods are

- ✔ Substance volume tracking

- ✔ Document management and shipping

- ✔ Bill of materials transfer

✔ Specification information system

✔ Phrase management

Substance volume tracking

This feature provides a structure for controlling the substance volumes needed for REACH and other regulatory reporting. It tracks substance volumes by monitoring the relevant material movements in the SAP system, exploding materials to base ingredients through bills of material, material-specification assignments, and compositions. It derives and aggregates required data for other relevant criteria, too, such as year, plant, and country. You can define threshold limits for each regulation and substance, and execute Web-based checks via other business processes, including purchasing, production, and sales. When the system determines that a regulatory limit has been met or exceeded, either it will send a warning or block the relevant business process.

Document management and shipping

The solution enables you to manually or automatically locate, generate, manipulate, organize, and ship high-quality documents and reports such as MSDSs, standard operating procedures, and labels in a variety of formats. Because the solution enables precise control of the amount and content of the data in your documents, you can create documents that are specific to your product and to both the destination countries and those through which the goods will travel. Multilingual documents and labels can be created, too, as can complex labels.

Your documents can hold all specification data, as well as graphics and other documents. Using a modified version of Microsoft Word (Windows Word Processor Integration [WWI]), you can define the exact document layout. Version and status management is also available for use with documents, including those that you import. You can search documents with user-friendly functions, via the Internet or your company intranet. Further, the solution can automatically determine whether an MSDS is required based on an order or delivery through SAP Sales and Distribution. After it has ascertained which MSDS (or bundles of MSDSs) it needs, the system automatically locates, produces, and distributes them, ensuring that all legal requirements are fulfilled.

Bill of materials transfer

You can use the bill of materials transfer solution to create the composition of a specification that is assigned to a material from your bill of material (BOM), either manually or automatically, creating new specifications and their compositions or changing existing ones during the process. The EH&S Expert automatically generates the data you need and converts units of measurement. The system also changes the composition of the specification accordingly if an item in the BOM changes. When specifications for a product are altered, the system can automatically ship the most current version to those who require it.

Specification information system

You can execute detailed searches for specifications and specification data using the specification information solution. For example, you can use any substance property as a search criterion. When you run a full-text search, the system runs through all short and long texts in all relevant languages simultaneously. If desired, you can customize the solution to extend the delivered search functionality. In addition, you can sharpen your results once a hit list is displayed and then distribute them using the SAP system, Microsoft Excel, or a browser using HTML format.

Phrase management

SAP EH&S uses text modules, called *phrases*, to assign texts to specification properties. Not only can you manage and translate phrases on demand, but also you can import commercial phrase libraries and then customize them to meet your specific needs. Phrases can be used in all of your documents, including your reports, MSDSs, labels, and technical data sheets.

Part IV
Managing the Flow of Information

The 5th Wave   By Rich Tennant

"We're using just-in-time inventory and just-in-time material flows which have saved us from implementing our just-in-time bankruptcy plan."

In this part . . .

You discover that when you come right down to it, GRC is all about the flow of information, both out to all your stakeholders in the important area of sustainability and across the enterprise — literally through its network pipes and out across the Internet, covered by the area of IT GRC and data governance. But the most important thing that a strong, integrated approach to GRC can do is improve your visibility into your business in a way that helps you run your business better and align corporate performance management (CPM) with GRC efforts. CPM and GRC are inextricably linked, and you'll see how GRC can help you find out things you didn't know before about your business — key information that can impact your strategic direction.

Chapter 13

Sustainability and Corporate Social Responsibility

In This Chapter

▶ A brief history of sustainability

▶ Why the current approach is a mess

▶ Some approaches to automation

Sustainability, long a mantra of environmentalists, has now firmly entered the vocabulary of the business world. Simply put, sustainability means meeting the needs of the present without compromising the needs of the future.

Corporate Social Responsibility (CSR) means that companies see the challenges of sustainability and realize that as a company, they have the responsibility to do something about that. CSR integrates social and environmental concerns into business operations and relationships with shareholders. Sometimes people refer to this concept as "corporate citizenship" or "corporate responsibility." All of these terms carry the same basic meaning: corporations must worry about more than bottom line profits. Now they must consider their environmental and social impact. This is often called "triple bottom line performance."

What's the triple bottom line? We're not going to abandon that first most popular bottom line (you know, the one about moolah), but now it's more complex. The *triple bottom line* includes three essential elements:

✔ Profits

✔ Environmental impact

✔ Social impact

How is your company going to practice CSR? That's where corporate sustainability comes in. It's a management philosophy that meets present goals for profits and growth without jeopardizing the company's future — and that means operating in an environment with more stakeholders, more variables, and higher expectations.

As we discuss in this chapter, sustainability also makes perfect sense as a business strategy. It encourages efficiency, good planning, and public goodwill — all key facets of success in an era of globalism. In this chapter, we discuss the myriad of advantages to taking a sustainable approach to your business. We also cover the challenges of sustainability reporting and make some suggestions for an automated solution.

Discovering the Great Power and Responsibility of Big Companies

Corporations now have unprecedented economic power. According to Bruce Piasecki's book *World Inc.*, 51 of the 100 largest economies in the world are corporations, not nations. The 100 largest multinational corporations now control 20 percent of global foreign assets. Only 21 nations have GDP markets larger than the annual sales revenue of each of the six largest multinational corporations.

Like Spider-Man says, "With great power, comes great responsibility." Corporations are expected to act as good global citizens and address social and environmental concerns that previously had been left to governments and non-governmental organizations (NGOs). Those that don't, face a backlash from consumers, investors, activists, and the media.

Consider these recent examples:

✔ In August 2007 Mattel, the world's largest toy maker, recalled 21 million toys in the U.S. because the products were covered in lead paint by manufacturers in China or contained magnets that could choke children. Mattel's safety checks — which include independent audits of facilities and ownership of many of its own factories in China — did not prevent the chain of events that led to the recall. The company's public image took a battering, and it faces lawsuits over the dangerous toys.

✔ Nike suffered worldwide criticism for employing child labor in third world countries, particularly at soccer ball factories in Pakistan. In 2001, the company issued its first corporate responsibility report and admitted that it "blew it" when it came to monitoring its production facilities. Its corporate responsibility report admitted, "Even when records keeping is more advanced, and hiring is carefully done, one mistake can brand a company like Nike as a purveyor of child labor."

Critics often portray globalism as freeing corporations from responsibility. In many ways, however, globalism has *increased* expectations on the corporation.

Now corporations must worry about more than pleasing their shareholders; they must answer to other stakeholders, such as government regulators, their customers, their employees, and activist groups. Companies that fail to act as good citizens now face substantial risks. They can squander consumer goodwill and undermine their own viability. They are accountable to customers at home and workers in Asia, Latin America, or Eastern Europe. If the latter are mistreated, the former may boycott. Similarly, corporations can't look at the environment as a local issue. It's no longer just a question of how a factory impacts local groundwater; now it must consider how its emissions might effect global warming.

CSR has become part of big business. More than 1,800 companies in 60 countries publish sustainability reports that detail nonfinancial areas, such as their employment in local communities and environmental impacts. About 1,000 companies around the world follow the sustainability reporting guidelines of the Global Reporting Initiative. In 2005, the *Economist* magazine declared, "Corporate Social Responsibility is now an industry in its own right."

Here are just a few examples:

- Automaker Toyota has an "Earth Charter," a worldwide environmental policy affecting every aspect of its operations.

- GE, the fifth largest U.S. company, launched its "ecoimagination" campaign to develop cleaner technologies such as solar energy, hybrid locomotives, fuel cells, lower emission aircraft engines, lighter and stronger materials, efficient lighting, and water purification technology. It vowed to reduce its own emissions by one percent and report publicly on meeting its sustainability goals.

- Interface, a floor covering and fabric manufacturer, has committed itself towards ambitious goals: eliminating waste, eliminating toxic substances, and moving toward renewable energy. The company issues an annual sustainability report following the standards from the Global Reporting Initiative.

Getting the Lowdown on Sustainability

The idea of sustainability has evolved over the last two decades. The first major milestone came in 1987 with the World Commission on Environment and Development. The U.N. created the commission to address growing concern "about the accelerating deterioration of the human environment and natural resources and the consequences of that deterioration for economic and social development." The commission was chaired by former Norwegian Prime Minister Gro Harlem Brundtland and the report "Our Common Future" came to be known as "The Brundtland Report." It established what continues to be the classic definition of sustainability:

"Sustainable development is development that meets the needs of the present without compromising the ability of future generations to meet their own needs."

This philosophy echoes the "seventh generation" philosophy of the Native American Iroquois Confederacy, which mandated that chiefs always consider how their actions would play out seven generations in the future.

In 1992, 178 governments endorsed the Rio Declaration on Environment and Development, also known as Agenda 21, an environmental summit in Brazil.

Sustainability in action: The Wal-Mart effect

Sustainability enhances the bottom line. Just ask the most notorious cost cutting behemoth of them all — Wal-Mart. When CEO Lee Scott took over in 2000, the company faced a series of PR woes: a class action lawsuit by female employees, opponents blocking new stores, criticism for its stingy wages and health benefits, and millions of dollars in fines for violating air- and water-pollution laws.

The company began a PR counterattack to polish its image. But then something funny happened — it found sustainability made good business sense too. Wal-Mart discovered that by eliminating excessive packaging on its Kid Connection toy line, it could save $2.4 million a year in shipping costs, 3,800 trees, and one million barrels of oil. Wal-Mart determined it could save $26 million a year in fuel costs for its fleet of 7,200 trucks merely by installing auxiliary power units that keep cabs warm or cool while drivers rest during mandatory ten-hour breaks from the road. Before that, drivers would let their engines idle, wasting fuel.

In 2006, Wal-Mart announced plans to invest $500 million in sustainability. It will double the efficiency of its vehicle fleet in ten years, reduce solid waste from US stores by 25 percent in three years, and cut energy consumption by 30 percent. Its stores also have boosted offerings of eco-friendly products: It's the biggest seller of organic milk and the biggest buyer of organic cotton in the world.

Wal-Mart operates 14 "sustainable value networks," made up of Wal-Mart executives, suppliers, environmental groups, and regulators that focus on areas such as facilities, internal operations, logistics, alternative fuels, packaging, chemicals, food and agriculture, electronics, textiles, forest products, jewelry, seafood, and climate change. The company opened dialogs with the World Wildlife Federation, the Natural Resources Defense Council, and Greenpeace. "Sustainability helped us develop the skills to listen to people who criticize us and to change where it's appropriate," Scott says.

The company is the biggest private user of electricity in the US — each of its 2,074 supercenters uses an average of 1.5 million kilowatts annually. It also has the nation's second-largest fleet of trucks, which travel a billion miles a year. By Wal-Mart's own admission, its U.S. operations were responsible for 15.3 million metric tons of carbon emissions in 2005 — more than the combined emissions of Bolivia and Cyprus.

But the sheer size of Wal-Mart means that even small changes have huge reverberations because its supply chain is so big. The environmental campaign that Scott admits started out as a "defensive strategy" was, in his view, "turning out to be precisely the opposite." Employees felt better about the company, the company saved money, and customers did, too. In short, sustainability turned out to be a bottom line strategy, too.

Later that year, the U.N. created the Commission on Sustainable Development to monitor and report on implementation of the agreements at the local, national, regional, and international levels.

The U.N. is now working with some of the world's largest financial institutions, pension funds, and research firms, representing more than $6 trillion in assets, to develop environmental, social, and governance (ESG) guidelines that will be more transparent to shareholders. These "Principles for Responsible Investment" include signatories, such as Citigroup, Bank of Tokyo, ABN AMRO, and hundreds of other financial institutions.

Meanwhile, changes also were afoot in the corporate world. Traditionally, companies had evaluated their performance on strictly financial measures, such as accounting figures and stock prices. In the 1980s and 1990s, they began to realize that their approach was too narrow. They began adopting new frameworks, such as the balanced scorecard to gain a more holistic and strategic picture of performance and strategy. New measurement systems began to include intangibles such as customer satisfaction, employee satisfaction, and product innovation. Research has shown that more balanced measurement systems are linked to better business performance.

Companies began issuing sustainability reports in the 1990s. In 1999, a coalition of activist groups, in cooperation with the United Nations, released the first sustainability reporting guidelines. This evolved into the Global Reporting Initiative (GRI). The GRI remains the de facto standard in sustainability reporting used by organizations in more than 60 countries. In 1990, virtually no corporations issued non-financial reports. Now more than 1,800 do so. The concern about sustainability is more than "do-goodism." Customers and investors increasingly demand that corporations act as good stewards — a mandate that companies ignore at their peril. In the U.S., socially responsible investment firms manage more than $2 trillion in assets. The market has recognized this ethic with new indexes, such as the Dow Jones Sustainability Index and FTSE4Good. According to Al Gore, cofounder of the investment firm Generation, "the full spectrum of value that represents a corporation's activities can only be understood if you look outside the narrow confines of financial reports."

This area continues to mature rapidly. The U.N. is now working with some of the world's largest financial institutions, pension funds, and research firms, representing more than $6 trillion in assets, to develop ESG guidelines that will be more transparent to shareholders. New automated solutions are under development. AMR Research predicts that 89 percent of companies in the U.S. and 62 percent of companies in Europe are going to invest in IT for sustainability between 2007 and 2009.

Without a doubt, sustainability is here to stay. But sustainability isn't just about doing what's right: It's also good for your business. In the next section, we show you how.

Discovering Why Sustainability Is Good Business

Businesses cannot operate as they did a generation ago. Until recently, corporations could operate with the attitude famously summed up by economist Milton Friedman, "The business of business is business." Of course, the business of business is *still* business — but the story doesn't end there. Now they operate in a more complicated, interconnected global economy. Businesses must integrate social and environmental concerns into their operations in order to be successful. In short, they must manage the "triple bottom line."

In the old fashioned view, the bottom line referred to only economic indicators like wages, profits or taxes. The new formula recognizes role of social factors such as investment in the local community, employee benefits or antidiscrimination policies and environmental ones like carbon emissions, the balance of renewable versus non-renewable energy sources and water consumption.

Say you're the CEO of a multinational corporation who's evaluating performance of plants in Latin America. The factory is no longer evaluated purely on productivity or profitability. Now executives ask new questions: What are its social investments in the surrounding community? What are its emissions of carbon dioxide and other greenhouse gases? What is the ethnic and gender diversity of the workforce? And how do all these things factor into the overall enterprise with 50 factories around the world?

Do you think these executives are doing this just to pander to the Sierra Club? Think again. Nearly three quarters of executives say economic factors are the leading drivers behind CSR. According to AMR Research, 51 percent of companies with sustainability initiatives reported gains in competitive advantage.

Managers recognize sustainability as a top priority

The changing ethos of business is reflected in the 2006 Global Survey of Business Executives conducted by the prestigious consulting firm McKinsey and Co. In the survey, only 16 percent of those surveyed said that the sole role of the corporation was to generate the highest returns. In contrast, 84 percent said companies should balance the quest for profits with contributions to the broader public good. Yet these same executives said the business world still hadn't lived up to the challenge: 70 percent agreed that "significant" or "substantial" improvements were needed.

Why do managers see this as a priority? The KPMG International Survey of Corporate Responsibility Reporting listed leading drivers of this movement cited by executives. Figure 13-1 shows the results of the survey.

Several forces are fueling the movement for corporate sustainability management. In the next few sections, we examine the most important ones.

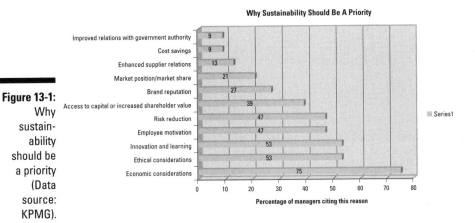

Figure 13-1: Why sustainability should be a priority (Data source: KPMG).

Data Source: KPMG International Survey of Corporate Responsibility Reporting

Stakeholders exert pressure

In the good old days, a CEO could go about his business while answering to relatively few stakeholders — namely the board of directors, shareholders, and customers. Now businesses have far more stakeholders, including customers, regulators, NGOs, vendors, competitors, and employees.

Who exactly is driving sustainability efforts can vary by region across the globe. One survey by the Economist Intelligent Unit (EIU) asked more than 1,200 executives around the world to name the stakeholders who were most influential in their sustainability efforts. In Western Europe, the top stakeholder was the customer (56 percent); in North America, it was the competitors (45 percent); and in Asia-Pacific it was government regulators (51 percent).

According to a survey by AMR Research, 27 percent of companies have business relationships dependent on their own environmental stance. But this appears to be scratching the surface: 57 percent expect such relationships to be dependent on their stance within the next two years. These stakeholders increasingly demand environmental stewardship and social responsibility. And they are more proactive about punishing those who fail to meet these expectations. In 1994, Greenpeace learned that Shell UK was planning to dispose of Brent Spar — a 453-foot-tall, 14,500 ton cylindrical oil storage facility — by dumping it in the North Sea. Environmentalists cried foul, and Greenpeace launched a major public relations offensive against the oil company. Greenpeace activists landed on Brent Spar by boat, occupied the platform for three weeks and generated ongoing news coverage before being expelled. Shell resorted to high-powered water cannons to keep a Greenpeace helicopter from approaching Brent Spar — providing more graphic television images.

Protests and boycotts against Shell broke out across Europe. Even the worker representatives on Shell Germany's supervisory board expressed "concern and outrage" at Shell's decision to "turn the sea into a trash pit." The mayor of Leipzig banned Shell gas in city vehicles. German economics minister Guenther Rexrodt announced that his ministry would join the boycott. Shell's German sales dropped 20 to 30 percent; in some areas they plummeted 40 percent.

Shell's response was uncoordinated and unfocused. Finally, the company had little choice but to give in. Shell UK announced that it would abandon plans to sink the Brent Spar and that it would instead dismantle the platform on land.

The episode proves a stark example of the power of these new stakeholders in influencing corporations. Some firms have learned to take proactive steps to reinforce a socially responsible image. British Petroleum (BP) has adopted such a strategy — at least insofar as an oil company is able to do so. BP has announced goals to reduce carbon dioxide emissions by 10 percent — one of the first big companies to take such a step. It also has vowed to reduce overall air, waste, and water emissions. It has built BP Solar International into one of the world's leading manufacturers of solar power generating equipment. The company signed a $30 million contract with the Philippine government to install over 1,000 packaged solar systems in 400 remote villages. BP also promised to eliminate *flaring*, the burning of natural gas generated in conjunction with crude oil production and a major source of carbon dioxide emissions. Chris Rose, deputy executive director of Greenpeace — the very group that vexed Shell during the Brent Spar episode — called BP one of "the good guys in this industry."

Activists increasingly see corporations as agents of social change. Instead of branding these companies as bogeymen, they often woo them as potential allies. In many cases, convincing a huge company such as Wal-Mart — with its giant supply chain and influence over its rivals — to alter its environmental policies may have a greater impact than lobbying for government regulations. As a 2007 article in the *Financial Times* observed, "Suppliers and activist groups that once dueled over government regulatory standards are battling instead to win over the Wal-Mart buyers who head its product-focused 'sustainability networks.'"

Customers increasingly shop green. One survey commissioned by British retailer Marks & Spencer shows consumers are thinking more about ethical and health issues when they buy clothing and food:

- ✓ Almost one-third said they had decided not to buy an item of clothing because they felt concerned about where it had come from or under what conditions it had been made.

- ✓ Fifty-nine percent said they had also avoided buying a food product due to similar concerns.

- ✓ Seventy-eight percent said they would like to know more about the way clothes are made including the conditions in the factories where they come from and the use of chemicals in their manufacture.

- ✓ Seventy-two percent of food shoppers said they were concerned about the future of fish stocks.

Think of CSR as a form of compliance. In strict sense, the term *compliance* refers to adhering to government regulations. But in broader sense, we can think of practicing CSR as compliance with stakeholder expectations.

Sustainable businesses have better access to capital

Investors and venture capitalists are demanding more sustainability. Companies that fail to recognize this trend risk losing out on a significant source of investment in the years ahead. The European Social Investment Forum (Eurosif) has a mission to "address sustainability through financial markets." The group estimates that the efforts will grow to Euro 1.25 billion by the end of 2006.

The Socially Responsible Investors (SRI) community now wields considerable clout. Nearly one out of every 10 dollars invested today falls under the category of socially responsible investment. These institutional and mutual fund investors are pushing for greater disclosure and challenging Generally Accepted Accounting Principles. Shareholder resolutions on social and environmental issues increased more than 16 percent from 299 proposals in 2003 to 348 in 2005. Institutional investors that filed or co-filed resolutions on social or environmental issues controlled nearly $703 billion in assets in 2005, a 57 percent rise over 2003.

Failing to live up to these standards can backfire. For example, the FTSE4Good semi-annual review resulted in the deletion of 17 companies from the index. A dozen were ejected for failing to meet environmental criteria, two for failing to adhere to labor standards in the supply chain, two for failing to meet anti-bribery standards, and one for owning a weapons company. Each company was named in the report.

Government regulations increasingly require it

Corporations now operate in a more complicated regulatory environment. In the U.S., the Sarbanes-Oxley Act was passed in the wake of the Enron collapse and other corporate scandals. Under Sarbanes-Oxley (SOX), environmental liabilities and risks are valuated, reported, and financially disclosed. CEOs or CFOs who fail to abide by Sarbanes-Oxley face severe penalties: up to $5 million in fines and/or up to 20 years in prison for willful certification of any statement not complying with the law.

The U.S. Securities & Exchange Commission is showing an interest in environmental enforcement. The SEC and independent financial auditors scrutinize environmental financial reporting like never before.

In the European Union, the new REACH guidelines (Registration, Evaluation, and Authorisation of Chemicals) makes the industry responsible for assessing and managing the risks posed by chemicals and providing appropriate safety information to users. All manufacturers and importers of chemicals must identify and manage risks linked to the substances they manufacture and market and document their actions with a registration dossier, which must be submitted to the European Chemicals Agency. (See Chapter 12 for more information on REACH.)

But why just be reactive to regulations? Government regulation is often a reaction to public pressure. Companies that practice effective sustainability can anticipate these challenges ahead of time. The trick is to be ahead of the curve — and that's what every business wants, right?

Sustainability helps you manage risk

Sustainability is a form of advanced risk management. One 2005 report by UBS Equity Research concluded that "Social risk is business risk; business risk translates into financial risk."

Corporations are waking up to the fact that costs are not as easily externalized as we used to think; selling products with associated health risks may translate into paying the costs for those health risks at some point in the future. The litigation that pummeled tobacco and asbestos companies in the U.S. may be a precursor of what other companies may face in the future. Nothing like a few multibillion dollar verdicts to change people's thinking.

More areas of potential big litigation loom on the horizon: Climate change, pollution, junk food, ozone depletion. The state of California sued six of the world's largest auto makers, saying that greenhouse gas emissions from their vehicles caused billions of dollars in damages.

The previously mentioned UBS Equity Research study notes that if a firm or an industry externalizes costs, the price is normally *not* negotiated at the time. Instead, the price may be renegotiated at a future date, and sometimes in a court of law. In other words, you can pay a fixed cost now for CSR or gamble on paying an unknown cost later — one that may be determined by trial lawyers and 12 angry men and women.

CSR protects your brand image

The reputation of the brand is one of the most valuable assets of any company. Corporations now operate in a globally networked world where information spreads within minutes. An environmental or social problem in a small village halfway around the world can influence the attitude of customers at the local Toys R Us. A hard-earned reputation can be damaged or destroyed in a day.

Corporations now come under great scrutiny from third-party groups. These may include environmental groups, human rights organizations, scientific alliances, and so on. The public is often biased more favorably towards these groups than corporations. In fact, the public can be downright skeptical towards big business. When an NGO gets into a dispute with a corporation, the burden of proof usually falls to the corporation.

CSR is a means to protect brand image. It shows the world you want to be a responsible citizen. When problems do arise, it shows you will correct them quickly and decisively and own up to your mistakes.

 Transparency has become a powerful brand differentiator and marketing tactic. British food retailer Marks & Spencer launched a major campaign called "look behind the label" to tell customers about how its products are sourced and made. For example, a package of crackers might list its environmental footprint, with CO_2 emissions, along with nutritional information. Such proactive tactics have generated many positive news items, according to an analysis by the Geneva-based ethical reputation research firm Covalence.

Two-thirds of chief financial officers at leading U.S. retailers say their company is actively involved with "green" or environmentally friendly practices, according to a new study by BDO Seidman, LLP. Among the 100 largest retailers, 83 percent are involved in green practices and 62 percent have increased their green investments during the past two years. When asked to identify the greatest motivator for this change, two-thirds of the CFOs cited the company's corporate image among consumers and shareholders. Tax breaks or tax incentives were only cited by 15 percent of the CFOs. In other words, brand image proved a much greater motivator than government policy.

It helps you attract and keep the best employees

Today corporations compete for the best workforce. Many people, especially those from younger generations, want more than just a high salary; they also want to *feel* good about their company. They want to work for an enterprise that makes meaningful contributions to the world. Your cafeteria food may be great, but if the news is full of reports about your company causing birth defects in the Third World, your employees are not going to have warm feelings about their employers.

Companies have become social institutions in their own right and they are accountable to their own employees. CSR shows the world you want to be a good global citizen and this helps recruitment and employee satisfaction, and lessens absenteeism and turnover.

CSR is ethical

Business leaders are just like the rest of us: They have moral values. In the KPMG International Survey of Corporate Responsibility Reporting, ethical considerations were cited by 53 percent of executives cited ethical considerations as the number two factor behind their sustainability initiatives, second only to economic considerations.

Take the example of Novo Nordisk. Like many western companies, it does business in China. But it also has taken on a pressing health problem — even though it may limit future growth. In China, diabetes is growing at a faster rate than the rest of the world due to the transition to a Western diet and lifestyle. Novo Nordisk has 60 percent of the Chinese market for insulin. If they succeed in reducing the effects of diabetes through education, presumably sales of insulin will not increase at the current rate. Yet the company believes that it's better to do the right thing rather than just seek profits. To that end, they're investing considerable effort into diabetes education, both for the public and for healthcare professionals.

It helps business planning and innovation

Sustainability reporting does more than assuage external stakeholders; it's also a management tool. It opens new windows into your operations. Imagine that your company wants to expand overseas production and is considering whether to invest in a factory in India and another in China. Sustainability reporting gives you an auditable database with benchmarks for examining key questions. How do the two factories compare in emissions of greenhouse gases? How about employee turnover? Investment in workers? Managers can get a fuller picture and make wiser decisions.

CSR increases profits

Finally, let's not forget the good old bottom line: profits. In the KPMG International Survey of Corporate Responsibility Reporting, economic factors were listed as the top driver behind this movement.

Sustainability helps companies reduce inefficiency and minimize lost profits. Saving resources and energy means reducing costs for both procurement and waste at the same time. Improvements in environmental, health, and safety measures have a real payoff: fewer accidents, fewer lost workdays, and fewer fines. Environmentally sound products gain more market share and earn more profits. Balancing social, environmental, and economic considerations contributes to long-term prosperity.

Sustainability management is good management. Pharmaceutical companies receiving above average EcoValue21(r) ratings have outperformed companies with below average ratings by approximately 17 percentage points (1700 basis points) since May 2001.

Similarly, a report by the Economist Intelligence Unit found a strong correlation between sustainability efforts and profits: Companies that rated their sustainability efforts most highly saw annual profit increases of 16 percent and share price growth of 45 percent. Those that ranked their own efforts poorly saw profits grow by only 7 percent and share price by 12 percent.

Business is still about the bottom line, but now there are three of them: profit, environmental impact, and social impact. Nearly 70 percent of chief executives of mid-sized to large companies believe that sustainability is vital to their profitability, and more than two-thirds say it will remain a high priority, according to recent global client surveys by Price Waterhouse Coopers. The business of business is *still* business — it just has to operate in a new climate. Sustainability is about adapting to a changing world. And, like Darwin told us, the ones who adapt best survive, and the ones who don't become extinct.

Consumers reward companies whose CSR programs:

- ✔ Have a good fit with the business mission and strategy.
- ✔ Demonstrate proactive versus reactive timing (regardless of whether motivation is profit or altruism).
- ✔ Make solid business sense. Sustainability is not about charity. If it is not good business, consumers are skeptical.

Discovering the Possible Downside of CSR

Still, sustainability has its share of skeptics in the business world. They point to a lack of empirical evidence of its effectiveness. Indeed, many of the arguments in its favor are theoretical and anecdotal. It's difficult to measure constructs, such as brand value or corporate reputation and tie them to sustainability initiatives.

In addition, costs are easily quantifiable whereas benefits of sustainability are more elusive. You look at the budget and see you invested $1 million on sustainability, but how does one measure the payoff in customer loyalty? Moreover, the benefits of sustainability initiatives often appear after a time lag. Companies that take a purely pragmatic approach may focus excessively on the downside of such initiatives — their cost — and underestimate their benefits.

Even worse, sustainability can backfire if not implemented wisely. If you've billed yourself as a green company and then get exposed for violating your own standards, you'll be branded as a hypocrite. The Center for Responsible Business at the University of California at Berkeley found that when social initiatives are not aligned with corporate objectives, CSR can "actually become a liability and diminish previously held beliefs about firms." Reporting must withstand the scrutiny of being audited. Under the watchful eyes of stakeholders around the world, corporations need to prove that their reporting is more than whitewash or — as it's known within environmental circles — greenwash.

Managing Sustainability Performance

After you've decided that sustainability is worthwhile, now comes the tough part: actually doing it. Unfortunately, managing corporate sustainability is largely a work in progress and standards and measures continue to evolve. These methods are still manual, time consuming, inefficient, and costly. Worse, the information gathered and reported often is not transparent or auditable. In short, these practices simply are not sustainable.

Sustainability is a global trend, but not a uniform one. Part of this rests on confusion about the meaning of sustainability itself. Businesses often are confused by new demands. They have trouble devising sustainability targets and aligning social and environmental objectives with financial ones. In the aforementioned EIU survey of more than 1,200 executives, only 53 percent of companies claimed to have a sustainability policy in place — and only half of those extended it beyond internal operations into their supply chains.

The current reporting process is a mess

Many companies borrow from templates, such as the Global Reporting Initiative. Yet standards vary and reports are often lean and labor intensive. In the EIU survey, only 22 percent of executives said their companies had formal procedures for triple bottom line reporting (although 40 percent planned to adopt them within the next five years).

Common problems with sustainability reporting include

- Information flows sequentially, and there are technical obstacles for each step.

- The whole process relies on manual operations. Information is typically exchanged by e-mail. Data is stored in Microsoft Excel spreadsheets. Validation and consolidation require considerable effort and time. The whole process is prone to errors.

- Whole teams spend weeks or months gathering the data, making sure that it's correct and consolidating it. Because this whole process is based on manual operations, many companies invest in third party assurance by hiring expensive auditing companies. Costs can reach two million euros per an annual report.

- Sustainability solutions often aren't integrated into other existing systems. According to a survey of 150 companies in the U.S. and Europe by AMR Research, less than one-third use their ERP systems to help manage CSR issues. Yet these enterprise-wide systems should be the very foundation of balancing environmental, social, and business objectives.

New tactics are required

Companies must move from reactive, uncoordinated *tactics* to proactive *strategy*. In other words, you must embed sustainability into your key business processes. Sustainable development then becomes a natural part of business development.

The benefits of such a shift include

- Competitive advantage. Sustainability monitoring can be cumbersome and time consuming. By doing it efficiently, you gain competitive advantage over rivals

- Long-term success. This depends not only on financial performance, but also on performance of non-financials, for instance, energy efficiency, carbon footprint, toxic substances in products, etc.

- Improved internal and external benchmarking. You gain more insight into your sustainability performance. This allows you to feed back information from internal or external benchmarks into your strategy management to help you identify opportunities to improve your business.

✔ Better informed investment decisions

✔ Reduced financial risk, stemming from reducing environmental and health risks

✔ Speed. Reporting requirements would be fulfilled more quickly

✔ Flexibility. An automated solution meets immediate needs and remains adaptable to future ones.

Discovering Why an Automated Solution Is Needed

The problem of manual, cumbersome sustainability reporting requires an automated solution, and, the AMR study cited earlier indicates that the market recognizes this as well, with the majority of companies in the US and in the EU planning to invest in IT for sustainability between 2007 and 2009. In the next few sections, we explore some of the reasons an IT solution is needed.

Sustainability reporting is a recurring problem

Sustainability reporting is becoming an increasingly important part of doing business. As it becomes more institutionalized, reporting requirements will only increase. Companies need a solution that doesn't have to be reinvented again and again.

Companies are regularly asked for sustainability data by various parties: their own executives, the press, NGOs, interest groups, and regulators. Under a manual system, this information must be calculated again and again. With an automated system, data is always up to date and can be gathered and customized with a few clicks.

Huge amounts of data are involved

Sustainability reporting is complex and undoubtedly will become even more so in the years ahead. It's simply impractical to manage so much data without a comprehensive solution. A solution must work across different business applications and must be able to draw data from systems of record. An integrated suite is critical.

Integration is a plus

A successful solution must integrate various back end systems. Such a solution leverages existing IT investments and builds upon existing infrastructure.

Sustainability cannot be viewed in isolation. To the contrary, it must be absorbed into the very heart of the enterprise. For example, sustainability is closely tied to risk management, governance, compliance, financials, and supply chain management, and thus should be integrated with all relevant software applications to ease sustainability metrics and reporting.

Such a solution would automatically pull relevant information from other systems of record. This would save the trouble of repeatedly hunting down bits of data and entering them manually. It also would be more efficient than building an entirely new system from scratch, which only introduces redundancy into the organization and creates problems with integration.

Key performance indicators could be displayed in some kind of dashboard or portal to give managers a quick snapshot. Managers could rest assured that they have an accurate picture that uses their best and most current data from other enterprise software.

Automation creates supply chain transparency

An automated solution helps solve one of the most vexing problems of sustainability efforts: the integrity of the supply chain. The supply chain is often a weak link in sustainability. In the Economist Intelligence Unit survey, about one fifth of executives admitted their company has performed poorly in setting standards for suppliers in environmental and human rights issues.

 Companies are being held accountable for problems in their supply chain — even when they are not directly responsible. For example, Mattel took a public beating when suppliers in China used lead paint on toys. In the mind of the consumer, it matters little where the problem originated; the buck stops with the name of the brand they see on the shelf.

Clearly, companies need more control over their own supply chains. This task has grown more complex in the era of globalism, when supply chains can stretch thousands of miles and involve hundreds of partners. Companies need sustainability software that interfaces with that of their suppliers. Ideally, a solution would "plug in" to the systems of supply chain partners. This would make the entire supply chain more transparent, which is something stakeholders have come to expect.

Automation means auditability

Companies are starting to require that their suppliers adhere to their sustainability requirements. In addition, the U.N. Global Compact and industry codes of conduct require members to ensure that suppliers are compliant. Currently this manual process involves a hodge-podge of emails, surveys, on site audits, and so on. A value chain sustainability application would analyze the requirements of, for example, regulations, industry groups or customers, and automate the audit, documentation, and response process. It would provide key performance indicators on sustainability programs and show what revenue is "at risk" by poor supply sustainability management.

For example, Wal-Mart has unveiled a "Sustainability 360" plan and has set a goal of one day using only renewable energy and creating no waste — and the giant retailer has challenged its suppliers, customers, and employees to do the same.

In 2007, Wal-Mart announced it will ask suppliers to measure and report greenhouse gas emissions incurred in the making of certain products. The company will start with a pilot group of about 30 manufacturers of seven common products, including toothpaste, soap, beer, milk, and DVDs. Wal-Mart plans to eventually widen the project to include about 68,000 suppliers. The move is part of an overall strategy that forces manufacturers and suppliers to comply with Wal-Mart standards or risk losing contracts. "This is an important first step toward reaching our goal of removing nonrenewable energy from products that Wal-Mart sells," John Fleming, Wal-Mart's chief merchandising officer, said in a statement.

Automation yields analytics and benchmarks

An IT solution provides a scorecard that can be tailored to many uses. Data can be customized for specific stakeholders or user groups. Value and units of measure could be converted from euros to dollars or kilos to pounds. Reporting units could be customized; an airline could compare plane types in terms of their environmental impact while a keyboard manufacturer could compare all its various types of keyboards in terms of the environmental impact of their component parts.

Consider a greenhouse gas management application. Many companies grapple with the problem of trying to quantify their carbon footprint. Such an application would automate the process by analyzing both the company's own direct "smokestack" emissions and indirect emissions from sources, such as travel, buildings, supply chain, and partners. Such an application could integrate ERP/manufacturing applications, sourcing, supply chain, and human resources. Executives could analyze key questions such as the potential for global warming or ozone depletion. They could compare performance in plants across the globe, drilling down and slicing data however they choose.

Features of a greenhouse gas management application could include:

  ✔ Changing query display options with one-click navigation. Change sorting, swap axes, change aggregation methods (sums, average) or change the display (ranked list, Olympic, cumulated. . .)

  ✔ Performance management

  ✔ Trend analysis

  ✔ Data mining

  ✔ Benchmarking

An IT solution speeds distribution of data

Different business regulations, complicated by regional differences, require access to information across disparate enterprise systems. An IT solution builds upon an integrated business applications environment that is cross-enterprise, and spans regional issues, business mandates, and industry regulations.

Chapter 14

IT GRC

So far, this book has been a general argument for instituting a Governance, Risk and Compliance regimen within your organization. In this chapter, we discuss the very significant role that IT plays in supporting and managing GRC efforts. IT must be appropriately monitored and up to the task at hand in order for the system to function and to comply with regulations, such as SOX.

What you don't know about IT GRC can and will come and bite you in the tuckus. Why? SOX and other regulatory initiatives, both financial and operational, have set responsibility for protecting the integrity of financial reporting on the shoulders of CEOs and directors, which we are sure is something you have heard ad nauseam.

The reality of this situation is that companies have had to initiate a host of policies, procedures, and internal controls to live up to that mandate. And although corporate officers cannot be expected to know every iota of detail about what is going on under the hood, they must have a depth of understanding of the efficiency of the company's internal controls, policies, and procedures in order to competently certify the company's financial reporting.

Simply saying, "Hey, we got IT all over the place" is not going to be enough if federal regulators and auditors come sniffing around the front door. To meet the requirement that you "competently certify the company's financial reporting," not to mention live up to a whole host of other regulations, such as those requiring data privacy, you must have effective controls in place, which means effective use of IT and policies surrounding technology. In this chapter, we cover the many tools you can use to protect data and secure IT assets.

Learned Hand: One man's control is another's negligence

A good question to ask yourself is, "I have policies and IT related controls in place, but are they enough to satisfy regulators and auditors if something goes wrong?" To answer that question, we need go no farther than one of the U.S.'s most celebrated and aptly named jurists — Learned Hand.

Learned Hand never made it to The Show — the Supreme Court of the United States — but he did make it as far as chief judge for the United States Court of Appeals for the Second Circuit, where he made two rulings he is now famous for.

The first relates to establishing negligence in a legal context. In the United States v. Carroll Towing, Hand established what is known as the "calculus of negligence," which, to paraphrase, says that if you can create benefits or mitigations at a low cost as compared to the amount of risk and its likelihood of occurring, and you don't, then you are negligent.

For example, if you operate a public storage warehouse, installing smoke detectors and a sprinkler system is a good way to respond to the risk of fire and avoid being sued for negligence.

As this relates to technology, most Internet service providers include spyware and antivirus protections as a means to reduce risk and avoid being accused of negligence. For a corporate CEO, maintaining a strong, proactive and enterprisewide GRC system is one way to live up to Hand's calculus of negligence should something go wrong and shareholders and regulators start making noises.

(Wondering about that second ruling Judge Hand made? It is indeed unrelated, so forgive the digression. The government had accused one taxpayer of avoiding taxes because this wily fellow used the tax code to his advantage to avoid paying as much taxes as he could. Hand ruled that it is not up to taxpayers to pay as much as they can, but that it is their right to pay as little as they can as long as they are following the tax code. This warms our hearts, especially around April 15.)

As with most GRC issues, with IT GRC, it makes sense to take an enterprisewide and integrated approach. However, managing risk and compliance issues has generally been made more difficult by the past tendency of companies to implement iterative and fragmented approaches to GRC, which in turn has led to fragmentation within the IT systems and infrastructure used to support GRC.

Further, compliance and risk have become more complex as customers and suppliers seek to hold businesses more accountable in how those relationships are carried out. An IT system must be able to handle this degree of complexity.

Getting a Handle on What IT GRC Is

Essentially, IT GRC encompasses the technical tools (software and hardware) and related policies and procedures used to support compliance and risk management efforts from an IT perspective based on established best practices. Specifically, Gartner, an IT research and advisory company, issued a report by Mark Nicolett and Paul E. Proctor in May of 2007 that delineates eight core IT GRC functions:

- ✔ **Controls and policy mapping:** IT controls and policies should be mapped into defined control objectives.

- ✔ **Policy distribution and attestation:** Policies should be broadly disseminated throughout the enterprise with a means for employees to attest that they have read them and will comply.

- ✔ **IT control self-assessment and measurement:** Assess your use of IT controls and collect data so that you can measure exactly how well you are doing and can note improvements over time.

- ✔ **GRC asset repository:** IT assets should be defined and grouped according to the business process they support and classified according to requirements for confidentiality, integrity, and availability.

- ✔ **Automated general computer control collection:** Essentially the status of computer controls can be collected from the source in an automated fashion.

- ✔ **Remediation and exception management:** Show where there were gaps in your process or problems (exceptions) and document how you addressed them so that you can show this information to auditors.

- ✔ **Basic compliance reporting:** Integrate compliance data in a form that is acceptable to auditors

- ✔ **Advanced IT risk evaluation and compliance dashboarding:** This helps the business make good decisions based on IT risk management and compliance information.

What Gartner is essentially saying is that IT GRC is about defining IT policies, processes, and controls so that they are based on best practices; making sure these policies are widely known throughout the enterprise; mapping the policies to technical controls; evaluating compliance issues and the risk of being noncompliant; and then automating the audit and regulatory reporting of your company's efforts.

Understanding IT Governance in Terms of Risk and Compliance

Simply put, IT governance is about how a company manages its IT landscape. It is governance directly tied to IT topics, so it involves fashioning IT policies and procedures that the company establishes in order to govern itself from a risk and compliance perspective.

Further, IT governance is aligned with the overall enterprise governance strategy so that every employee and every process complies with prescribed IT policies. Examples could be password policies and rules around how passwords are used, mandatory IT training, rules for e-mail usage, IT governance related documentation, and so on.

In terms of risk

When it comes to risk, IT GRC is fairly straightforward. It essentially deals with how to set policies and procedures that minimize risks to the network, applications, and data.

Information security involves ensuring the integrity and privacy of corporate data. So naturally IT GRC must ensure that adequate security measures are in place to protect information both from internal and external attack (as well as snafus resulting from plain old human error). But there are other considerations as well.

Suppose that the company is going to do an upgrade to the system that generates financial reports. In this instance, what are the documented policies and procedures for backing up the existing system? Who is in charge of checking the various components of the system? And who is testing — and what pieces are they testing — to make sure the components are actually going to support the business needs the system is designed to address?

Then there is the area of disaster recovery. Katrina is the oft- and overused example of this kind of thing, but when the hurricane struck it put every worst-case IT risk scenario to the test. Those companies that were prepared managed to recover because they understood the need to have disaster recovery systems in place that could mitigate the impact of a hurricane hitting the Gulf Coast.

The threat doesn't necessarily have to be a large-scale catastrophe, such as Katrina. A heavy snowfall, rain causing a roof to collapse, or a mouse chewing on some wires causing a fire are all examples of possible disasters. In either event, the company that has considered its IT risks and established the means to respond to them will survive both the immense hurricane and the tiny mouse.

Your disaster recovery plan needs to include not only your company's physical location, but also that of your backup site. For example, say that your company is located in an area that is geologically secure, far enough north to avoid hurricanes, and far enough south to never have more than a gentle sprinkling of rain or dusting of snow. However, if it is using an offsite vendor to back up data or has located its data recovery center in another geographic region, what are the policies for managing a storm or fire or some other event that could threaten that data? Also, has there been a study to measure the risk associated with that site as compared with others?

If a vendor is responsible for managing data, is there a system of accountability for what happens if an incident occurs? An example could be stipulations — such as penalties or assurances — dealing directly with such issues in a service level agreement.

Other risks that require policies in order to deal with the potential for such a scenario playing out include loss of intellectual property, leaking of customer information, and more. We discuss these issues in greater detail later in the chapter, but the larger point here is that governance as it concerns risk is about ensuring business continuity and mitigation of financial risks based on and with regard to the IT resources of the company.

In terms of compliance

If your company operates across state and national boundaries, or it hopes to one day do so, compliance extends far beyond SOX or even HIPAA (the Health Insurance Portability and Accountability Act). Here's a quick rundown of some of the data privacy regulations around the world. Remember that, to date, the U.S. takes this topic less seriously than other regions:

- ✔ **Europe:** The European Data Protection Directive, which has shaped legislation in each member country
- ✔ **Canada:** Personal Information Protection and Electronic Documents Act
- ✔ **Japan:** Personal Information Privacy Act

States within the U.S. are also getting into the act to shore up protections they may feel the federal government is moving too slowly on. For example, according to the Data Governance Institute (DGI), the California Security Breach Information Act requires state agencies, nonprofit institutions, and companies, regardless of geographic location, to notify their California customers if personal information maintained in digital format has been compromised. (The DGI is a very good resource for those interested in learning more on IT compliance issues. For more info, see their Web site www.datagovernance.com).

The California Security Breach Information Act means that if you do business via the Internet on your Web site hosted in, say, Massachusetts and you collect shipping addresses and credit card information in order to send and process orders and you believe that your security was compromised, you have to notify each customer in California who may have been affected. Simply placing an ad in the newspaper is not enough. California is not the only state with such a law — Arkansas, Connecticut, New York, Delaware, and many others have passed their own versions.

There is no doubt, then, that the scope of managing compliance as it relates to your IT systems is a rather daunting task. This is where the control frameworks come into play, including COBIT and COSO (see the next two sections). These control frameworks provide an outline of the issues you need to look at, as well as providing some nice four- and five-letter acronyms for you to add to your alphabet soup.

COBIT

Published by the IT Governance Institute and the Information Systems Audit and Control Association (ISACA), COBIT (Control Objectives for Information and Related Technologies) is an open source standard that provides an IT governance framework to manage risk and compliance issues based on best practices.

According to ISACA, the bottom-line function for IT is to support the business goals for the company. To do that, COBIT supports an IT governance framework that helps a company make sure that its IT systems are aligned with the business, that IT enables the business and maximizes IT's benefits to the business, that IT resources are used responsibly, and IT risks are managed appropriately. For more information, go to the ISACA Web site at www. isaca.org.

COSO

The full name for COSO (www.coso.org) is the Committee of Sponsoring Organizations of the Treadway Commission, and it is a voluntary private sector organization dedicated to improving the quality of financial reporting through business ethics, effective internal controls, and corporate governance.

As such, the organization has created an internal control framework known as the COSOS-Enterprise Risk Management Framework. According to a COSO publication titled "Enterprise Risk Management — Integrated Framework: Executive Summary," the framework is based on eight interrelated components by which to evaluate the company's risk management strategy:

- Internal Environment
- Objective Setting
- Event Identification
- Risk Assessment
- Risk Response
- Control Activities
- Information & Communication
- Monitoring

However, COBIT and COSO, while they are helpful, have something of a one-size-fits-all feel to them and may not be specific enough to get your company to its desired scenario, ensuring that all is well under the hood.

Therefore, to augment these frameworks, it is advisable to bring in an independent auditor to identify critical transactions and examine whether the company has the right controls around those from an IT perspective.

The frameworks may be too generic to rely on entirely, but if your company has a breach of security, you would at least be in a position to say that you have a documented structure in place: You have performed due diligence. Further, these frameworks can serve as an organizing principle around which you can develop your compliance initiatives, ensuring that all the bases are covered.

Keeping up with the pace of change

A properly functioning IT governance framework recognizes the constantly changing nature of IT. Such a framework would frequently evaluate current processes against a changing landscape — new threats, risks, laws, and evolving technologies in order to keep the calculus of negligence tilted in your favor.

Your company may have come up with a better mouse trap five years ago, but unfortunately the mouse has gotten a lot bigger and a heck of a lot smarter. Within the brief evolutionary cycle of risk and compliance, it is very easy to neglect to recognize the true threat posed by the mouse and adequately adapt your systems.

Perspective is key, and one of the best ways to gain a good perspective is to look outside of your company to experts that can help you see with clarity what your industry expects, what your customers and vendors expect of you, and what regulatory agencies expect of you. Challenging your own assumptions about how up-to-date and correct your systems are may require looking to an auditor to gain much needed perspective.

If you do this due diligence, in a pinch, you will be able to look at the norms and exceptions (for example, the tolerances and when you may have exceeded them) for your spend management systems and clearly declare whether your reporting is complete, accurate, and valid as measured against the industry and aligned with the company's risk and compliance profile.

Securing Your Software Applications

Applications are software that is designed to perform some meaningful function. For a company, application software could be any one of the enterprise systems such as enterprise resource planning, supply chain management, or customer relationship management, or the databases that maintain information on everything from products to customers to the financial transactions of the company.

Therefore, application security directly relates to making sure those assets perform properly and are not vulnerable to attack by hackers or misused internally by employees.

Generally, application security has been widely recognized as a good thing that everybody must have, but it has also commonly been interpreted as solely the province of the IT department. With the passage of SOX (yes, we know, more about SOX), CEOs and directors are more accountable than ever for what goes on under the hood of their companies, so ignoring application security comes with a significant set of perils. Simply put, IT may run and manage this function, but the CEO needs to understand what they are doing and how they are doing it.

Taking basic application security measures

The tools of application security are the same kinds of controls used in nearly every other aspect of GRC: software, hardware, and guidelines establishing set policies and procedures for employees to follow. Further, because of the recognized risk of being hacked, application developers are building security measures into their software, and application security should be an evaluation point for software purchases.

Some of the most basic and elemental application security measures are items that have reached a high degree of ubiquity throughout society, such as firewalls, anti-virus software, and anti-spyware software. Routers can also get into the act by making sure that internal IP addresses can be hidden and ensuring that packets with internal IP addresses do not come into the firewall from the outside (an attack technique called IP spoofing). Other measures can include encryption of information as it travels from one point to another or biometric authentication tools that ensure the user is certified to access certain data or use a particular piece of hardware.

Application security can be enhanced through a practice known as *threat modeling*, which can include a wide range of possible scenarios such as a failure of the application to operate properly, a malicious action taken by an internal or external player, or some other form of attack that either exposes the data held by the application, allows unauthorized individuals to use the application, or crashes it.

As with the governing frameworks discussed above, companies need to assess their unique risk and compliance needs when establishing a threat model, but here are some general rules of the road as a starting point:

- ✔ Understand the business objectives the application is used to support. After all, spend management applications fulfill different roles from customer relationship management.
- ✔ Determine who uses the application and the roles those people are performing.
- ✔ Know in a fairly precise sense the data used by the application and place a value on that data. Is it a database with credit card numbers or is it inventory control software?
- ✔ Understand when the application is used. Does it manage vendor payments or keep track of the number of SKUs held in a warehouse?
- ✔ Precisely understand how the application works. What are its mechanics?
- ✔ Use the above information to identify potential threats and vulnerabilities.
- ✔ Assess the likelihood of the identified threats and the potential impact to the company (financial, brand, compliance).
- ✔ Create procedures and policies around responses to potential threat scenarios.
- ✔ Consider the words of Learned Hand and install or create appropriate counter measures to protect the applications from the threats. (For more on the aptly named jurist, see the "Learned Hand: One man's control is another's negligence" sidebar elsewhere in this chapter.)

- ✔ As with every recipe in this book, stir in a rounded cup of regularly-update-all-of-the-above.

Consolidating security solutions

Obviously the level and number of possible threats and risks to your applications has grown over the years. First it was hackers, then along came viruses, followed by spyware, and on and on. In addition, with each iteration, your company wisely thought it prudent to integrate some form of countermeasures — such as firewalls, anti-virus software, and so on — and then policies to enhance the technical countermeasures — such as "Don't open e-mail attachments from unidentified or unknown sources." In addition, each of these was targeted toward a specific and/or emerging threat.

Over the years, these countermeasures and policies have accumulated. Some are still in use even as the company seeks the next best mousetrap and others have been cast aside as their utility faded or they were replaced by something else.

These various solutions have likely worked fairly well at keeping the company's applications and network safe from various threats. However, as you seek to gain a better idea of your inventory and start poking around the garage, the basement, and the attic, you may begin to realize that your application security tools and policies lack a common approach or oversight. Therefore, it is important to take a look and see if this is true for your company and if so, implement a plan to bring uniformity to the company's approach based on accepted best practices.

Consolidating the IT infrastructure makes sense, particularly for global companies. For example, IBM is consolidating its back office functions and moving them into global regions — procurement in China, service delivery in India — and building shared service centers and centers of excellence as a way to improve efficiencies and develop new products and services. To do all this, IBM overhauled its management culture. By consolidating these functions, they can be optimized so that they cost less and also more consistently managed. Managing compliance in one location is obviously much more efficient than managing it in many locations around the world.

Making friends with the IT department

As you begin to look at the various frameworks upon which the company could build its own system, dig into threat modeling, and consider how to defragment your security assets and policies, it's also a good time to bridge what can often be a rather large gap between the IT and business sides of the business. The following points, taken from "New Era of Corporate Governance: Application Security Implications of Sarbanes-Oxley Act of 2002 and Proposals to Securities and Exchange Commission," by Gary Dickhart, should help by providing a starting point for those efforts:

- Make sure that there is a process to facilitate knowledge sharing between the business and IT sides
- Simplify technical information so that it is accessible to non-IT personnel
- Application security counter measures — policies and technical tools — should be a part of daily life for managers
- People close to the daily operations of the company should handle security-related activities in order to best monitor trends
- Align all processes, policies, and countermeasures with best practices

> ✔ The board and CEO should integrate policies, processes and counter measures into a unified approach covering physical security, information security, information privacy, fraud detection, a means for employees to report issues, and ethics training.

Keeping the Kimono Closed: Data Privacy

If there was a hit parade of IT GRC issues, data privacy would top the charts. It has become a hot area for government regulation and has received an immense amount of media attention, which means it is being considered beyond business circles and is generally out in the public consciousness. In fact, public awareness of the risk of identity theft has sparked increased use of shredders at home, firewalls on personal computers, as well as a whole host of other counter measures to protect private information.

Public policy setters, being the keen observers that they are, have been busy looking for ways to enforce the public's wish that government agencies, nonprofits, and the business community take steps to protect all forms of information.

HIPAA (the Health Insurance Portability and Accountability Act) is but one example of efforts to hold organizations accountable for protecting private information. Not only does the law protect health information, but billing information as well. Further, national standards have been set for maintaining the security of this information, which specify a series of administrative, technical, and physical security procedures to assure the confidentiality of health information stored electronically.

HIPAA is but one example of laws requiring organizations to take steps to assure the integrity of their information systems in order to protect consumers' e-mail addresses, Social Security numbers, contact information, credit card numbers, bank account numbers, and on and on.

With the attention this one issue has received by the media, there is also a certain amount of corporate peer pressure being applied. Consider for a moment the hit your brand and reputation would take if it were to become public knowledge that someone lost a laptop with thousands of credit card numbers.

Generally speaking, protecting this information has landed on the CIO's desk because this role is responsible for and has direct jurisdiction over digital assets. However, accountability, unlike water, generally flows up, so it is important for business side executives and board members to take an active interest in the measures being taken to secure data.

Protecting employee information: Data loss at HP

In August 2006, *Computerworld* reported on the results of a survey conducted by Ponemon Institute LLC and Vontu Inc., a San Francisco-based provider of data loss prevention products. The survey concluded that 81 percent of reporting companies had experienced a theft or loss of sensitive employee information — items such as names, addresses, and social security numbers. In most cases, the sensitive data was on company laptops that had been stolen or gone missing. One company that experienced such a loss was HP.

In HP's case, the laptop in this case was owned by Fidelity. It contained data on approximately 200,000 HP employees and was to be used to showcase new software that Fidelity said would help HP in certain administrative tasks related to HP's retirement plan. According to an article in the *Register*, Fidelity didn't brief HP beforehand that the data was to be used to showcase the software in question. But the *Register* went on to say that the loss of the laptop was, according to HP, due to "human error." Was the "human error" a case of an employee leaving the laptop unattended, thereby resulting in its theft?

How did such an error occur, and who was responsible for the loss of Fidelity's laptop?

These questions raise issues of oversight and accountability, especially at Fidelity. A March 2006 *CNet* article mentions that no abuses of the employee information had thus far occurred, and that employee PIN numbers for the Fidelity accounts were not part of the missing data. This would seem to indicate that the accounts wouldn't be easily breached by anyone with malicious intentions.

So many companies report a loss of employee data (81 percent as cited earlier) that this IT GRC issue should raise serious concern for security and IT professionals in all companies, even those with small employee databases. Best practices in the area of data protection must be considered, both for employee data and for client data (which is really the problem in many cases, including HP's).

Protecting Key Corporate Assets: Intellectual Property

What if your company loses a laptop holding proprietary information, such as CAD drawings of your next big idea or other forms of intellectual property? The key to your success as a company is typically associated with protecting key corporate assets and those assets are at least in part digital (if you are a software company, they may be entirely digital). This is not strictly about data privacy, but it is about data protection: keeping information from falling into the wrong hands.

Cinching up the kimono

So, how is a company supposed to manage all of its information? Digitally mark every bit of proprietary information? Digital signatures? Watermarking?

Encrypted and password protected files? Have some form of IT security guard escort this data throughout the organization and its partners? And how do you make these efforts universal throughout the organization on a highly granular or granular enough level or align it with corporate security policies?

In large part, this is a challenge with a lot of ideas and possibilities, but without a defining technology or method. According to the Gartner report mentioned earlier, and others in the field, there is no definitive IT GRC product — yet. It is an emerging market and as time goes on, products will emerge or a core of applications used for existing needs will be leveraged into an end-to-end IT GRC solution.

However, as you begin to consider how your company handles IT GRC, there is one overarching thought that could help you create a context within which to target your efforts — leveraging the network.

Leveraging the network

A company's network is the one place that all of its data and applications come into contact with each other and the conduit through which information travels throughout the enterprise and beyond. Therefore, thinking in terms of a

---

The buddy system: Keeping track of partners

Control of information often extends beyond the company's walls: Suppliers and partners often receive sensitive information, so it is important to consider what measures are being taken to ensure these people act responsibly too. As a starting point, it would be wise to consider:

✔ Setting and documenting policies defining who the partners are and which partners should have access to what and what can be shared with a partner.

✔ Ensuring that partners' internal policies should match your goals with regard to IT GRC and protecting information. This can be accomplished via a service level agreement stating what each side must live up to.

✔ Collaborating carefully. There is also the issue of federated websites and the means by which partners gain access behind the

curtain. Protocols should be established that are protective and create an auditable trail, but allow for an efficient workflow.

✔ Integrating the GRC framework with underlying network technology to prevent data leakage.

✔ Enforcing data transfer policies.

✔ Encrypting communications and other forms of IP data transfer.

The partner's IT environment should have the capacity to be able to support your company's IT GRC goals. Especially for key partners, a site visit is in order to evaluate how well what the partner says matches what it does (for example, how easy is it to gain physical access to servers?).

single platform approach rather than trying to react to each technology threat and/or risk scenario is a very important message.

If you think of the possible risks in terms of IT assets — such as laptop computers, cell phones, BlackBerries, and the like — and sending data from one point to another electronically, these risks have an important factor in common. The common point of data departure is from the network — a hacker breaks into the network to gain access, a device is connected to the network to access and download data, or information is sent via the network. Therefore, rather than attempt to come up with a multitude of countermeasures, protections can be placed at the network level.

To begin, most companies carry volumes of data with a range from high to low sensitivity. Therefore, considering the amount of data, it's helpful to establish policies and procedures to delineate the level of importance for certain types of information. For example, customer credit card or social security numbers should hold a much higher priority than other types of information. High value information should receive an elevated degree of protection such as being encrypted, strict password protection, and other controls.

Other ways data can walk away

Go into a store and at the checkout line among the flashlights and gum, you'll see a jump drive. This tiny device connects via a USB port and allows data to be moved between computers. It also allows product specifications, intellectual property, and customer information to leave the building without passing through the network (necessarily). This particular type of threat indicates that certain data must receive special protection, or classification. Such data should not be allowed to walk out of the building via a jump drive or another device, such as an iPod. Data protection is another important issue.

Ultimately, employees must be trained to handle data properly depending on their role and privileges. You must determine who handles sensitive data and ensure that they are aware of the policies surrounding it, have a legitimate reason for being given access to it, and do not have conflicting roles (see Chapter 6) that could compromise their ability to be objective with regard to handling the data. For this latter issue, access control could provide an appropriate resource. As an example, access control could be used to ensure that an IT administrator with access to credit card numbers is unable to correlate those numbers with customer names and other information.

In all, the intent is to add an extra layer of protection and risk prevention in order to prevent problems or quickly resolve them if they occur.

Protecting IT assets

As the means to carry information have evolved to include devices such as cell phones, BlackBerries, laptops, jump drives, and so on, controlling whether someone can walk away with sensitive information is something of a whole new world. It's not enough to simply restrict access to the building, but to consider that even a properly credentialed employee could load work-related information onto a jump drive or laptop and have it stolen or misplace it.

In a perfect world, every access point in the network would recognize when a foreign device has been connected to it. This may be accomplished when a device is connected directly to the network, for example the system would recognize a jump drive has been connected and would issue a report and/or require a password in order for data to be downloaded.

Also, because certain types of information have been given a high value, there could be a lock preventing, say, CAD designs (intellectual property) or Social Security numbers from being downloaded to any mobile device. This lock could also prevent data from coming into a database storing this information so that the information's integrity would not be compromised.

However, frequently, authorized employees download information onto a laptop. You may want them to be able to do that, but you would also want to prevent a jump drive or other device from being able to attach to the laptop. Further, with RFID (Radio Frequency Identification) tags, it would be possible to monitor whether laptops leave their assigned workstations and even if someone walks out the front door with them. It could also be possible to place a chip on the laptop that wipes it clean should it move from a certain area.

As cell phones have gone from a means to communicate to data carrying and management tools (smart phones), they also represent a risk. Therefore, countermeasures such as requiring passwords for phones every 10 to 20 minutes could prevent a misplaced or stolen phone from being used for access to all kinds of data. The same holds true for BlackBerries and any other mobile devices employees use to do their jobs.

In general, it is important to seek out solutions that enforce guidelines no matter what technology is in use. For example, if a foreign device is trying to download information, it should be noticed and prevented from doing so. Uploading information should also be monitored, so that when the next protocol arrives (like BitTorrent) or the next Web 2.0 innovation arrives (such as wikis), data leaving the network this way is monitored as well.

Although technology can help with some of these issues, strong IT governance must align with these goals. For example, there should be policies surrounding the use of passwords, restrictions on USB usage, restricting where assets can be moved to, policies on how IT assets can be handled, access to server rooms, elimination of SoD issues, policies about how certain types of information can be handled, policies requiring employees to use company cell phones or other mobile devices, and so on.

And enforcement of these policies should be done at the network layer when possible.

Communication

Information doesn't have to travel outside of the company on a mobile device. E-mail, file transfer, conference calls, and other means to communicate also present a challenge.

And when considering the volume of these communications, preventing all of the imaginable risk scenarios can seem like a rather daunting prospect.

The first step is to take a rather surgical approach to it. For example, data with a high level of sensitivity should receive a higher level of protection when it travels across or outside of the network. In the case of an email, packet scanning would identify if an email has a high value attachment and the network could block it from traveling to an outside IP address or from being sent at all. Emails and other correspondence could be scanned for certain code words such as those relating to an impending merger or large scale business initiative.

Pattern recognition technology is another control that could be applied. Essentially, these are IT solutions that look at usage patterns and can determine when usage exceeds or contrasts in some way with a defined pattern, such as "Why are we sending more encrypted emails to one address or set of addresses than is normal?" or "Why is someone browsing around our databases that carry customer information?" Once identified, the user can be logged out and/or an e-mail sent to an appropriate person to determine what is going on and if necessary initiate a response.

When considering communications such as conference calls and video conferencing, all of which enable a higher level of collaboration, it is important to ensure these interactions are secure, but also that they happen efficiently so they can facilitate collaboration. Manual controls such as policies establishing how these conversations are to occur — use of secure call conferencing and passwords — could be employed. There is also the idea of application-to-application security, which could prevent connections to nonapproved conferencing technology.

In short, policies and the network should be in the position of being able to identify what is coming in and going out and to assure that when sensitive data travels, it has the appropriate credentials to do so.

Chapter 15

Turning On the Lights with GRC and CPM

*I*n this chapter, we look at the relationship between corporate performance management (CPM) and GRC. The goal of our analysis is to show how creating processes for collecting and analyzing the data that is used for GRC overlaps to a significant extent with CPM. If you think about both GRC and CPM at the same time when you are designing ways to gather and make sense of information, you can cut costs and create a flow of high-quality data that helps run the business better (which is the goal of CPM), while at the same time achieving the goals of GRC.

If you've slogged through this book's coverage about the many different ways of complying, managing risk, and governing your company, it should be clear that making GRC processes work effectively is quite a bit of work. The same thing is true of improving CPM processes to get better information. Although some of this work is mandatory and other tasks just make good sense, one thing is clear — most companies' investment in GRC is a major one, so companies must maximize the benefit by making every step meet as many needs as possible.

The fundamental idea is that GRC or CPM shouldn't be addressed in a narrow way. When you approach either topic, you are looking at a business process and how it needs to be monitored and controlled. What kind of information must be provided to evaluate operation efficiency, levels of risk, and compliance with regulations? A full set of requirements involves tracking the aspects of the process that may be useful for both CPM and GRC. This chapter examines the things these two processes have in common and recommends some ways of thinking about both topics at the same time.

Turning On the Lights with CPM

As companies have grown larger and more complex, the demand for actionable information has grown dramatically. Boards of directors, CEOs, CFOs, and executives at all levels want an accurate view of the performance of the business. Outsourcing has also driven the need for more detailed information. A company that hires another company to perform a task seeks to keep track of how the work is going, which is especially important because under most regulatory schemes, the company using the outsourcer is liable for what the outsourcer does. The world moves fast, and serious operational risks can appear in a blink.

 As with most common needs of business, this desire for information has been recognized, studied, and analyzed. The name given for the large number of activities that take place to provide better information to managers is called *corporate performance management*, or CPM. To understand how CPM and GRC are two sides of the same coin, you first must look at the different parts of CPM.

CPM has evolved from financial budgeting and consolidation to a complete 360-degree view of performance management for an organization. This panoramic view adds in strategy management and profitability management to optimize the basics of financial budgeting and consolidation. Although CPM has been covered in many books, white papers, seminars, and conferences, it can be accurately simplified into the following dimensions:

- **Strategy management:** This part of CPM concerns itself with translating corporate goals into initiatives and key performance indicators, which provide guidance that align actions across the organization. Strategy management also encompasses monitoring the performance of the corporation to see if the strategy that has been set forth is being achieved. The mechanisms of strategy management are initiatives, KPIs (key performance indicators), and high-level analysis techniques like the balanced scorecard that organizes important indicators of a company's performance. One important idea behind strategy management is that the company must understand its behavior not only in financial terms but also in terms of the other sorts of public and private value that is created. The challenge of strategy management is to ensure that all employees understand the impact that their actions have on the performance of the organization. Therefore, key performance indicators must be chosen carefully and calculated from accurate data.

- **Planning:** With a strategy clearly in place, planning can begin. But you shouldn't think of planning only in terms of budgets. Planning is about strategic resource allocation. What resources does each part of the business need to do its job? How are resources going to be allocated according to the strategy? How will the company know if the resources are being used properly? What are measures of success for each department? What performance is expected according to those measures? What are the potential risks to the plan?

✔ **Reporting and consolidation:** In this phase of CPM, you take financial results and consolidate them for various purposes. For example, the results are consolidated both for financial reporting (to the SEC), known as statutory consolidation, and for management reporting (in such a case, consolidation by business unit or product line makes more sense).

✔ **Revenue, cost, and profitability modeling:** Understanding the profitability of your business activities provides perspective and guidance for your strategic planning cycle. As you create a strategy — a plan — and execute it, it is vital to understand the profits and losses associated with customers, channels, products, and other business activities. To do this, you must be able to predict and track revenue and costs. Accurate models for these numbers enable you to forecast profits, which becomes an important factor in understanding the success of a corporate strategy and helps you compare alternatives when allocating resources.

If we take a step back, it is easy to see a parallel between the general shape and patterns of activity in CPM and GRC. Both disciplines have a strong top-down component. Strategy in CPM sets the broad picture. Governance in GRC does the same thing. Strategy is of course related to governance. Strategy is the *what;* governance is the *how.*

In fact, the components of CPM and GRC are, in most cases, two halves of the same coin. Strategy management lays out the goals of the organization as well as initiatives for turning those goals into action. Governance provides the rules, policies, and applicable regulations that must govern those actions. Business planning is more effective when it is informed about material risks to the business, and resources for mitigating those risks are allocated appropriately — and risks must be analyzed in the context of business plans in order to establish relevance and material impact. Financial results need to be consolidated in a way that ensures compliance in order to be reportable. In each case, parallel business processes are utilizing the same data for separate but related purposes.

The planning stage moves to a more detailed level. In CPM, resources are allocated and KPIs are created. In GRC, some of those same KPIs may be used to identify and manage risks or to help identify improper behavior. Some KPIs may be called Key Risk Indicators (KRIs), but they are usually numbers that can be used for many purposes if they are meaningful.

In the reporting and consolidation stage, the convergence becomes stronger. Neither CPM nor GRC can be effective without accurate data. Financial reporting, referred to as *statutory* reporting, must obviously be compliant with generally accepted accounting principles and other applicable regulations. The certifiability of the numbers being reported depends in large measure on GRC activities such as segregation of duties. If this groundwork has been laid, executives can have confidence in their statutory reporting. Although CPM is concerned with the meaning of the numbers, GRC is concerned with the traceability and auditability of the processes used to create those numbers.

With respect to modeling, both CPM and GRC create many models of correct or desired activity and then detect and measure variances from the model.

The core components of CPM and GRC are correlated. They are so similar and have so many overlapping aspects that it seems obvious that they should be addressed in a synchronized and integrated manner. But in practice, this is rarely the case for a variety of reasons. In the next section, we explore the case for an integrated approach to CPM and GRC and the barriers in the way.

Making the Case for CPM and GRC Integration

The case for an integrated approach to CPM and GRC amounts to the following argument:

- ✔ Both CPM and GRC are involved with monitoring business activity.
- ✔ Both CPM and GRC are part of virtually every business process in the enterprise.
- ✔ When designing a business process, the needs of both CPM and GRC should be incorporated so that monitoring, compliance, and risk management are part of the normal way of doing business.
- ✔ Addressing CPM and GRC in an integrated fashion will result in cost savings, better information, and improvements in the quality of both CPM and GRC processes.

Companies set their overall business strategy and have a need to tie in key risks associated with the overall strategy. For example, say that a company's key strategy is to enter the Chinese market. The KPI for this objective is to grow market share in China by 10 percent of the company's overall revenue by only investing $5 million on the overall plan. Before the company executes on this key objective of entering the Chinese market, management needs to know what risks are involved, such as infrastructure, resources, market conditions, and regulations. In addition, besides evaluating the risks of entering the Chinese market, how will the company track against the $5 million plan and ensure profitability against its budget? In this example, you can see the need to tie in CPM (for planning, profitability, and actuals against budgets) with GRC (for measuring risk and monitoring regulations).

Although this argument is theoretically compelling to most people, in practice, CPM and GRC are frequently not integrated.

Understanding obstacles to integration

The convergence of CPM and GRC faces a variety of obstacles. First of all, both CPM and GRC are in their early stage of definition and acceptance. Just a short time ago, CPM and GRC were only addressed by point solutions that handled a single area, such as managing Sarbanes-Oxley compliance. Now, point solutions compete with integrated suites that address the whole problem. The notion of an integrated suite of solutions that addresses both CPM and GRC is only just starting to appear on the horizon. Many analysts predict that this convergence will happen quickly and CPM and GRC will soon be thought of together, but this idea is still in its infancy.

Another obstacle is that the integrated approach may run into organizational and political barriers. If a department is in charge of GRC, it may not want to become part of the CPM department, or vice versa. If someone is in control of a niche function, she may not want to see it integrated into another department. This sort of barrier is common to many efforts at improving business processes.

The tendency to think of GRC, and to a lesser extent CPM, as pass/fail activities also reduces the appetite for pursuing an integrated approach. The "tone at the top," meaning the attitude management expresses about the importance of an activity, is an important element of a successful program. When the goal is to focus only on compliance at the lowest possible cost, opportunities for integration are hard to pursue.

Competition for resources can also slow any progress toward pursuing an integrated approach. CPM and GRC are often seen only to produce enterprise-wide benefits, which means that it may sometimes be hard to find advocates for improving these processes. Although high-quality information is of benefit to every level of a company, unless a specific champion for it emerges at some level, an integrated approach will not be pursued.

Past efforts at creating dashboards for executives can also be a barrier. Some of these efforts failed to live up to expectations and left senior executives with a lasting sense of disappointment. Even though service-oriented architecture (with its ability to refresh data frequently across the network) and improved enterprise software makes information more accessible, some executives are reluctant to pursue such projects because of past failures.

The negative effect of excessive scrutiny is another objection to increased monitoring of the sort that comes with an integrated approach to CPM and GRC. Some companies argue that they don't want to make employees feel that Big Brother is watching them as they pursue their activities. Although it may be true that expressing distrust of employees can be damaging to morale, collecting more information doesn't have to be negative. Expressing clear KPIs and KRIs along with targets for performance can provide employees with a sense of relief because they have clear guidance about what is expected of them.

Instrumenting the enterprise

Perhaps the best way to understand the convergence of CPM and GRC is to step back and take an abstract view. The goal of both CPM and GRC is to monitor other activities and then provide information to help improve their effectiveness, efficiency, and form. Both CPM and GRC collect data that summarizes the activity of the business processes of the enterprise. To a large extent, CPM is looking to quantify certain activities (How much revenue? How much expense? How efficient was a process?). GRC is frequently looking to see that certain activities took place (Was a credit check obtained and was the process followed?) as well as quantities (Is too much purchasing flowing through a single supplier, creating a risk?).

In both cases, after the information is gathered and analyzed, a process of informing someone may be initiated that reports on the failure or success of the business process in meeting its goals. In this way, the information collected by both CPM and GRC leads to the creation and execution of new processes for reporting and problem resolution.

The goal of most efforts at improving CPM and GRC is also the same; that is, to take point activities and merge them into an integrated whole. The information both CPM and GRC provide is much more valuable when it is timely. But in many cases, information for both CPM and GRC is collected through manual processes that create data that is stale, weeks or months behind the actual performance of the enterprise. Using such data is like attempting to drive a car by looking in the rearview mirror.

To avoid delays in creating high-quality information, the process of collecting the data must be built into the business processes. This is the goal of most improvement programs for CPM and GRC. But the highest level of efficiency is obtained when the needs of both CPM and GRC are taken into account when designing a fully instrumented business process. When this happens, information about both CPM and GRC is available as soon as possible, which allows quick reaction time to solve problems or manage risks. Efficiencies from this integrated approach result from the fact that common data, activities, and people are leveraged across both CPM and GRC.

Often improvements in GRC are promoted based on the goal of "keeping the CFO out of jail." But this narrow perspective obscures the larger benefit of improved instrumentation of a business. In the fast changing modern marketplace where risks can appear in a flash, running your business based on numbers that are stale and old is worse than going to jail (okay, some may argue this point). For this reason, some CFOs have stopped attributing investments in better instrumentation to compliance. Getting better data about the business in a timely fashion helps both compliance and running the business. How can you tell the difference between data for compliance and data for performance? Some CFOs say you can't tell the difference and have stopped trying to make this distinction.

So, from a high level, the value and efficiencies of integrated CPM and GRC are clear. But business happens at the level of detail. How will an integrated approach improve my day-to-day operations? Read on to find out.

Collecting the payoff from CPM and GRC integration

A variety of benefits flow from an integrated approach. Perhaps the most profound is a sense of security. When CPM and GRC are integrated, you are looking at reports and dashboards that reflect the current state of the business. Answers to the following questions are readily available: How are we performing? Are we in compliance? Are our risks growing? Without integration of CPM and GRC, the answers to such questions are only available in hindsight. How are we doing? We won't know for a month.

Providing immediate access to performance and compliance data also improves the payoff in groups dedicated to performance. These groups stop acting as human integrators who manually assemble needed information. They cease to be in reactive mode, jumping to address problems, and are more often seeking out new kinds of problems. Risk can be sought out systematically, not discovered after the fact.

The clock speed of a business can also move faster. If you know that you have an accurate view of the performance of your business and your risks are being monitored, you can devolve responsibility to the edges of the business and let everything run faster in a more distributed manner.

Some analysts see the integration and automation of CPM and GRC as the only remedy to the faster pace of change and higher risk profile of the modern business environment. These analysts suggest we have reached an inflection point for most large businesses. The complexity of the modern enterprise has outstripped the informal performance and compliance approaches of the previous generation. One simple formulation of this viewpoint comes in the recommendation to integrate, take an enterprise perspective, and then automate

CPM and GRC processes. The enterprise must be fully instrumented not as a luxury but as the only way to steer the car. To revisit our driving analogy, instead of looking in the rear view mirror, integrated CPM and GRC turns the lights on and allows you to see obstacles and risks sooner and to drive faster.

In the next couple of sections, we look at two examples that help illustrate the practical benefits of integrated CPM and GRC.

Supplier concentration

Imagine that you work in a manufacturing firm and that your ability to produce certain products depends on delivery of components from suppliers. As part of your GRC program, you institute a search for concentration in specific suppliers of key components so you can identify potential vulnerabilities.

In the typical nonintegrated approach to GRC, you might have analysts examine the bill of materials for products being manufactured, enter the key components into a spreadsheet, sort them by supplier, and then identify the suppliers that pose the most risk. Then a program could be initiated to find alternative suppliers. For that moment in time, you understand your supplier concentration and have mitigated the risk.

An integrated approach would recognize that the concentration of risk in suppliers will change over time. Identifying and managing concentration would be made part of routine operations. Here's how this might work:

- ✔ The bill of materials for each product would be extracted on a monthly basis into an automated report that would sort the components by supplier to reveal any concentration. Concentrations above a certain level would trigger an event that would notify the appropriate executives.

- ✔ The report and any events would be reviewed during a monthly GRC meeting to determine how they should be remediated.

- ✔ The task of finding a new supplier, redesigning products to reduce concentration, or improving the service-level agreement with the supplier would be assigned to the appropriate executives.

- ✔ Product design staff would be part of the team managing concentration so that new product design could be performed in such a way to avoid excessive concentration in one supplier.

In this way, the management of a specific risk, supplier concentration, has become part of an improved process that provides the company with more information about supplier concentration to meet CPM objectives and has baked risk remediation processes into standard operating procedure.

Loan processing

Loan processing offers another example of the convergence of CPM and GRC. The process of making loans in most financial institutions is highly distributed. Hundreds or thousands of people are involved in evaluating the risk in each loan application and determining whether the loan meets the acceptable parameters. The acceptable parameters change constantly as interest rates and market conditions change.

Much of the processing of loans can be automated to improve the performance of a company. In automating loan processing and approval, the loan must be evaluated to determine if it meets certain parameters. One compliance issue related to such automation called "configuration persistence." It can be possible for someone to change the parameters in a system and then run a loan through that is improper, fraudulent, or perhaps a legitimate exception. The process of automation, which was introduced to increase performance, could be supplemented by a compliance event that is raised each time the configuration parameters are changed. If the change is not approved by an appropriate person within a certain amount of time, it would be escalated to more senior executives. In this way, automation to improve performance is extended to address compliance.

Seeing CPM and GRC Integration in Practice

In the next few sections, we look at a few more detailed examples that illustrate the opportunity of CPM and GRC integration.

The intersection of actuals

CPM and GRC take a different view of *actuals*, the numbers that reflect the financial and operational performance of a business. To CPM, the quantity of these numbers is the important thing. (How much revenue? How much expense? How much income?). To GRC, the traceability and auditability of the numbers are primary. The best quality information is both accurate and auditable.

But as anyone who has worked in accounting knows, no automated system always gets everything right. Accountants and bookkeepers are always making journal entries to correct the information collected about the business. But as recent scandals have shown, journal entries may also be abused to fraudulently influence financial reports.

So the best integration of CPM and GRC would be one that addresses the intersection. Processes must be in place to allow journal entries to be made to increase the accuracy of the numbers, but these journal entries must be scrutinized and audited as an enforced policy to make sure that no fraud is taking place. A good GRC system will also enforce segregation of duties to mitigate the risk of fraud. The faster the journal entries can be made, while still ensuring good governance, the better information a company will have — with minimal external audit expenses.

Strategy, risk, and planning

Almost all strategic plans include an expected scenario along with pessimistic and optimistic variants. Why? Because every strategy faces risks and obstacles that may slow it down, resulting in the pessimistic scenario. Or perhaps things will go better than expected, resulting in the optimistic scenario.

An integrated approach to CPM and GRC puts KPIs and key risk indicators (KRIs) in place to measure the risks and in effect determine which scenario is accurate. From a CPM perspective, the measures help determine what the performance is and how close or far the company is from its expected scenario. From a GRC perspective, the measures indicate magnitude of risks that a company is facing. From both perspectives, having a clear picture allows the right remediation to be taken in a timely manner.

For example, if a company decides to change its strategy from acquiring new customers to increasing the share of wallet from existing customers, the KPIs that define success also change. Revenue per customer becomes more important than new customers added each quarter. The risks change as well. An integrated program of CPM and GRC allows the focus to shift not just at a high level, but at the level of instrumentation that gives specific guidance to those carrying out the change in strategy.

Governance and strategy

Strategy reflects what the business is intending to do; that is, what decisions or choices the business is going to make to achieve whatever it has decided to achieve. In this way, strategy reflects the *what* of an organization's goals. CPM has historically focused on measuring how well the *what* is being achieved. Governance really reflects the *how* — the codes of conduct and the policies and frameworks that reflect how the strategy should be realized.

The case for integration of CPM and GRC is based on the convergence of the *what* and the *how*. The mechanisms to keep track of each overlap in many ways that must be balanced. The focus on *what* over *how* leads to the kinds of errors that have been reported in recent scandals, where the pressure to produce results overcame governance mechanisms. Overemphasis of *how* over *what* can lead to an organization focused on compliance at the expense of performance. At its worst, this means a company has perfectly clean audits but goes out of business.

Discovering the Reusable Technology of GRC

One of the benefits of taking a serious approach to GRC is that new capabilities are brought into an organization. GRC processes and supporting software exist to monitor activities of a business. What is less well understood is that the software platform that supports GRC is actually a framework that can be used for many other purposes besides GRC, including CPM, business intelligence, process optimization, and automating processes for problem resolution.

Right now, GRC software is a bit further along in its maturity, so this section briefly describes the aspects of the software platform that supports GRC. In the past, this same layer of software has sometimes been referred to as the GRC foundation. Whatever it is called, a GRC platform usually provides the following capabilities that have multiple uses.

Repository

A GRC platform must have a repository that stores unstructured items such as documents and also structured information that describes controls, processes, events, and so on. The repository must have some sort of retention management so that auditors can see how information changed over time and who changed it. All sorts of information can be stored in the repository, including predefined parameters and process descriptions that tailor the GRC application to a particular industry or purpose.

Document management

Documents that describe strategy, policies, controls, and reports delivered to regulators all must be kept in a central location with versions and a historical archive. A GRC platform must have a document management solution to perform this function. Frequently, this solution is implemented through a standard that allows any document management system that meets the standard to be used for the repository. An integrated approach to GRC and CPM leverages the documentation in a shared repository from strategy creation all the way down to spend compliance of the budget against the strategy.

Case management

When a task or issue arises, people are assigned to address it. Case management functionality in a GRC platform provides an environment for tracking the work done on a case and supporting other forms of collaboration. A case ties GRC and CPM together when, for example, someone in finance makes several journal entry reversals that could impact the actuals for the quarter. Such an occurrence would automatically send the CFO or VP of Finance a case alerting them about the compliance risk and providing them with overall reporting visibility.

Workflow

GRC platforms frequently support defined workflows for approvals, case management, and other tasks that require participate of many people in a series of well-defined steps. With the addition of CPM in the process, the workflow can also be tied to all the steps in the month-end closing process along with any GRC-related substeps.

Process modeling

GRC platforms frequently support forms of business modeling that can be used to describe the processes in a company. These models are then used to analyze the efficiency of processes and to determine where and how to implement controls. In CPM, the business templates can tie into GRC to expedite key processes such as month-end close. In addition, CPM has a predictive engine that shows the root cause and effect of issues that can also be tied into GRC business modeling.

Policy engine

A *policy engine* is part of a GRC platform that allows declarative expression of policies that are implemented in the systems to enforce certain activities using mechanisms of the GRC platform and of enterprise applications. CPM also has processes and documentation, such as how to close the books at year end that are tied to GRC policy engine.

Rule engine

A *rule engine* is a way of expressing rules that govern the behavior of the GRC platform. Rules can be used to determine how to handle events, what to do if a control is violated, how to distribute reports, and so on. Expressing automation as rules allows a large number of people to participate in determining the behavior of the GRC platform. In CPM, rules are set for activities, such as cost allocation per headcount for each facility that resides in the rules engine. When the value for a rule is above the threshold, a case is created and assigned to the relevant user. The user is then referred back to the documentation or policy engine for information on how to fix the broken process.

Controls

A GRC platform provides an environment for expressing the design of a system of controls and implementing and tracking the information gathered from them. Preventative or detective controls can be implemented in the GRC platform or at the direction of the GRC platform in enterprise applications, the network, or through other means. Any portion of CPM, whether it's budgeting, booking of actuals, the consolidation process, setting of the overall strategy, or monitoring and measuring profitability can be tied to a control within GRC. For example, if a product profit margin is below 10 percent, a control can be put in place in GRC, allowing the user to be alerted if the profit margin becomes too thin.

Reporting

GRC platforms usually are able to produce reports as part of their basic functionality as well as exporting data to data marts or data warehouses for more advanced analysis. The marriage of CPM with GRC reporting enables the production of optimal analytics for performance as well as the ability to measure the effectiveness of governance and compliance in the organization.

Standardized interfaces to components

A GRC platform usually implements many of its components, such as databases, data warehouses, and document repositories using standardized interfaces that allow the implementation to be provisioned by any product that implements the standard. CPM also ties into these key interfaces and enables companies to leverage their underlying systems to extract master data and leverage it for these components.

Composite apps on the platform

All of these components of GRC and CPM can be combined to create new applications to automate processes or provide environments for special kinds of analysis. Such composite applications can be used for GRC, CPM, or any purpose that is required, such as optimization or management of specific processes or line of business.

Part V
The Part of Tens

The 5th Wave   By Rich Tennant

"I always assumed elves just naturally dresssed like this. I never imagined it was a condition of employment."

In this part . . .

Your favorite part of any Dummies book might be, as ours is, the Part of Tens. You'll find first and foremost a Part of Ten to help drive your GRC success, providing lessons learned from successful GRC implementations. The ever-complex global trade area gets its own Part of Ten to sum up what to do in this arena. And for your continued GRC edification and entertainment, we lead you to some great resources for additional reading, surfing, and reference.

Chapter 16

Top Ten GRC Strategies

*A*re you eager to get started with GRC? This chapter details the strategies used in the most successful GRC projects.

Evaluate Which of the Most Prevalent GRC Issues Apply to You

The most prevalent GRC issues facing companies include audit compliance, segregation of duties, and internal productivity and resource availability.

For audit compliance, you should

- ✔ Establish an approach and process to manage risks.
- ✔ Pinpoint sources of deficiencies and data sources to identify preventative measures.
- ✔ Eliminate conflicting testing methods and reconciliations.

For segregation of duties, you'll want to

- ✔ Identify business functions that produce risks when executed by one person.
- ✔ Gain risk visibility on 100 percent of user population.
- ✔ Perform risk analysis before committing and approving changes to access controls.

To improve internal productivity and resource availability

- ✔ **Focus on prevention.** It's better to prevent bad things from happening in the first place than to simply detect them after the fact.

- ✔ **Document test results and violations by business process and organization.** Doing so will give you a scorecard of what's happening in various business processes and units.

- ✔ **Select controls and tolerances concurrent with organization policies, procedures, and regulations.** In other words, you don't want alarms going off all the time — just when something warrants further investigation.

Adopt Best Practices

The 2006 SAP GRC Benchmarking Survey identified seven best practices for GRC:

- ✔ **Document well and store the documentation centrally.** All processes should be well-documented and stored in a central repository, including the documentation of policies, work papers, and evidence to meet requirements of Sarbanes-Oxley sections 302 and 404.

- ✔ **Automate as many controls as possible.** The majority of process control testing is automated and can be scheduled for appropriate locations, business units, or legal entities.

- ✔ **Automate the flow of manual controls to keep them moving.** Manual control testing is streamlined with automated task assignments, guided procedures, and workflows.

- ✔ **Find segregation of duties (SoD) violations automatically.** SoD risk identification and remediation should be performed automatically, across multiple ERP environments and instances.

- ✔ **Automate user provisioning and changes.** User access administration and change management should be automated with approval notification and mandatory compliance verification.

- ✔ **Make business people responsible.** Business process managers should be accountable for control documentation and testing, not Internal Audit or IT.

- ✔ **Audit yourself.** Internal Audit should regularly perform audits to cover the effectiveness and efficiency of operations, the reliability of financial reporting, compliance with applicable laws and regulations, and safeguarding of assets.

Implement Key GRC Strategies

You can reduce risks, time, and cost by putting these plays into your GRC playbook:

✔ Promote effective business personnel participation.

✔ Reduce effort by automating.

✔ Segregate business and technical issues.

✔ Attack the sources of problems to promote prevention.

✔ Leverage processes to integrate best practices into the organization.

Set Yourself Up for Success

Here are some success factors that can help you ensure the success of your GRC implementation project:

✔ Identify the right people to help:

- Active executive participation
- A good project manager
- Decision makers
- People who can encourage collaboration among all parties
- People who have deep knowledge of the business processes

✔ Employee and company knowledge are essential.

✔ Don't wait for the perfect time or future functionality.

✔ Focus on priorities and methodologies.

✔ Focus on high-risk areas, not all risks.

Watch Out for Danger Signs

Just like you work to ensure success, you have to watch out to look for signs of the following problems as well:

✔ **A big bang approach.** Don't be overly ambitious. Do not implement all the products at one time.

✔ **Unrealistic expectations.** Make sure that management doesn't believe compliance can be achieved in a few weeks or when the project ends.

✔ **The project staff is made up of contractors only.** Make sure key internal staff works on the project as well. Having only contractors assigned to the project means that little knowledge transfer will take place. Furthermore, contractors don't have a relationship with the business and won't know the unique circumstances and challenges your company faces.

✔ **No authority.** Project leaders are given little decision-making authority and are simply told to just keep doing things the way we've always done them. Successful GRC implementations require lots of input as well as latitude to make important changes.

Define GRC Roles and Responsibilities

A successful GRC implementation requires broad participation. So the first question you may hear is "What do I have to do?" Table 16-1 contains some answers, depending on who asks the question.

Table 16-1	GRC Roles and Responsibilities
Role	*Their Responsibilities*
Business process owners and business analysts	Identify risks and approve risks for monitoring
	Approve user role assignments
	Design alternative controls for mitigating risks
	Communicate access assignments or role changes to users
	Architect business processes
	Identify configuration alternatives
	Conduct gap analysis on current processes
	Explain the key control integration into the processes
Senior officers	Arbitrate conflicts between business areas

Role	Their Responsibilities
	Approve key controls and mitigating controls for high risks
Security administrator and role owners	Ownership of SAP solutions for GRC and security process
	Design and maintain rules to identify risk conditions
	Maintain the technical integrity of the roles' business purpose
	Decision maker for role changes
SAP Application Support and Compliance Team	Identify key controls
	Review automated controls for applicability of deployment
	Document processes, controls, and testing methods
	Complete surveys for control designs
Auditors and regulators	Perform risk assessment on a regular basis
	Provide specific requirements for audit purposes
	Perform periodic testing of processes and key control points
SoD Rule Keeper	Maintain controls over rules to ensure integrity

Shake Down the People Who Know

Have policy building sessions to emphasize commitment and collaboration between business, technical, and audit personnel. Cover the following topics and make sure you get the deliverables mentioned in Table 16-2.

Table 16-2	Suggested Guidelines for Policy Building Sessions	
Participants	*Topics*	*Deliverables*
Executives	Sensitive information and transactions	Sensitive transactions and data
Process Managers	Process risks and process overlaps	Segregation of duties risks between processes
Auditors	Segregation of duties and internal controls	Risks and control omissions
Security Administrators	Security design and processes	Naming conventions and approval processes

Move to Strategic Adoption of Automated Controls

Manual controls can only check a sample of transactions, and the controls have to be tested every day. Automatic controls check every transaction, and after initial testing, can simply run, allowing you to manage by exception. Not all controls can be automated controls, but the more automated controls you put in place, the easier your job becomes.

Adopt Strategies for Cleaning Up Access Control

Segregation of duties violations are largely prevented through effective access control. Because these problems have evolved over time, you'll need to get everyone on board in cleaning up this area.

Be sure to separate technical and business issues:

- Roles and profiles belong to IT.
- User assignments and circumstances belong to business.
- Collaboration of both required to validate results.

Segregate role cleanup from user cleanup:

- ✔ Roles must not contain conflicts.

- ✔ Business managers can then take unneeded access away from particular roles or specify an alternative if the access must be kept, such as additional supervision.

Sometimes changing a business process or responsibilities is much easier than trying to build roles around the process.

Eliminate risks and use mitigation for exceptions:

- ✔ Investigate and implement controls to eliminate the risk.

- ✔ Ensure users only have the access they need.

- ✔ When you need to make exceptions, identify alternative controls, and decide who will monitor them.

Getting Your GRC Project Going and Keeping It Going

Begin your GRC efforts by having some business workshops to launch the project. Here are some things to do at those workshops:

- ✔ Identify risks to be monitored.

- ✔ Discuss industry-specific risks.

- ✔ Look at which areas of the business currently have role conflicts that must be resolved (hint: IT and risk management professionals may already know what these are and can point them out).

- ✔ Start thinking about mitigating controls.

Like any effort, the focus on GRC can fizzle if not nurtured. Have a quarterly business meeting to keep the GRC effort going:

- ✔ After initial implementations, quarterly meetings help reinforce GRC efforts.

- ✔ Provides assurance new risks are recognized as changes occur.

- ✔ Risk identification and recognition becomes routine.

Chapter 17

Ten Best Practices in Global Trade

*G*lobalization means a lot more of us are involved in global trade these days. Here are ten best practices to help you navigate these complicated waters. (And don't forget to read Chapter 8 for much more information.)

Automate or Else

Global importing and exporting has grown so complex it's absolutely crucial to automate your import and export processes. Dozens of countries, hundreds of regulations, and thousands of orders can quickly create a mountain of paperwork. More importantly, it's simply not feasible to hand check each order to ensure it complies with global trade regulations. Rolling the dice can have major consequences for companies — large fines and public disgrace. The best solution is to put in place a software system — such as SAP GRC Global Trade Services — that automates all of the essential import and export tasks.

Don't Go to Pieces

Remember the old war between VHS and Beta? Customers who bought one system couldn't use tapes from the other and vice versa. It was a big mess. Today, some companies handle global trade the same way. Different departments within each company often manage imports and exports using processes and tools that are not necessarily compatible company wide. Doing this is a recipe for disorder, inefficiency, and mistakes. The best way to handle importing and exporting is to create a central repository for all of your global trade data and standardize on best practices for global trade.

Make Sure You Can Trust Your Partners

You might spend months centralizing your efforts and setting up the perfect global trade system, but your hard work can easily be compromised by the companies to which you outsource key importing and exporting tasks. A law firm might misclassify your product or a customs broker might not file import documents properly. Choosing partners who are as committed to excellence as you are is important. Check their background and research their reputation before hiring them.

Avoid Importing Delays

The old cliché is especially true when it comes to importing. Delays at the border can have major costs. Goods may not arrive in time for the all-important holiday shopping season. Parts arriving late can bring manufacturing to a halt and the uncertainty of when goods will arrive means expensive safety stock must be kept on hand. A clearly delineated importing plan is the best way to stave off these border snags. The plan should feature a good customs broker (if needed), a system for processing documents, classifying goods, and clearing goods through Customs.

Get On Board with the Government's High-Tech Documenting Processes

The government is not usually known for its tech savvy, but one area where it has made strides in the last decade or so is in importing and exporting documentation. In fact, many trade documents are required to be filed electronically with the U.S. government. Even though some companies have shirked these new regulations, it's critical to have a software system in place to file these documents, rather than pay a third party an arm and a leg to handle it for you.

Know Who Is Allowed at the Party

We all know people who can ruin a good party, so we don't invite them. It's no different in the export business. More and more countries and government agencies maintain growing lists of "restricted parties" that can not be shipped to. These bans are usually on terrorist-related groups and can change daily. In addition, shipping some goods to countries that are embargoed or are sanctioned is illegal. Needless to say, violating these restrictions can result in major penalties, bad press, and jail time. The best way to avoid these pitfalls is to implement an automated system to flag shipments that might violate embargoes, "restricted parties" lists, or other government regulations.

Know Who You're Shipping to

Security can be tricky to navigate in the post-September 11 world. One of the trickiest aspects for exporters is making sure that their goods don't fall into the wrong hands. Under global trade regulations, a shipper can be held responsible if terrorists use its goods for nefarious purposes — even if the goods are used in a way that the company never intended. (For example, coffee filters were used by terrorists to sift anthrax, a use coffee filter makers never anticipated.) Companies can sidestep these potential headaches by setting up a system to flag goods that could possibly cause problems if they are exported.

Get the Right Licenses

It seems like there is a license for everything these days. Exports, it turns out, are no different. The licenses aren't just required for obvious goods like firearms, but for advanced technology, medical devices, and other classes of goods. Failing to get a proper license can result in major fines.

Take the Free Money

Companies leave millions of dollars on the table each year by not taking advantage of international trade agreements. The North American Free Trade Agreement (NAFTA), the Central America-Dominican Republic-United States

Free Trade Agreement (CAFTA-DR) and others offer companies breaks on tariffs, if their products qualify for the program. It can be a headache to determine if your products meet the standards, but software can make the task much simpler. Why throw away free money?

Leave a Paper Trail

An international shipment can create as many as 35 different documents as an item travels to its destination. Saving and keeping track of these documents may be a hassle, but it has become absolutely crucial. Because companies can be held liable for shipping dangerous items to terrorists or even for terrorists misusing their items for bad purposes, it's important to have a paper trail documenting the precautions you took to follow international trade regulations. In addition, accounting regulations enacted in the wake of the Enron collapse mean companies must keep detailed financial records of importing and exporting transactions. Audit trails are important to keeping your company, not to mention the regulators, happy.

Chapter 18

Ten Groups of GRC Thought Leadership Resources

As you've seen already if you've read this book from cover to cover, GRC covers a lot of ground. Don't hold it against us if we give you a few more than ten resources in this Part of Ten. Instead, how about ten categories of resources?

GRC Resources

In this section, we detail some all-around GRC resources, including some links to information about SAP's GRC solutions.

Web sites

Here are some general Web sites devoted to GRC:

- ✔ SAP solutions for GRC: The official Web site. www.sap.com/solutions/grc/index.epx

- ✔ SAP Developer Network (SDN) includes a community for GRC, the Governance Risk and Compliance BPX Community. This online community provides blogs, forums, articles, and more on the topic of GRC: www.sdn.sap.com/irj/sdn/bpx-grc

✔ Open Compliance and Ethics Group (OCEG), a nonprofit that provides GRC guidelines and standards, a community for GRC professionals, information about GRC events, and publishes *Compliance Weekly*: `www.oceg.org/`

✔ GRC Roundtable, a community for end-users and others seeking help with GRC-related issues: `www.grcroundtable.org/`

Blogs

Following is a list of GRC-related blogs:

✔ Corporate Integrity LLC's GRC Pundit blog, authored by Michael Rasmussen: `http://corp-integrity.blogspot.com/`

✔ Ahmad Shahzad's blog: `http://blogs.bluehammock.com/blog/8`

✔ The Village View by Mark Crofton: `http://mhjcsoftware.blogspot.com/`

✔ Amit Chatterjee's blog: `http://amitchatterjee.com/`

✔ James Governor's GRC blogs: `www.redmonk.com/jgovernor/topic/grc/`

✔ Thomas Otter's blog, Vendorprisey: `http://theotherthomasotter.wordpress.com/?s=grc`

✔ AccMan's blog regularly covers compliance issues: `www.accmanpro.com/category/compliance/`

✔ Sometimes Dennis Howlett blogs on SDN as well: "What are we missing in GRC?": `www.sdn.sap.com/irj/sdn/weblogs?blog=/pub/wlg/7730`

✔ On his Deal Architect blog, Vinnie Mirchandani frequently writes about compliance (the rest of his blog is interesting as well): `http://dealarchitect.typepad.com/deal_architect/compliance_sox_others/index.html`

Online journals

You may find the following online journals helpful as well:

✔ Compliance Executive: `www.complianceexecutive.com/`

✔ Compliance Week: `www.complianceweek.com/`

✔ The CRO (Corporate Responsibility Officer): `www.thecro.com/`

Risk Resources

Enterprise risk management is a fascinating topic, and you'll find a wealth of information that lets you learn from the experience of others and build up your risk management expertise.

Web sites

Here are some risk management Web sites:

- ✔ SAP GRC Risk Management: `www.sap.com/solutions/grc/riskmanagement/index.epx`
- ✔ Risk and Insurance Management Society. Conferences, articles, white papers, and much more: `www.rims.org`
- ✔ Operational risk. Sounds narrow, but it's a very rich site: `http://oprisk.austega.com/index.php`
- ✔ Risk Television. News and, as implied, video: `http://risk.mashnetworks.com/newsroom.aspx`

Blogs

These are some good risk management blogs:

- ✔ "Risk management ... links to business value" by Amit Chatterjee: `www.sdn.sap.com/irj/sdn/weblogs?blog=/pub/wlg/6680`
- ✔ David Rowe's Risk Management blog: `www.sungard.com/blogs/riskManagement/`

Books

Yes, we still like those old-fashioned things with pages, too. (After all, you're holding this one, aren't you?):

- ✔ Peter L. Bernstein. *Against the Gods: The Remarkable Story of Risk*. John Wiley & Sons, Inc., 1996.
- ✔ Beaumont Vance and Joanna Makomaski. *Enterprise Risk Management For Dummies*. John Wiley & Sons, Inc., 2008

- Barton, Thomas L., Shenkir, William G, and Walker, *Paul L. Making Enterprise Risk Management Pay Off: How Leading Companies Implement Risk Management.* FT Press, 2002.

SOX Resources

When people think of compliance, they often think of SOX. If you're looking for more information about SOX, here are some places to dig in.

Web sites and forums

Some SOX-related Web sites:

- Sarbanes-Oxley Act. Purely informative, section by section, searchable version of the law itself: `www.sarbanes-oxley.com/search.php?q=404`

- SOX Online. There aren't too many sites you can hit for both information and entertainment. This, believe it or not, is one of the best: `www.sox-online.com/`

- SOX TV: `http://sox.mashnetworks.com/newsroom.aspx`

- The Sarbanes-Oxley Act Forum: `www.sarbanes-oxley-forum.com/index.php`

Books

A list of SOX-related books:

- Scott Green, *Manager's Guide to the Sarbanes-Oxley Act: Improving Internal Controls to Prevent Fraud*, John Wiley & Sons, Inc., 2004.

- Jill Gilbert Welytok. *Sarbanes-Oxley For Dummies*, 2nd Edition. John Wiley & Sons, Inc., 2008.

- Stephen M. Bainbridge, *The Complete Guide to Sarbanes-Oxley*, p. 12, June 12, 2007 Adams Media: Trade Paperback ISBN: 1-59869-267-9

Financial Compliance Resources

As we've discussed, there's more to compliance than just SOX. Here are some resources for complying with regulations in other countries, as well as resources on the Corrupt Foreign Practices Act.

J-SOX

Some resources on J-SOX (J-SOX is the Japanese law comparable to SOX in the US.):

- ✔ J-SOX Insights. Frequently Asked Questions about J-SOX. A FAQ about J-SOX from Protiviti Independent Risk Consulting: `www.sdn.sap.com/irj/sdn/go/portal/prtroot/docs/library/uuid/40d44037-09 aa-2910-e5b0-edd182ed9cec`

- ✔ J-SOX Flash Report. On November 21, 2006, the Financial Services Agency (FSA) of Japan released a 93 page draft of "Implementation Standards for Evaluation and Audit of Internal Control over Financial Reporting." This report provides detailed information on this legislation: `www.sdn.sap.com/irj/sdn/go/portal/prtroot/docs/library/ uuid/209c60c7-06aa-2910-ed82-84f6f93155c4`

- ✔ Compliance Week article on J-SOX. "Japan Takes First Step Into J-SOX World" by Yuriko Nagano, September 25, 2007: `www.complianceweek. com/index.cfm?fuseaction=article.viewArticle&article_ ID=3712`

Basel II

An article by Dan Ilett that explains Basel II with humor and style: `www. silicon.com/financialservices/0,3800010322,39161667,00.htm`

Foreign Corrupt Practices Act

Under the Foreign Corrupt Practices Act, companies are responsible for the behavior of their partners, especially in areas such as bribery. For a 1977 act, this law has seen a sudden burst of prosecutions since 2005:

- ✔ Foreign Corrupt Practices Act (FCPA). Information from the US Department of Justice: `www.usdoj.gov/criminal/fraud/fcpa/`

- ✔ An article that summarizes the trend toward FCPA prosecutions very well: "United States: The Foreign Corrupt Practices Act: The Next Corporate Scandal?" By Christopher J. Steskal, Fenwick & West LLP, 29 January 2008: (`www.mondaq.com/article.asp?articleid=56616`)

- ✔ The FCPA Blog: `http://fcpablog.blogspot.com/`

Access Control and Process Control Resources

Access control and process control are key areas for any GRC implementation.

Web sites

Some control-related Web sites:

- ✓ SAP GRC Access Control helps identify and prevent access and authorization risks: www.sap.com/solutions/grc/accessand authorization/index.epx
- ✓ SAP GRC Process Control helps optimize business operations and ensure compliance by centrally monitoring key controls for business processes and cross-enterprise IT systems: www.sap.com/solutions/ grc/grcprocesscontrol/index.epx

Articles

Check out the following articles for more information on controls:

- ✓ SAP Best Practices for GRC Access Control: http://help.sap.com/ bp_grcv152/GRC_US/HTML/index.htm
- ✓ SAP GRC Access Control: Offline-Mode Risk Analysis Article: www.sdn.sap.com/irj/sdn/go/portal/prtroot/docs/library/ uuid/20a06e3f-24b6-2a10-dba0-e8174339c47c
- ✓ Introduction to SAP Governance Risk and Compliance by Vikas Chauhan: www.sdn.sap.com/irj/sdn/weblogs?blog=/pub/wlg/6298

Wikis

SAP GRC Access Control How-to guides. You can find a wealth of materials about SAP's access control product on this page of the SDN wiki: https:// wiki.sdn.sap.com/wiki/x/_so

IT GRC Resources

The following Web sites offer a number of important tips on IT GRC:

- ✔ The Data Governance Institute provides a wealth of information about IT GRC issues: www.datagovernance.com/

- ✔ ITC Compliance Institute. Provides compliance webcasts, publishes the *IT Compliance Journal*, has a white paper archive and a regulations library, all of which are searchable: www.itcinstitute.com/

Blogs

Some blogs focused on IT GRC:

- ✔ Alan Calder is the author of *IT Governance: a Manager's Guide to Data Security and BS7799/ISO17799*, now in its third edition. http://alancalder.blogspot.com/

- ✔ HIPAA blog by Jeff Drummond. http://hipaablog.blogspot.com/

Global Trade Resources

Global Trade is one of the most complex areas of all, as you'll see by the sheer number of government Web sites we list.

Web sites

The following are resources on global trade:

- ✔ SAP GRC Global Trade Services – Manage all foreign trade processes with a comprehensive platform to ensure trade compliance, expedited cross-border transactions, and optimum utilization of trade agreements: www.sap.com/solutions/grc/globaltradeservices/index.epx

- ✔ The Bureau of Industry and Security's web site provides news as well as a host of useful resources about importing and exporting in the U.S.: www.bis.doc.gov/index.htm

- ✔ U.S. Customs and Border Protection: www.cbp.gov/

- ✔ U.S. International Trade Commission: www.usitc.gov/

✔ U.S. Customs and Border Protection: www.cbp.gov/

✔ U.S. International Trade Commission: www.usitc.gov/

✔ U.S. Department of Treasury: www.treas.gov

✔ U.S. Directorate of Defense Trade Controls: http://pmddtc.state.gov

✔ Office of U.S. Trade Representative: www.ustr.gov/

✔ Export.gov: www.export.gov/index.asp

✔ European Commission Tariff and Customs: http://ec.europa.eu/

✔ U.S. Office of Regional Security and Arms Control: www.state.gov/t/pm/rsat/

✔ Office of Foreign Asset Control: www.treasury.gov/offices/enforcement/ofac/

✔ C-TPAT information: http://www.geosbush.com/ctpat.htm

✔ C-TPAT press release: www.customs.gov/xp/cgov/newsroom/news_releases/01312008.xml

Blogs

Some global trade related blogs:

✔ Denied Party Mayhem by Ahmad Shahzad: http://blogs.bluehammock.com/node/43

✔ A Hong Kong-based blog on global trade issues: http://policynetwork.blogs.com/ipnhongkong/

✔ Free Trade Blog. A study on the impact of FTAs on IT-based business, with a focus on the DR-CAFTA agreement. A project of the AHRC Research Centre for Studies in Intellectual Property and Technology law in the School of Law at the University of Edinburgh, Scotland: http://freetrade.opencontentlaw.org/

✔ Global Trade Blog. Matt Babcock's blog on global trade and business topics: http://globaltradeblog.blogspot.com/

Employee Health and Safety Resources

Let's face it: all companies have employees, so everyone has to worry about employee safety (ok, maybe razor blade factories have to worry a little more than most).

Web sites and online journals

Here are some employee health and safety Web sites and online journals:

- US Occupational Health and Safety Administration: `www.osha.gov/`
- Occupational Health and Safety Online: `www.ohsonline.com` (magazine)

Blogs

The following are safety-related blogs:

- Safe Workplace and OSHA VPP Blog: `www.safe-workplace.com/safety-blog/`
- Root Cause Analysis Blog. Root cause analysis is a methodology that examines why an incident happened in an attempt to improve safety: `www.taproot.com/wordpress/index.php`
- The safety blog. This blog discusses forklift safety, among other topics (and it's serious, unlike that viral German forklift safety video which was serious too, but is quite humorous): `http://blog.safetyservices ompany.com/`

Articles

For more information, check out this article on workplace safety: "CII: Making Zero Accidents a Reality" by John Mathis and Jimmy Hinze. An interesting research study on the CDC's site: `www.cdc.gov/elcosh/docs/d0500/d000518/d000518.html`

Going Green Resources

Environmental compliance is a complex issue, but it's one with an upside. It's not just about following rules: Going green is about saving the planet.

Web sites

Some helpful Web sites on various environmental compliance:

- REACH resources. The main site for this emerging regulation: `http://ec.europa.eu/environment/chemicals/reach/reach_intro.htm`

- Independent Liquid Terminals Association. An informative page on REACH by an organization whose members are affected by the legislation: `www.ilta.org/LegislativeandRegulatory/Reach/Reachinfo.htm`

- Information on GHS, Globally Harmonized System of Classification and Labelling of Chemicals, a UN initiative to standardize definitions of hazardous chemicals: `www.unece.org/trans/danger/publi/ghs/ghs_welcome_e.html`

- GHS and OSHA's HCS compared by OSHA: `www.osha.gov/dsg/hazcom/GHSOSHAComparison.html`

- Earth Policy Institute, with information from author Lester R. Brown: `www.earth-policy.org`

Wikis

Check out SAP's Green 2.0 wiki:
`https://wiki.sdn.sap.com/wiki/x/FOQ`

Articles

Take a look at the following articles about companies going green:

- An article about the greening of Wal-Mart. "Soft soap?" by Jonathan Birchall, *Financial Times*, 9 September 2007: `www.ft.com/cms/s/2/fcb62b30-5eff-11dc-837c-0000779fd2ac.html`

- Wal-Mart pushes suppliers to 'go green' Company uses business-as-usual tactics to drive environmental agenda: (`www.msnbc.msn.com/id/18056716/`)

- A look at going green in the hotel industry. This article is one in a series of related articles. "Are There Good Business Reasons To Go Green?" by Arthur B. Weissman, Ph.D., President and CEO, Green Seal, Inc.: `www.hotelexecutive.com/bus_rev/pub/002/132.asp`

- "Why it pays for firms to go green. Small firms can worry about the potential extra cost of being more environmentally friendly." BBC News, Dr. Martin Gibson, President of Envirowise: `http://news.bbc.co.uk/1/hi/business/6658677.stm`

✔ LEED and green buildings: "Going green for sustainable reasons" by Dennis Domrzalski, New Mexico Business Weekly, 5/11/2007 `http://sanantonio.bizjournals.com/albuquerque/stories/2007/05/14/focus1.html?jst=s_cn_hl`

Blogs

For blogs on environmental business issues, check out the following:

✔ Andreas Vogel's blog on Green 2.0: `http://andreasonsoftware.blogspot.com/`

✔ Greenmonk Associates' blog covers a wide variety of green issues: `http://greenmonk.net/`

✔ Joel Makower's blog, Two Steps Forward, covers green business: `http://makower.typepad.com/joel_makower`. Makower contributed to the *State of Green Business 2008*, a research report downloadable from `www.stateofgreenbusiness.com/`

Books

Lester R. Brown, *Plan B 3.0: Mobilizing to Save Civilization*, W.W. Norton & Company, 2007.

Sustainability Resources

Sustainability encompasses environmental concerns, but then adds ethics, workplace diversity, and much more to the mix.

Web sites

For online resources related to sustainability, check these out:

✔ The Global Reporting Initiative's site provides a wealth of information on sustainability, including the GRI's guidelines (G3): `www.globalreporting.org/`

✔ Corporate Social Responsibility and Sustainability Wiki on SDN: `https://wiki.sdn.sap.com/wiki/x/AtY`

✔ Corporate Social Responsibility and Sustainability BPX Community: `www.sdn.sap.com/irj/sdn/bpx-csr`

Articles

For more info on sustainability, see the following articles:

- ✔ "Laying the Foundations for Sustainability with Environmental Compliance," Thursday, August 16, 2007, Simon Jacobson and Colin Masson, `www.amrresearch.com/Content/View.asp?pmillid=20644`

- ✔ "Risk and Opportunity in a Green and Sustainable World" Tuesday, June 05, 2007, John Davies `www.amrresearch.com/Content/View.asp?pmillid=20462`

Blogs and books

Check out the following blogs and books related to sustainability:

- ✔ CSR and Sustainability blogs on SDN: `www.sdn.sap.com/irj/sdn/weblogs?blog=/weblogs/topic/86`

- ✔ *World Inc.* by Bruce Piasecki: `worldincbook.com`

- ✔ *Lean and Green: Profit for Your Workplace and the Environment* by Pamela J Gordon

Glossary

access control: Access control refers to what a person can do in a computer system or application once she has signed on. Role-based access control defines a person's access to transactions according to their job function.

accounting controls: Procedures and documentation concerned with safeguarding of assets, the conduct and recording of financial transactions, and the reliability of financial records.

audit: An independent examination of a company's books to ensure that the information recorded is correct and complete.

audit committee: A committee, often including members of the board of directors, responsible for overseeing financial reporting and internal controls.

audit trail: A record of a sequence of transactions that enables an auditor to see what took place.

automated controls: Internal controls that are executed automatically by computer systems. Manual controls are executed by a person charged with that task and are typically performed on a subset of transactions. Automated controls can be executed on every relevant transaction, ensuring greater accuracy with less effort.

Basel II: An international standard for banking that regulators can use when making regulations on how much capital banks must have to offset potential risk. The more risk a bank has, the more capital it should have in place to ensure that it stays solvent. The regulation was the second such standard issued by the Basel Committee on Banking Supervision, and hence the name Basel II.

board of directors: Publicly traded companies must have a board of directors. The members of company's board of directors are elected by its shareholders. The board of directors is responsible for looking out for the interests of the shareholders as well as other stakeholders such as employees.

C-11: A 2005 Canadian law that establishes a procedure for the disclosure of wrongdoings in the public sector and ensures protection for the person who discloses them.

CAFTA-DR: Dominican Republic-Central America–United States Free Trade Agreement. According to the USDA's web site, "CAFTA–DR is a comprehensive trade agreement among Costa Rica, the Dominican Republic, El Salvador, Guatemala, Honduras, Nicaragua, and the United States."

carbon footprint: A measurement in units of CO_2 used to keep track of carbon dioxide equivalent embedded in a product or activity. Companies and individuals can reduce their carbon footprint by taking fewer business trips, for example.

CCO (Chief Compliance Officer): A corporate official in charge of overseeing and managing compliance issues within an organization, ensuring that a company is complying with regulatory requirements, and that the company is complying with internal policies and procedures.

CEO (Chief Executive Officer): Usually (but not always) the president of a company. The CEO directly reports to the board of directors.

CFO (Chief Financial Officer): Responsible for a company's finances, the CFO typically reports to the CEO and is a member of the company's board of directors.

change control: When key enterprise software is upgraded, a company's operations can be disrupted. Following a program of change control allows changes to be documented and tested before they are deployed and rolled back, in most cases, if they are unsuccessful.

chart of accounts: A list of all accounts tracked by a single accounting system. Most charts of accounts classify each account into one of five categories: Assets, Liabilities, Equity, Income, or Expenses.

CIO (Chief Information Officer): An executive who is responsible for a company's IT strategy and infrastructure. The CIO may or may not sit on the company's board of directors and typically reports to the CEO. Some organizations have two related roles: the CIO and the CTO (chief technology officer), putting the former in charge of the flow of information and the latter in charge of IT infrastructure.

classification: The act of determining the tariff schedule category that an article falls under and the applicable duty rate. People who prepare entry papers (such as importers and Customs brokers) must ensure that the merchandise is classified.

Clause 49: An Indian law enacted in 2005 that regulates companies that trade on the Indian Stock Exchange. It requires that companies establish risk management processes, report on their internal controls (and unlike SOX, all internal controls, not just financial internal controls must be certified), have an appropriate number of independent directors, establish a code of conduct, and issue a compliance report.

Clean Air Act (CAA): A U.S. law first passed in 1963 and amended most recently in 1990. The Clean Air Act is enforced by the Environmental Protection Agency (EPA) to help control and reduce smog and air pollution.

Clean Water Act (CWA): A U.S. law enforced by the EPA, the CWA is the foundation of surface water quality protection in the U.S. today.

CLERP 9: An Australian law comparable to, though less stringent than, SOX. CLERP 9 is part of the Corporate Law Economic Reform Program (CLERP).

COBIT: Published by the IT Governance Institute and the Information Systems Audit and Control Association (ISACA), COBIT (Control Objectives for Information and Related Technologies) provides an IT governance framework to manage risk and compliance issues based on best practices.

compliance: The C in GRC, compliance is the act of adhering to and demonstrating adherence with laws, regulations, or policies. Compliance relates not just to financial regulations but also to regulations in a host of other areas including the environment, global trade, worker safety and privacy.

COO (Chief Operating Officer): Also called a Chief Operations Officer, an executive in charge of the company's day-to-day operations.

corrective controls: Internal controls that come into play once a problem is discovered. An example would be removing access from users who have excessive privileges or executing a backup and recovery plan after a physical disaster has occurred.

COSO (Committee of Sponsoring Organizations): COSO was formed in 1985 to sponsor the National Commission on Fraudulent Financial Reporting, an independent private sector initiative that studied the causal factors that can lead to fraudulent financial reporting and developed recommendations for public companies, the SEC and other regulators, and educational institutions.

CPM (Corporate Performance Management): A combination of strategy management, planning, reporting and consolidation, and revenue, cost, and profitability modeling that enables companies to measure their performance and improve it.

CRM (Customer Relationship Management): An enterprise software application that allows companies to track their relationships with and provide better service.

CRO (Chief Risk Officer): Sometimes also called the Chief Risk Management Officer, an executive in charge of enterprise risk management and the compliance efforts of a company.

CSO (Chief Sustainability Officer): An executive in charge of the company's emphasis on sustainability.

CSR (Corporate Social Responsibility): Through the practice of sustainability, companies practice a commitment to sustainable growth and ethics and promote the health and well-being of all stakeholders, including the community in which they are situated.

customs value: The value assigned to merchandise at the time of entry. It is used as the basis for assessing the amount of duty and taxes owed and for other purposes. It can be calculated in a number of ways, but the preferred method of valuation is transaction value.

data privacy: Keeping data confidential requires protecting data, sometimes through security measures such as encryption. Data privacy is increasingly being regulated, especially as it relates to personal information that could be used to perpetrate crimes such as identity theft.

denied persons list: Also referred to as a denied parties list. Technically, a list that used to be referenced in the U.S. Export Administration Regulations, of specific persons who have been denied export privileges, in whole or in part. This term can also refer to a consolidated list of all restricted entities published by many different U.S., UN, and EU bodies.

detective controls: Internal controls that determine whether a bad event has already happened. For example, when a bank statement is received, it is reconciled to the customer's records to detect processing errors by the bank or customer.

directive: A model law that the European Union sets out. Directives are implemented into specific laws by member nations.

duty: A tax imposed on imports by the Customs authority of a country. Duties are generally based on the value of the goods (ad valorem duties), other factors such as weight or quantity (specific duties), or a combination of value and other factors (compound duties).

duty drawback process: Customs regulations typically allow the recovery of the majority (99 percent in the U. S.) of the duty paid upon importation if the merchandise is subsequently exported. To recover the duty, the appropriate import and export information and supporting documents must be available and a drawback claim must be filed with Customs.

ECA (European Chemicals Agency): An organization based in Helsinki, Finland that oversees the enforcement of REACH (Regulation on Registration, Evaluation, Authorisation and Restriction of Chemicals).

ERP (Enterprise Resource Planning): Enterprise software for managing nearly every area of a business, including such elements as accounting, purchasing, and human resources.

EUP (Energy Use in Products): An EU directive that requires companies to design products to use less energy.

European Directive on Data Protection: One of the first and most important pieces of data privacy legislation that specifically addresses Internet privacy.

export: To send or transport merchandise out of a country, especially for trade or sale.

fair market value: The price at which merchandise is sold in the manufacturer's home market.

FASB (Financial Accounting Standards Board): The official rulemaking body in the accounting profession.

FCPA (Foreign Corrupt Practices Act): A U.S. law enacted in 1977 but increasingly enforced in the 1980s and 1990s. Cases brought under the act doubled between 2006 and 2007. Under the act, companies can be prosecuted for their business partners' corrupt practices such as, bribing local officials. It includes anti-bribery provisions as well as provisions relating to the accounting of partner firms, both in terms of internal accounting controls and the keeping of books and records.

Federal Trade Commission: An agency of the U.S. government that promotes fair trade. Among other things, the FTC enforces antitrust regulations and educates the public about identity theft.

financial compliance: Compliance relating to accounting-related laws such as Sarbanes-Oxley. Other types of compliance include global trade compliance and environmental compliance.

financial risks: Relating to the effect of external factors such as credit, foreign exchange rates, interest rates, and other market events.

fraud: Intentional deception for unlawful gain. Fraud is difficult to prosecute in many cases because prosecution entails proving intent.

GAAP (Generally Accepted Accounting Principles): The standard framework of guidelines for financial accounting. It includes the standards, conventions, and rules accountants follow in recording and summarizing transactions and in the preparation of financial statements.

GHG (Green House Gases): Greenhouse gas emissions are increasingly the subject of emissions laws. Greenhouse gases include not only CO_2, but also CH_4, N_2O, HFCs, PFCs, and SF_6 as specified by the Kyoto Protocol.

governance: In business, governance develops and manages consistent, cohesive policies, processes, and decision-rights for a given area of responsibility. For example, managing issues at a corporate level such as privacy, internal investment, and the use of data.

GRAS (Generally recognized as safe): A U.S. Food and Drug Administration designation for food additives.

GRC (Governance, Risk, and Compliance): Risk management, governance, and compliance with regulations have traditionally been separate corporate functions. GRC seeks to integrate these functions into a holistic framework.

GRI (Global Reporting Initiative): An international group that has created the G3 framework for sustainability reporting.

HCS (Hazard Communication Standard): An OSHA regulation that relates to handling and classification of hazardous materials.

HIPAA (Health Insurance Portability and Accountability Act): A 1996 U.S. regulation requiring all participants in the healthcare field to increase electronic communication and security of personal data. HIPAA also provides portability of health coverage for individuals.

HMR (Hazardous Materials Regulations): Issued by the U.S. Department of Transportation (USDOT) to regulate the transport of hazardous materials in the U.S. and for goods leaving or entering the U.S.

HTS (Harmonized Tariff System): An international, multipurpose classification system designed to improve the collection of import and export statistics. It is harmonized with the tariff schedules of the major trading nations of the world in that it follows a basic structure and has the same basic language. The rates of duty and the specific provisions vary from country to country.

IASB (International Accounting Standards Board): The international body governing the accounting profession.

ICS (Integrated Cargo System): The Australian Customs Service's electronic customs initiative.

identity theft: The act of impersonating another for financial gain.

import: To bring in goods from another country.

import license: A document required and issued by some national governments that authorizes goods to be imported into their individual countries.

import restrictions: Any one of a series of tariff and non-tariff barriers imposed by an importing nation to control the volume of goods coming into the country from other countries.

incident: In risk management, when a risk becomes a reality it is an incident. From the standpoint of employee, health, and safety, an accident or a near-miss is an incident.

internal control: A test designed to verify that a business process is achieving its goals efficiently and is protected from fraud and other forms of abuse.

IT GRC: Encompasses the software and hardware and related policies and procedures used to support compliance and risk management efforts from an IT perspective based on established best practices.

ITIL (IT Infrastructure Library): A framework of best practices for IT by the U.K.'s Office of Government Commerce.

J-SOX: The nickname for Japan's Financial Instruments and Exchange Law, which was modeled on SOX.

KPI (Key Performance Indicator): A statistical measure of how well an organization is doing. KPIs represent quantifiable goals or targets established in a business's strategic plan.

KRI (Key Risk Indicator): A statistical measure of risk that links directly to a unique or key corporate goal and initiative. This is the way risk is assessed for the goal and associated initiative.

KonTraG: The Act on Control and Transparency in Enterprises: A German law that specifies that companies must perform risk management in a way that allows them to address risks before they turn into incidents and in a way that aligns with their corporate objectives.

Kyoto Protocol: An international treaty regarding reduction of greenhouse gases. Some 170 nations have ratified the treaty, which is legally binding, but the U.S. is not among them.

LEED (Leadership in Energy and Environmental Design): A rating system created by the United States Green Building Council (USGBC) for green building and green renovation.

line of business: A particular type of business that a company engages in. For example, a company may sell cameras, printers, and software. Each of these would be considered a line of business.

material weakness: A weakness that would be likely to affect the financial status of the corporation and thus the stock's price once the weakness becomes known by the public.

mitigating controls: Controls that have an element of supervision in place to reduce risk. For example, a typical rule is that the same person should not be able to create a vendor and cut a check. In smaller branch offices, a person may have many such conflicting duties. To manage this, companies put in a mitigating control, such as having a supervisor review the transactions.

mitigation: Reducing the risk associated with a particular activity.

MSDS (Material Safety Data Sheet): A document required by OSHA that must accompany hazardous materials. The MSDS describes how to handle such a substance in transit, for example.

NAFTA (North American Free Trade Agreement): If certain requirements are met, goods exported from Canada or Mexico into the United States will qualify for reduced rates of duty (or may be duty-free) and may not require quota or visa.

negligence: A crime involving the failure to do something that was required. Negligence, unlike fraud, is easy to prove because intent is not required.

objective: A concise statement describing the specific things an organization must do well in order to execute its strategy. Objectives often begin with action verbs such as increase, reduce, improve, or achieve.

OCEG (Open Compliance and Ethics Group): A nonprofit offering comprehensive guidance, standards, benchmarks, and tools for integrating GRC processes.

operational risks: Risks relating to the people, processes, and systems required to achieve a firm's mission and objectives.

PCAOB (Public Company Accounting Oversight Board): A private nonprofit that was created to oversee implementation of Sarbanes-Oxley.

Personal Information Privacy Act: A Japanese data privacy law.

Personal Information Protection and Electronic Documents Act: A Canadian data privacy law.

privacy: The right of an individual not to have data about them disclosed or used without consent.

process control: The concept of inserting internal controls into business processes so that they become part of the normal execution of that process.

REACH (Registration, Evaluation and Authorization of Chemicals): A European law that went into effect in June 2007 (though its provisions are being phased in over time). Companies must register substances that they produce in quantities of more than 1 ton per hear. Alternatives should be substituted for dangerous chemicals where possible. The aim is to protect the quality of life of Europe's citizens and its environments by tracking and setting limits on chemicals that come into the continent.

restatement: The resubmission of financial reports because of errors or misstatements found during the audit process.

risk: Anything that impacts the achievement of an organization's objectives. Types of risks include operational risks (fraud, for example), risks of noncompliance (not filing the proper documents to comply with legislation), and strategic risks (such as an incident that affects a brand's reputation).

risk analysis: A systematic use of available information to determine how often specified events may occur and the magnitude of their consequences.

risk appetite: Risk appetite is the amount of risk an entity is willing to accept in pursuit of objectives. It reflects that organization's risk management philosophy and influences the organization's culture and operating style.

risk management framework: A formalized process for managing risk on an explicit basis. The framework consists of a risk assessment, response, and accountability for the risk and mitigation activities around it.

risk mitigation: The processes built into the controls environment, such as policies, frameworks, and accountabilities, to reduce a risk.

risk response: The decision to accept a risk, decline a risk, treat or mitigate a risk, or share a risk with another party.

RoHS (Reduction of Hazardous Substances): A European directive that regulates the use of six substances: lead, mercury, cadmium, hexavalent chromium, polybrominated biphenyls, and polybrominated diphenyl ether.

SCM (Supply Chain Management): Enterprise software for managing a company's supply chain.

SEC (Securities and Exchange Commission): Publicly traded U.S. companies must file annual reports with the SEC.

segregation of duties: Taking a process that is too valuable for one person to carry it out and separating the tasks so that different users perform key steps in the process. Segregation of duties helps to eliminate fraud.

shareholder: A person that owns stock in a publicly traded company.

sick building syndrome: Negative health effects that result from a building's design, construction, or state of cleanliness.

SIEF (Substance Information Exchange Forum): An organization tasked with providing data to companies to help them achieve REACH compliance.

SOX (Sarbanes-Oxley Act): U.S. legislation enacted in response to the high-profile Enron and WorldCom financial scandals to protect shareholders and the general public from accounting errors and fraudulent practices in the enterprise. Applies to companies that trade publicly in the U.S.

stakeholder: A person or entity with an interest in a company. Although shareholders have a financial interest, employees, nongovernmental organizations, and local citizens are among corporate stakeholders.

strategic risks: Relating to strategic objectives such as political factors, competition, customer priorities, and brand or reputation.

substance: A substance (usually a chemical) that is used to make another chemical or product and is regulated due to its toxic or hazardous properties

supply chain: The supply chain represents the flow of materials, information, and finances as they move in a process from supplier to manufacturer to wholesaler to retailer to consumer.

sustainability: Meeting the needs of the present without compromising the needs of the future.

SVHC (Substances of Very High Concern): Substances that are particularly harmful to humans and the environment. The European law REACH aims to phase out these substances in Europe.

system of record: A software system in which key business data is kept.

transparency: Visibility into the data held in an organization.

TSCA (Toxic Substances Control Act): An EPA law that regulates the use of certain chemicals in the U.S.. The law particularly applies to lead, radon, asbestos, and PCBs.

WEEE (Waste Electrical and Electronic Equipment): A European directive for the disposal of electrical and electronic wastes.

Index

• D •